The
HOENGSONG VALLEY MASSACRE

Command Collapse or Cover-up?

ARTHUR SHARP

outskirts
press

The Hoengsong Valley Massacre
Command Collapse or Cover-up?
All Rights Reserved.
Copyright © 2022 Arthur Sharp
v3.0

The opinions expressed in this manuscript are solely the opinions of the author and do not represent the opinions or thoughts of the publisher. The author has represented and warranted full ownership and/or legal right to publish all the materials in this book.

This book may not be reproduced, transmitted, or stored in whole or in part by any means, including graphic, electronic, or mechanical without the express written consent of the publisher except in the case of brief quotations embodied in critical articles and reviews.

Outskirts Press, Inc.
http://www.outskirtspress.com

ISBN: 978-1-9772-5341-5

Cover Photo © 2022 www.gettyimages.com. All rights reserved - used with permission.

Outskirts Press and the "OP" logo are trademarks belonging to Outskirts Press, Inc.

PRINTED IN THE UNITED STATES OF AMERICA

Overview

For the first three months after their October 1950 entry into the Korean War the Chinese pretty much pushed the allied forces around at will. By the end of the year U.S. Eighth Army Commander Matthew Ridgway had had enough of withdrawing and being chased by the enemy. Fortunately, the Chinese had to take a break too.

In January 1951 they broke off their attacks to resupply and reinforce their troops and assess their transportation capabilities. Ridgway took advantage of the lull to consolidate his lines. He had not quite finished the task when the Chinese renewed their attacks around Chip'yong-ni and Wonju.

They began their operation at Hoengsong against the Republic of Korea (ROK) 3rd and 8th Divisions, which were spread out too widely to effectively repel Chinese attacks. Worse, their haphazard dispersal left X Corps' left flank vulnerable, which the Chinese capitalized on. (X Corps included the 1st Marine Division, the U.S. Army 7th Infantry Division, and other U.S. Army units.) They rolled up the ROKs' flank, advanced rapidly toward Hoengsong, and cut off the Main Supply Route (MSR), which was their only route of escape.

Consequently, all the allied forces north and west of the town were hemmed in, blocking their tanks, artillery, and vehicles from getting through the Chinese roadblock. And, because the roads were flanked by steep hills and gullies on both sides, the infantry troops were caught in the open as well. That was the situation on February 11, 1951—the day the massacre began.

Dedication

This book is dedicated to the men and women of the American and allied armed services who participated in the Korean War, the United Nations' first war aimed at stopping the spread of Communism from east to west—especially to the 36,574 killed in action, 4,714 who became prisoners of war, and the 7,500 who were missing in action and are still unaccounted for.**

**36,574 is the number of U.S. warfighters killed in action during the Korean War whose names are etched on the Wall of Remembrance that was dedicated at the Korean War Veterans Memorial in Washington D.C. in 2022.

The other numbers are approximate, especially the missing in action personnel. The remains of many of them have been recovered and identified by the Defense POW/MIA Accounting Agency (DPAA) in recent years.

Acknowledgments

Thanks to the large number of people who shared their personal experiences about the Hoengsong massacre, the folks who prepared the command reports that became sources, and the many other contributors such as Korean War combat correspondents who knowingly or unknowingly helped construct the story.

Caveat

This is not intended to be a complete play-by-play summary of the battle at Hoengsong. It is a snapshot of the chaos that prevailed in the valley as the Communists sprung their trap and tried to annihilate allied troops that stumbled into it.

There is probably no way to document fully what happened in Hoengsong Valley during the February 11-13, 1951 timeframe. The best historians can do is to produce an overview to give readers an idea of what happened as units of both sides moved backwards and forwards during the ebb and flow of combat. This book is such an overview.

Table of Contents

Introduction i

Chapter 1: Why Hoengsong? 1

Chapter 2: Dying For Your Country—And Your Clothing 10

Chapter 3: Massacre, Murder, And Mayhem:
   Never Pleasant Either Way 26

Chapter 4: Setting Up The Story 45

Chapter 5: The 36 Stratagems 53

Chapter 6: Hiding Hordes Around Hoengsong 67

Chapter 7: The Hoengsong Shuffle 76

Chapter 8: ROK Army History: Anything But Spectacular 81

Chapter 9: February 11th: Springing The Trap 95

Chapter 10: Time On Your Hands 101

Chapter 11: Held After Hoengsong 109

Chapter 12: Run, ROKs, Run 117

Chapter 13: February 12, 1951: Caught In A Crossfire 122

Chapter 14: Diddling, Dawdling, And Dying 128

Chapter 15: Too Many Ribbons, Too Few FOs—
And A Lack Of Intelligence 136

Chapter 16: No Bang For The Buck—Or Any Other Price 145

Chapter 17: The Best Defense Is A Good Offense 155

Chapter 18: The Chinese Were Devious And Daring 163

Chapter 19: General Ruffner Assumes Command Of The
General Confusion 169

Chapter 20: Never Go Back The Way You Came 175

Chapter 21: The Netherlands Detachment At Hoengsong 184

Chapter 22: Goosens Gads About 194

Chapter 23: Survivors 201

Chapter 24: Hope Springs Eternal 213

Chapter 25: It's No One's Fault 219

Epilogue 232

Appendix A 235

Appendix B 245

Appendix C 248

Appendix D 250

Sources 252

Introduction

"The bodies have been removed. But all along the road on both sides are the helmets of the dead American soldiers and the fur-lined caps of South Koreans and Chinese. It is astonishing how many there are.

A French war correspondent looked and shook his head. "In France," he said, "where we have had many battles we have an expression for this. It is 'trop de chapeaux—too many hats'."

THE OPENING PARAGRAPH in a March 2, 1951 AP newspaper report account of a Korean War battle sounded innocuous. It read in part: "Tank-led Marines of the First Division drove into Hoengsong unopposed at 2:40 p.m. (12:40 a.m. EST) after smashing Chinese Reds in a two-day battle on dominating ridges nearby. Infantrymen followed the Leathernecks."

The next line was more telling: "Field dispatches said they found the rubbled highway hub littered with the frozen bodies of earlier allied casualties and scores of wrecked Army trucks and jeeps. Hoengsong was virtually deserted."

The following day's headline proclaimed in bold print, "Marines find Red ambush victims."

"The bodies of an undisclosed number of American soldiers were found today sprawled in mud and water where they had been shot down three weeks ago by ambushing Chinese communists two miles north of Hoengsong. Most of the bodies had been looted for shoes and other wearing apparel. Several of the men had been bound and shot in the back, according to the Marines who found them."

An important word in that account is "undisclosed." Military commanders were reluctant to reveal the true magnitude of the massacre, although later reports set the number of dead around 300, which turned out to be a gross under-calculation. Those same reports noted that approximately one-half of the 2,400 men in the regiment involved were unaccounted for. The U.S. Army 2d Division history makes no mention of the battle on its website, as if Hoengsong never existed. Yet, eyewitness and newspaper accounts make it clear that it did—and that a heinous affair took place there.

Here is the pertinent information about the time period from the 2nd ID History:

"With the outbreak of hostilities in Korea during the summer of 1950, the 2nd Infantry Division was quickly alerted for movement to the Far East Command. The division arrived in Korea, via Pusan on 23 July 1950, becoming the first unit to reach Korea directly from the United States. Initially employed piecemeal, the entire division was committed as a unit on 24 August 1950, relieving the 24th Infantry Division at the Naktong River Line.

"The first big test came when the North Koreans struck in a desperate human wave attack on the night of 31 August 1950. In the 16-day battle that followed, the division's clerks, bandsmen, technical and supply personnel joined in the fight to defend against the attackers. Shortly thereafter, the Warrior Division was the first unit to break

INTRODUCTION

out of the Pusan Perimeter and they led the Eighth Army drive to the Manchurian border. The division became the first UN force to enter the North Korean Capital of Pyongyang.

"When the Chinese entered the war on 26 November 1950, soldiers of the 2nd Infantry Division were given the mission of protecting the rear and right flank of the Eighth Army as it retired to the South. Fighting around Kunu-ri cost the division nearly one third of its strength, but was ten times more costly to the enemy and the way was kept open.

"On 5 February 1951, the 23rd Regimental Combat Team moved into the narrow valley of Chip'yong-ni. Colonel Paul Freeman, the 23rd Regimental Combat Team Commander, realized that he occupied a salient in front of the main defensive line and requested permission to fall back, however; Lieutenant General Matthew Ridgway, the Eighth United States Army Commanding General, ordered the 23rd Regimental Combat Team to make a stand against Communist Chinese Forces."

This would nominally be the place where the Hoengsong portion of the battle should be mentioned. However, it is left blank for some reason. The history continues:

"On 13 February 1951, the 23rd Regimental Combat Team, with the attached French Battalion, was cut off and surrounded by three Chinese divisions. As the surrounded 23rd Regimental Combat Team exhausted supplies due to intense fighting, air drops were conducted to restock the ammunition, ration, medical and equipment supply dumps. The Air Force conducted over 131 sorties utilizing Napalm to demoralize and destroy the Communist Chinese Forces. For more than three days the 23rd Regimental Combat Team bravely fought in freezing weather killing over 5,000 Chinese and causing the Communist Chinese Forces to withdraw. The Battle of Chip'yong-ni was the first major defeat for the Chinese and proved to be the turning point of the Korean War."

That, at least, deserves mentioning.

One Marine, Bob Hall, remembered the first time he drove through the site of the massacre "as I was taking the daily ammo report to 1st Marine Division headquarters and seeing fingers and toes alongside the road. I don't recall whether there were still any damaged vehicles in the area, but there could have been."

His conclusion was telling: "What a tragedy, especially for those involved. It's no wonder news did not leak out for quite some time."

Hall was not alone in believing that the Army was not particularly keen on releasing news of the massacre. His fellow Marine, Walt Duffet, averred that somebody knew about the massacre.

"I was a Marine Corporal at the time and the reason I remember that place is we pulled into Hoengsong at dusk and we dug in our positions. It was on March 10, 1951, my 21st birthday!

"My unit was the 1st Tank Bn., 1st Marine Division. I started digging my hole in what turned out to be ground behind a row of tall trees. I soon found out why it was easy digging. I dug into a mass grave of dead Chinese soldiers. That would address the question, "Did they exact a cost from the Chinese..?"

"My sergeant, "Scotty" Davis, had gone farther up the road from where I was located and came back to say, "There are hundreds of dead doggies still in their trucks who must have been overrun." He also told me the officers reported the hills were full of Chinese!

"So, we set up every machine gun available, plus some tanks in a firing line across this valley we were in. I remember thinking, "Not even a piss ant could get through our line of fire that night." The Chinese did not attack.

"I can say with certainty that the Marines knew of this massacre on March 10th, 1951. Perhaps some units knew of it before then. I can't say how long it took for other divisions to know about it.

INTRODUCTION

"I'm not sure, but I think that I recall that it was the 2nd Division that the Chinese caught in that convoy."

Neither Hall nor Duffet were specific about numbers. Nor was anyone else until war correspondents with the Marines, realizing that the Army was covering up a big fiasco, began filing stories critical of the massacre.

Years later historian and Korean War veteran Anthony Sobieski presented some startling—and extremely precise—statistics:

"February 12-13 were two hard days to be in Korea in 1951. The 12th was the most deadly day of the year, with 565 men killed. The next day was the second deadliest. There were another 430 killed that day. Five units in particular bore the brunt of these deaths due to the envelopment.

"The 38th Infantry Regiment was decimated, with 469 men listed as KIA.

"Next came the 15th Field Artillery Battalion, which was overrun and suffered 208 artillerymen KIA. The 3rd Battalion of the 9th Infantry Regiment (mostly from 'K' Company) lost 104 men. 'A' Battery of the 503rd Field Artillery Battalion suffered 56 men killed. Finally, the 82nd Anti-Aircraft Artillery Battalion incurred 36 deaths.

"Another 381 men died before things calmed down to 'light' combat operations by the middle of the month."

The total was 1,780, which was more in line with eyewitnesses' refutation of the initial numbers and war correspondents' guesses. Sobieski added a caveat: "...the way the U.S. military tracked and reported its losses necessitated that the date of capture or wounded would be used as the initial date of loss. A vast number of men who are listed as KIA between the 12th through the 15th actually died later while in captivity, mostly between April and June 1951, at the infamous 'Bean Camp' (an old Japanese forced labor camp from WWII), or while force-marched to the camp or from it to other camps."

However the numbers were counted, they far exceeded the original 300 cited. Numbers aside, battle-hardened Marine eyewitnesses found it difficult to process what they saw in the valley and questioned the 300 number bandied about. Marine tank commander Sgt. Virgil Street, said, "There may be more. We have counted something like *(censored)* bodies already," he said. "Most were around the convoy and some were up in the hills where the men ran to get away. And I don't think we've found all of them yet."

He was spot on. Some of what they found was appalling, For example:

- The naked bodies of 30 American soldiers killed by the Chinese, who then stole their clothes. (It is significant to note that the Chinese may have taken the clothes more out of necessity than spite or savagery.) As Dutch Korean War veteran and historian Elie Van Schilt wrote in his account of the Netherlands Detachment at Hoengsong:

"Still, the Chinese have a damned hard life, they are sent again and again to attack, daily they are exposed to air raids with napalm, fragmentation bombs and other items designed to annihilate them. There are just a few volunteers among them, some of them don't even know exactly where they are. They are sent onto the field with a baglet full of rice and an ammunition belt."

- 10 bodies in a ditch beside a village house. They had been stripped of their winter clothing.
- Another 10 bodies were found piled beyond the house; more corpses were scattered over the cluttered area.
- An American described as elderly, who had been knifed to death, lay near a bridge just north of the town of Saemal. His uniform was gone.
- Two young GIs lay in a muddy rice paddy beside their

- knocked-out tank.
- Three trucks, two of them overturned and burned, littered the roadside. The third was minus its engine and front axle.

Similar scenes were found along the road for miles. Mine clearance team leader William Parks provided a distressing description:

"I led a patrol through the lines up the road aways. We came to a blown-out bridge, where a jeep had made it down the left side. The driver and an officer were still sitting upright in the jeep. The driver was charred, and had his head tilted back. His mouth was full of snow.

"I will never forget this. Up on top, personal gear was scattered. I saw a Second Army patch among the personal effects. There were soldiers lying everywhere. Some looked like they were crawling. Most all of them were stripped of winter clothing.

"One soldier was lying in the middle of the road. He had been run over several times. We continued down the road with jeeps until we came to a house on the left side of the road. There were two South Korean soldiers inside the house. Both were wounded.

"They were loaded in the jeep. The officer in charge stayed a little while at the house, then we left."

Marine lieutenant W. R. Abell, one of the first officers on the scene, expressed the same surprise and shock his troops felt when they encountered the sights. His description was not for the squeamish.

"There were bodies scattered everywhere. In the trucks, under them, and on both sides of the road. The first truck had been carrying a field kitchen. Four men were in the back. They had been killed before they could begin to move.

"The trucks were not bunched together, but were strung out one by one, with many yards between them. You could see how the Chinese had done it. On one side of the road a dike went out at almost a right angle. On the other side there was a wall that served the same purpose. The Chinese had got behind these barricades and simply waited for the convoy to come by in the night.

"I was with the Marines up north at Hagaru and Yudam [at the Chosin Reservoir]. That was horrible enough, but this was worse than anything I ever saw up there. Some of the Americans were killed in fair fighting. They and the Chinese they had killed lay together in small heaps around the trucks. But other Americans apparently had been murdered. They must have been the wounded ones. I saw two GIs who had been hit with mortar shrapnel but probably not fatally.

"Their trousers had been taken off and their ankles tied together. They had bullet holes in the temples. I can't understand what happened to the field guns. There were five or six 155 mm. Howitzers. They were terribly wrecked.

"Some of their tubes had been exploded and their muzzles were cracked and spread out wide. I don't know whether the American gunners managed to destroy their guns before they were killed or whether the Chinese destroyed them later to keep the Americans from recapturing them."

What was more appalling to Abell was the civilian loss of life. He saw a dead baby lying on the ditch bank beside the road near a Korean woman who was apparently the mother. Numerous other civilians lay dead there too, well away from the road. Abell said it was as if they had moved to the side of the road to let the trucks pass, but had been caught in the path of the Chinese machine gun fire.

If there was any good news it was that the Marines found four survivors, two Americans and two South Koreans, all of whom were taken to hospitals. One of the Americans was wounded; the other was suffering from frostbite. They reported that they were in a U.S. Army 2nd Division convoy retreating on February 12th due to an overwhelming Chinese attack on the central front. The convoy comprised 25 trucks,

INTRODUCTION

3 tanks, 2 armored halftracks and several jeeps. The survivors said the Chinese ambushed them at night in the valley north of Hoengsong with mortars, machine guns, and rifles.

Flash back almost three weeks earlier. On February 13th AP correspondents reported that "Two American units of undisclosed size were reported cut off north of Hoengsong. They were fighting to crack enemy road blocks that extended two miles along the road south of them. An American relief force was battling up from the south. A South Korean regiment also was reported cut off northeast of Hoengsong."

What happened between that day and March 2nd is one of the more guarded secrets of the Korean War in particular and U.S. military history in general. If it weren't for the massacre Hoengsong probably would have remained just another sleepy Korean village along rural transportation routes in Central Korea. The bodies the Marines discovered placed it on the map as the scene of one of the most significant massacres in U.S. military history.

CHAPTER I

Why Hoengsong?

"Deep wedge driven into Allied lines... Field dispatches said the situation was confused and serious." (AP, 2/12/51)

HOENGSONG WAS A critical town to hold for UN and communist troops because it sat along the route about fifteen miles northwest of Hongchon, a key to the Chinese central defense line and their local assembly center. Ironically, one newspaper reporter at the time wrote, "Hoengsong, a wrecked no-man's land, was not considered of any military value by the attacking Allies."

Yet, the article continued, "Brig. Gen. Lewis B. "Chesty" Puller's First Marine Division smashed into heavy enemy resistance at the outset of the attack. The leathernecks, moving up both sides of the Twinnam River, struck toward a mountain pass. Through the pass, the main highway leads northwest from Hoengsong to Hongchon." Whether Hoengsong was a key objective or of no military value to the allies is moot: either way it will remain an essential part of U.S. military history, albeit in a negative sense.

Why those KIA (killed in action) allied troops' bodies were still on the battlefield two weeks later is a mystery, especially for the United

States, a country whose military branches pride themselves on never leaving a dead comrade behind if humanly possible. The answer to that question is the central point of this book. Why the massacre occurred can be explained in terms of military significance. Why the evidence of it that remained on the battlefield for weeks thereafter cannot.

Massacres are hard to define and even harder to hide. Eventually, in most cases, somebody has to take the blame for them. That was the case with the "Hoengsong Massacre" that took place February 11-13 1951, of which Marine Lt. Col. Harry T. Milne said, "It's as bad as anything I've ever seen. It was horrible."

Milne, who commanded a Marine tank battalion, spoke from experience. He was a survivor of the Chosin Reservoir campaign three months earlier, the most heralded military evacuation in U.S. history, when almost 15,000 American and Allied troops, outnumbered 10 to 1 by their Chinese enemy sworn to annihilate them, escaped the communist trap. The campaign was particularly devastating for elements of the U.S. Army's 7th Infantry Division, particularly Task Force Faith, which were all but wiped out on the east side of the reservoir. (The Marines operated mostly on the western side.)

The price those members of Task Force Faith paid at Chosin was steep but, unlike that paid by their counterparts who would die at Hoengsong, it had some redeeming value. The soldiers who died at Chinese hands at Chosin fought hard and bought some time for the Marines to bolster their defenses before the full Chinese onslaught began. And, many of the few Task Force Faith survivors joined with the Marines to fight their way out of the trap. That was dubious glory, but there was not even much of that for the soldiers massacred at Hoengsong two months later.

There were striking similarities between Chosin and Hoengsong. First, the Chosin campaign was the result of significant U.S. military leadership blunders, particularly by Generals MacArthur and Almond, who refused to accept intelligence reports revealing that the Chinese had crossed the Yalu River, the dividing line between Manchuria and North Korea, in large numbers. Then, they underestimated the fighting prowess of the Chinese troops.

Second, the weather and topographical conditions at Hoengsong bore a resemblance to Chosin. The village, fifty miles southeast of Seoul, was located in rugged hill country, precisely the type of terrain in which the Chinese were most comfortable fighting, although not as mountainous. The roads, such as they were, were narrow, which inhibited the allies' ability to travel.

There were two mountain passes south of Hoengsong, but they were pretty much restricted to one-way travel. As one reporter put it, "The Communists move along these icy precipitous roads like mountain goats, but transport is dangerous for the mechanized allied forces."

To top it off, the temperatures in the area had dropped off to zero. That was twenty to thirty degrees warmer than it had been at Chosin, but it was still less than ideal for military operations. Indeed, it was a recipe for disaster.

In the case of the Hoengsong massacre, which had a far deadlier outcome for the allied forces than did Chosin, no one was ever found culpable for what turned out to be a military debacle of the highest order, despite an investigation into the causes. According to Korean War veteran and historian Tom Moore:

"It would seem the main cause was an experiment from General MacArthur's office in Japan, and enforced by X Corps commander Lt. Gen. Almond. Support Force-21 (SF-21), was attached to the 8th.ROK Division, a command structure that required the total dependence on the ROK's "command and control." The experiment was later regretted.

"LTC. Robert G. Fergusson of G-2 (Intelligence), gave Gen. Almond a full report that X Corps would be CCF's "prime target." The allied commanders looked for the enemy to attack in great force (4 Chinese, and 2 North Korean Divisions) on or about February 15, 1951. With this alert in mind, many commanding officers believed Lt. Gen. Almond would have withdrawn to the well-prepared American defensive positions in Wonju. Instead, Gen. Almond pressed north, repeating a mistake he and General MacArthur had made at the Chosin Reservoir three months earlier.

"After the battle, the Army seemed to try to cover up the huge losses. Casualties; ROK-9,844—US and UN-2,018—Total-11,862. The numbers were hardly reported in American newspapers. The Chinese, however, knew how badly they had mauled the UN forces at Hoengsong—and how badly they had treated some of them.

NOTE: Not all of the KIA warfighters were left on the battlefield. The troops the Marines found in early March 1951 represented only a small percentage of the total number killed.

"Later in the spring, some slain CCF soldiers were wearing U.S. Army shirts and jackets with 2nd Inf. Div. patches. In the pockets were letters and photos from GIs' families. The U.S. troops were ordered to turn this material over to their company officers, and not to say a word about the matter ever. The Chinese made up for the silence: they proclaimed the battle of Hoengsong as their biggest victory against foreign troops ever.

"General Ridgway ordered an official investigation by Gen. George C. Stewart, 2nd Inf. Division. Stewart, recognizing that his Corps commander was the main fault, realized that his assignment was politically perilous. He tried to get out of it, but could not.

"The testimony he took was not under oath. His report placed blame on the Korean commanders. With Gen. Almond, and all other Americans absolved of blame, there could be no court-martials. Nevertheless, Gen. Ridgway continued to blame Gen. Almond. He remembered that elements of the 2nd Division were not mutually supporting each other, and for that reason they got caught."

Caught, but not blamed. That accounted in part for why the Army attempted a cover-up, and why the definition of massacre came into play in discussions of what happened. According to Moore, many historians and veterans now believe that when the U.S. Marines came into the valley 25 days after the battle and coined the phrase "Massacre Valley" they meant by massacre to convey shambles or a large-scale overwhelming defeat, not an atrocity. What else could it have been other than an atrocity?

The Marines found hundreds of dead soldiers in the valley. Most of them had been stripped of their winter clothes and boots by the Chinese. A few of the soldiers had been executed with their hands tied behind their backs and stripped of clothes. War correspondents with the U.S. Marines realized the Army had covered up the death count.

An article that appeared in "Time" magazine did not do much to downplay the notion of an atrocity.

"Forty half burned trucks and jeeps, and the blown-out barrels of six 155 millimeter field pieces were scattered along the road. In the vehicles, and under them lay the burned and decomposed bodies of U.S. and South Korean soldiers. Other bodies, stripped of their uniforms, sprawled by the roadside. This was the sight met by advancing U.S. Marines, two miles northwest of Hoengsong. It was part of the most horribly concentrated display of American dead since the Korean War began."

No wonder Hoengsong is a word that dredges up some bad memories for Korean War veterans, instills puzzlement in military historians, and creates embarrassment for U.S. Army leaders. Hoengsong was not, and is not, listed among the U.S. Army's finest moments—and it has had some great ones—for obvious reasons, as this book suggests.

THE HOENGSONG VALLEY MASSACRE

To read some accounts of the battle fought around Hoengsong, Korea in February 1951 some people might infer that it was simply a skirmish between small numbers of enemy combatants, after which both sides went on their way and the war continued. Indeed, that is the way James F. Schnabel portrayed it in his history, *United States Army In The Korean War: Policy And Direction, The First Year*, written for the Center Of Military History, United States Army.

Schnabel described the battle in terse, innocuous terms.

"On the night of 11-12 February, two Chinese armies (three divisions to an Army) and a North Korean corps (three divisions to a corps) struck the central front, scattered three ROK divisions, and forced the troops in this sector to abandon Hoengsong and withdraw southward toward Wonju. (At full strength these numbers would approximate 150,000 to 200,000 enemy troops.) The enemy was obviously aiming his attack at the communications centers of Wonju, near the center, and Chip'yong-ni, near the west flank of the X Corps sector; whose seizure would assist further advances to the south and west.

"General Ridgway [the commander of the U.S. Eighth Army at the time] therefore resolved that Wonju and Chip'yong-ni would be held."

Schnabel's description of the operation leaves a lot unsaid. He acknowledged that there was a military operation around Hoengsong in early February 1951 involving Chinese and North Korean Army units versus Republic of Korea (ROK), American, and Dutch troops. And, the latter units abandoned the area. He failed to mention that the UN forces left behind almost 2,000 dead comrades, many shot execution style, and lost large numbers of supplies and equipment which the Chinese and North Koreans put to good use for themselves, starting with the decisive Battle of Chip'yong-ni a few days later and continuing into and through the ensuing months.

Unlike Schnabel and other historians, U.S. Marine Jack M. Witter, one of the first people to reach the grisly scene of the massacre, got right to the heart of the matter. (Witter may have been off with his numbers as later accounts in this book suggest. And, he refers only to American casualties.)

"On February 11, 1951, units of the 2nd Infantry Division were ordered to withdraw from the area of Chanbong-ni and Saemal, Korea in the face of a Chinese attack. As the affected units did so, they became trapped in a valley two miles northwest of Hoengsong, Korea and there suffered a terrible defeat which became known as the 'Hoengsong Massacre' and 'Massacre Valley.'

"In early March 1951, I was a young Marine and one of the first to re-enter the area of that ambush. I saw the wreckage and the bodies left behind. In fact, I participated in the rescue of some of our wounded soldiers who had been left behind by the Chinese because they did not walk with the other prisoners taken north.

"In addition to losing numerous vehicles, equipment and artillery pieces, we lost 413 killed in action, 18 died of wounds, 392 died while POWs, 104 died while missing in action, and 690 were wounded in action. 268 other men were captured and later returned to our military control. A total of 1,895 casualties were suffered during the period of February 11-13, 1951 at this site."

Note that Witter arrived on the scene about two weeks after the massacre ended—and there were still troops needing assistance. No wonder, as he continued, "Reporters were ordered not to report or take photographs of what they saw and this incident has gone unreported or written about all of these years. In fact, evidence reflects that great attempts were made to even cover it up at the time it took place."

The Chinese did not try to keep the event quiet. They made a very loud statement about it in the form of artillery rounds. The Chinese employed artillery they captured intact at Hoengsong against UN troops at the ensuing battle of Chip'yong-ni in mid-February. The guns were taken from the U.S. Army's 15th Field Artillery Battalion and its attached Battery A of the 503d Field Artillery Battalion, which was supporting one of the ROK Divisions until it was cut off and overwhelmed by Chinese troops. About 75 percent of the battalion's members, including its commander, were killed at Hoengsong. Many more were captured.

For months after the battle U.S. Marines were encountering Chinese soldiers wearing the uniforms stripped from U.S. 2d Infantry Division troops massacred at Hoengsong. The Marines did not treat those Chinese soldiers well, but their attempts to avenge their infantry brethren were hollow. The damage had been done, and the incident left a sour taste in their mouths that no retaliation could eradicate.

Questions abound to this day about the battle at Hoengsong—especially among the few remaining survivors of the battle. Almost all of them express amazement upon learning what happened there. A common refrain is, "The Army never told me that."

Simply put, the Army didn't tell too many people much at all about the battle, and possibly would not have said anything about it all at all if a couple war journalists had not picked up the story for home-based publications such as Time Magazine and placed blame where it lay. The Staff Section Report of G-3, 2d Infantry Division, called the operation at Hoengsong, "the calamitous employment of support forces with ROK units."

Deliberately or not, Army officials treated the massacre at Hoengsong as a "forgotten battle" in a "forgotten war." They treated it as one part of the larger battle for Chip'yong-ni, rather than single it out as a separate action. That way they could mask the seriousness of the carnage. Only in recent years are survivors and first responders talking about what they experienced or saw afterwards. In the process, they are learning about what really happened at Hoengsong—seven decades later.

In all fairness to the U.S. Army, UN forces were at the time of the massacre fighting a battle across a 25-mile front in central Korea. They were stretched thin. The 2d Infantry Division alone was 4,700 troops short of its authorized strength of 18,800 soldiers. Worse, it suffered from a serious shortage of basic infantrymen and artillerymen and noncommissioned and junior officers (both 1st and 2nd lieutenants) who were qualified for leadership in the combat elements.

Some of the ROK divisions were either crumbling or out of service due to battle losses. The UN forces' lack of numbers resulted in gaps in their flanks for which they had no reserves to fill. The best they could do was rearrange units to meet exigencies—which the enemy forces created in abundance.

The communists were adept at probing for the inevitable gaps in the UN lines and then slipping troops through in small or large numbers, depending on their targets and missions. In light of the constant enemy probes and attacks, the lack of reserves, and the large area of land which the UN was defending, the "unpleasantness" at Hoengsong can be described as just one small part of a large battle. To do so, however, is rationalization. Nearly 12,000 UN soldiers died in a funnel between Hongch'on and Hoengsong, a story which cannot be sloughed off as simply a small part of a large battle.

The facts regarding the results were clear: bodies and carnage were not discovered for 25 days—and by Marines, not Army troops! Why was that the case? What went wrong at Hoengsong? Why did it take so long for anyone to reach the site? How long would those bodies have lain unrecovered if the Marines had not retaken the valley? Why did the Army try to cover up what has become known as the Hoengsong Massacre? Or did it? Let's find out.

CHAPTER 2

Dying For Your Country— And Your Clothing

"The peaceful valley through which the road meanders up from Hoengsong looks at first glance like a perfect place for a picnic. The hills are splashed with the delicate pastel of newly budded trees. A mountain brook rollicks over the smooth worn stones. Now and then a bird chirps a welcome." (United Press)

THE CONDITIONS DESCRIBED above may have been true on March 2, 1951 when U.S. Marines from D Co., 2nd Bn., 7th Regiment (D-2-7), 1st Marine Division stumbled across an incredible sight in the Hoengsong Valley in Central Korea during a routine patrol. They encountered the corpses of hundreds of dead, frozen UN soldiers, many stripped to their underwear or naked and shot in the backs of their heads.

For most of these battle-hardened Marines the eerie scene was a sad sight at best. For some, it was unbearable. They quickly inscribed a sign on a ration box that read, "You are now entering massacre valley." Another put up a sign saying, "Massacre Valley, Scene of Harry S. Truman's Police action. Nice going, Harry." Political statements aside, there was no better way to describe the site.

Many of the first responders to the scene remembered it with disgust and did not want to discuss it. But, as D/2/7 member Fred Frankville said, "Talking and writing about what we saw releases some of the demons combat Soldiers and Marines have." That was doubly true for members of the regiment who encountered a similar scene, albeit on a lesser scale, just three months later.

Grisly Scenes Affect Grizzled Veterans

The Marines of the 7th Regiment were no strangers to grisly scenes. In fact, such scenes on a smaller scale were not new in Korea, especially in the early stages, when members of almost every U.S. unit on the front line of the Pusan Perimeter experienced atrocities at the hands of their North Korean enemies. The Chinese did not enter the war en masse until late October 1950. They, too, were brutal at times, but unpredictable in their brutality, as the following news story involving the 7th Marine Regiment attests.

"Two Marines, Cpls. William S. Blair, 7th Marines, and Bernard W. Insco, an artillery observer with the 1st Korean Marine Regiment, were captured at different points across the central front on April 23, 1951 by the Chinese. Their captors forced them to sign petitions demanding that President Truman and Secretary of Defense Louis A. Johnson be ousted.

"Apparently the Chinese did not know that Johnson was no longer the Secretary of Defense. The Marines also said that the petitions called for the UN to leave Korea and the U.S. Seventh Fleet leave the Formosa area. The Chinese interrogated them intensely about other matters, such as how much property they owned in the U.S., if they had ever raped any Korean women, and whether the Japanese were going to take part in the fighting in Korea.

"The Chinese held on to Blair, Insco, and several other POWs for twenty days. They traveled on foot at night and hid with their captors in caves and dugouts by day. Blair recalled seeing several American prisoners being used to drive Chinese trucks. Then, on May 9, the Chinese gave the prisoners haircuts, handed them safe-conduct passes, and provided them with a guide for the long trek south. The guide and guards stayed with them until they neared UN lines.

"On the night of May 11, the group spotted searchlights on the front lines near Chunchon. An Army patrol found them the next day. The prisoners were well-fed and in good physical condition. They enjoyed a far different outcome than many of the POWs interned in Communist camps. There was simply no way of predicting how POWs would fare under Chinese control."

Brutality and murder apparently were perpetrated according to the communists' whims. On 12 September 1950, north of Taegu, the U.S. 1st Cavalry and 1st ROK counterattacked the 13th and 1st North Korean Divisions. The 3rd Bn, 7th Cav fought a particularly fierce battle for Hill 314, during which it lost half its strength in hand-to-hand fighting. (Hills were named according to their heights in meters.) They took the hill nonetheless—and found the bodies of 700 American and South Korean soldiers who had been murdered after being captured. That was only one of many such atrocities that UN troops discovered during the first year of fighting.

There was some speculation about why the North Koreans did what they did. Some people believed the North Korean atrocities were simply acts of sadism. Others believed they were perpetrated for their psychological impact. It was a matter of eastern vs. western military philosophy, although some UN troops, including Americans, responded in kind at times.

The North Koreans believed that defeating an enemy without fighting was a form of psychological superiority. To achieve this goal, they strove to weaken their opponents' will. Fear was an excellent way to do this in their way of thinking. One event that occurred on the night of August 30-31, 1950 epitomized their approach to warfare.

Some U.S. Army cooks were ambushed while bringing hot food forward from the 35th Regiment's trains to front line troops. The attack took place on a road that one soldier, Sam Holliday, had used four times that day without any incidents. Two of the cooks escaped the ambush. Later, they heard the screams of those being tortured. When they reached a nearby American unit, they told the troops what had happened. The unit sent a relief team, but by the time they reached the ambush site the North Koreans had gone. They left the bodies of the slain cooks behind to make sure they were discovered.

Holliday arrived on the scene ten minutes after the relief team, before the bodies had been moved. The slain soldiers' hands were tied. All of them had been shot in the back of the head execution style. Some had their tongues cut out. Others had feet or fingers cut off. The head cook had been castrated, and his testicles stuffed in his mouth.

As appalling as these atrocities were, they did not deter the UN troops from pursuing their mission to drive the North Koreans back over the 38th Parallel into their own territory. They did so, eventually—but the Chinese who reinforced them displayed some of the same inhumane tactics as their North Korean allies. That is what the Marines of the 7th Regiment discovered at Hoengsong.

On March 6, 1951 they were engaged with the Chinese near Hoengsong. Dog Company got a free pass in the fighting for once. The objectives they attacked were not defended. The members of the company knew that was not going to last long. At that point they were just a little south and west of Hoengsong, which was their objective for the next day.

The Marines gathered pine cones to start a small and near-smokeless fire to cook hamburgers which they had recently "liberated" from the officers' mess. The weather was nice. It was just a few degrees below freezing and there was no wind. That was to be their last respite for a while.

The next day the weather changed. There was light snow during the night and early morning. The snow came straight down since there was no wind. With the pine trees covered with snow, it was very picturesque. Dog Company had a sack of mail to drop off to E/2/7 (Easy Company, 7th Marine Regiment) as they passed through their positions on their way to Hoengsong, which was in the valley below them.

When Dog Company reached Easy Company's position, the members found their comrades in a firefight with a heavily defended enemy position on a hill between the two mountain ranges that blocked the approach to Hoengsong. Dog Company watched the firefight from a short distance. The members could see black figures falling in the snow, which they identified sadly as their Easy Company buddies.

As they watched, four Navy A1 Sky Raiders showed up and "napalmed" the enemy-held hill. All resistance stopped after the air attack. Dog Company moved up the hill with the mail. As they did, they walked by a half-dozen or so Marine casualties covered with ponchos. As sad as that sight was, it hardly prepared them for what lay ahead.

The Navy A1s took about five minutes to destroy the enemy positions at a cost of just a few gallons of gasoline. As combat veterans can attest, to survive in fighting is a matter of luck and timing. Frankville noted, "For instance, the position that our platoon assaulted the day before was not defended. If the air assault had arrived sooner at Easy Company's position, there would have been fewer—or no—Marine casualties in their firefight."

As Dog Company climbed the hill, they walked through the trenches in which the Chinese the pilots hit with napalm had taken shelter. Frankville described it as a scene out of Dante's Inferno:

"The Chinese defenders were turned into charcoal statues. They were killed instantly while aiming rifles toward the attacking Marines. The statues were looking down the barrels of what used to be rifles; the napalm had consumed the wood in the stock. The Chinese in the trenches were also black statues. The Chinese that were away from the trench were burned black and red with their skin rolled up."

As Marines had learned on Saipan in World War II, where napalm was first used, and Frankville reiterated, "What a horrible weapon napalm is." Horrible it may have been, but U.S. forces used it liberally in the Korean War to good effect. Its use may have caused some of the communists' brutality as a bit of revenge.

Napalm, a sticky gasoline gel derived from aluminum naphthenic and palmitic acids, was developed in 1943 by Louis F. Fieser, a chemistry professor at Harvard University. It spread farther, stuck to the target, was safer for its dispenser, and was cheaper to manufacture than other incendiary weapons.

U.S. aircraft dropped about 5,000 tons of napalm during WWII. Approximately two-thirds of it was used in the Pacific Theater. Its use by UN forces was increased considerably in Korea to negate the numerical superiority held by the Chinese. Napalm, by all accounts, was the one U.S. weapon the Chinese feared the most—and for good reason.

On an average day in the Korean War the U.S. Air Force dropped around 45,000 gallons of napalm, the U.S. Navy released around 12,000 gallons, and the U.S. Marine Corps delivered around 5,000 gallons to targets. Napalm was also used as land mines and in 55-gallon drums connected to explosive charges and detonators. It was used to burn off vegetation, as well as in many other useful military efforts.

The use of napalm in Korea got off to a rocky start. In the summer of 1950, shortly after the war started, UN forces experienced problems with napalm ignitions. They resolved the problem quickly. Tacticians also developed the strategy of "Golden Rain," in which a napalm mixture was sprayed in the air above enemy troops, showering them with flame.

Once the problems with ignition and delivery were resolved, UN forces used napalm liberally. They dropped it on enemy troops, communications centers, dams, factories, power-plants, and industrial centers. Five major North Korean cities suffered heavy napalm bombing: Chinnampo, Pyongyang, Rashin, Seishin, and Wonsan. The bombing over those cities was so effective it almost forced the people living in them to cease functioning above ground because of fires and suffocation. It was a weapon of terror—but an effective one.

Dog Company dropped off the mail for Easy Company and started down the valley, with Frankville's fire team in the point. "We walked toward Route 29, an elevated road that went through Hoengsong," he recalled. "In the distance we could see vehicles and artillery lying in different positions along the roadside. As we got closer, we also saw tanks in the ditch."

Neither he nor his fellow Marines were prepared for what they saw. Frankville wrote, "As we got next to the trucks, we started seeing bodies stripped to their underwear. There were lots of bodies. We were in shock. We kept asking each other, 'How could this happen?'"

One company member, Tom Cassis, the machine gun section leader in Frankville's platoon, recounted that he saw fifty bodies lying in one group, left only in their underwear. The Chinese and North Koreans had stripped the bodies of their cold weather clothing. The Marines realized that the soldiers who had surrendered were executed simply for their cold weather gear. Some of the Chinese wearing the dead soldiers' clothing would pay dearly later for their actions.

Frankville described the eerie scene as one almost beyond words. "In this cold weather, the battlefield had been preserved and frozen in time. This action had taken place approximately 25 days before we arrived. The stripped bodies were laid out on the road like railroad ties in near perfect rows. It looked like a mile of bodies."

There was one piece of irony in the scene among the intermingled bodies of Chinese, American, and South Korean dead. Marine Technical Staff Sergeant James C. Jones noted one slain Chinese soldier lying on his back, arms and hands raised to the sky as if he were praying.

"Next to him—I don't know where it came from—there was an American hymn book," Jones recalled. "The wind rustled the hymnal's pages. On the open page was the title, 'Master, Let Me Walk With Thee.'

A war correspondent for the United Press put a human face on the scene by relating some of the mementoes Marines found among the carnage:

"Here beside the road is a snapshot, twisted and curled by the capricious mountain weather. A chubby child smiles from the picture, and across the bottom is scrawled "to daddy."

"Grandma had written to one of the men of the 2nd Division, and it is here now for any passerby to read: "I do hope the war will soon be over, and the boys can get home. But many will not return."

"The crumpled page of a magazine lies against a sheltering stone. On it was a horoscope reading. One sentence said "A journey undertaken this week will have to be postponed, or might bring you some curious experience."

"A wife longing for her husband's return wrote, "There isn't much we can do but wait with patience and put all our trust In the Lord."

The pathos was overwhelming.

Frankville observed that most of the soldiers may have been killed in combat, but it looked like many were executed. "The roadway looked like corduroy with the bodies covered with light snow," he continued. "Some tanks came up the road and stopped where we were standing at the head of the bodies. We milled around in shock at the massacre."

Without warning, the lead tank started moving and ran over several bodies before we could stop it. The bright red flesh between the tank treads looked just like the ground beef we had cooked the night before. We threw away what was left of the hamburger. Our appetite for it was gone!"

Dale Erickson, a member of Weapons Company/2/7, had similar memories. He was one of the Marines who was never able to forget it. As he recalled, W/2/7 was advancing along with the rest of the 2nd Battalion of the 7th Marines to a new position in east central Korea near the little village of Hoengsong.

"We had been on the move for two or three hours on foot when we spotted some American bodies along the road out in a rice paddy," he noted. "Then we saw another body and another somewhat closer to the road. As we walked on, more bodies showed up."

The number of bodies was astounding. "We started seeing bodies all over by the hundreds. We had no warning. Then we came on a truck with U.S. Army marking in which we saw four frozen bodies. All were American soldiers."

It got worse. They spotted more trucks and tanks. "We started seeing bodies all over the place," Erickson observed. "Some of them were burned and naked." But, he emphasized, there was evidence that the Americans had put up a fight, albeit a hopeless one. "For every ten American bodies there was one Chinese body," he guessed.

Frankville said the Marines' usual macho banter stopped as they surveyed the scene. "Even the toughest men of the 7th Marine regiment—and we had some tough ones—looked the other way, which didn't help much, since there were bodies in every direction." The Marines realized they were seeing something different. They began to converse in hushed tones, as if they were in church."

Charles Hughes, a rifleman with H-3-7, experienced a similar reaction. He wrote in his book *Accordion War: Korea 1951 – Life and Death in a Marine Rifle Company* (p. 130):

"What we saw and smelled on this day drove home the realization that it is much easier to look upon the dead "them" than the dead "us." These were Americans who had died here. This realization fell on us like a pall. All banter stopped as we marched through the valley. We looked quietly to the left and right as we passed through the scenes of destruction, each man deep in his own thoughts."

Erickson described the scene in similar solemn terms. "We had our own vehicles, trucks and tanks moving with us on the same road," he said. "We came to a place where the road dropped off sharply on one side; the other side had a rock wall. We saw bodies that were frozen on and beside the road." It was far from pleasant for the Marines, who kept moving at first.

"We had to walk along alongside our own trucks and tanks while our vehicles crushed the bodies with wheels and threads creating a crimson carnage that repulsed the souls of everyone that witnessed it," Erickson commented. "It was the most horrifying scene that anyone can imagine."

Erickson continued begrudgingly. "As we walked along, there was not much space between the trucks and the tanks and the rock wall. We could not take a step without stepping on a face, an arm, or a hand. The road was thick with this carnage, and my boots were covered with blood."

It was too much for him.

"I could not bear to see this anymore," he stated. "I grabbed onto the shoulder of the Marine ahead of me, closed my eyes and stumbled along with him. I do not know for how long."

In fact, after that point, he lost track of everything.

"I must have blacked out, because I do not remember what happened after that," he concluded. When he woke up he was aboard a Navy hospital ship, USS Repose (AH-16).

Remarkably, he had participated in a battle two days after their experience at Hoengsong, and his company even took casualties. "I did not find this out till later because I woke up on Repose," Erickson revealed. He had a simple explanation for his reaction.

"My body must have reached its limits and it took me out. It was too much to see," he said. "I could take all the death and dead bodies, but I could never get the blood off my boots after that."

Sadly, he was never able to forget what he saw at Hoengsong. "Part of that experience has stayed with me all of my life," he acknowledged. Erickson was not alone in that regard.

Paul G. McCoy, a member of the U.S. Army's 82nd AAA, B Battery, remembered clearly what he saw and experienced at Hoengsong, which he described in his contribution to The Patriot, a Library of Congress website dedicated to the preservation of military history.

"On 11 February, prior to midnight, we received word that the 8th ROK Division was under severe attack by Chinese forces. This soon turned into a collapse of the ROK units. Support Force 21 (SF-21) started a delayed effort to load vehicles and attempt our own withdrawal. Our delay was caused by the complete loss of communications with the ROK unit we were supporting and a lack of control of SF-21 by U.S. Forces. Our withdrawal did not start until 0200 hours, 12 February. By this time, the Changbong-ni area was inundated with fleeing ROK forces being closely followed by elements of several Chinese divisions.

"By the time our column started its withdrawal, it came under sporadic machine gun fire and, as the intensity of the fire increased, the movement of the column became more disparate. At this time, I was 'ranked' out of the front seat of my jeep by Captain Joyce, who was acting as assistant to Captain Stevens, our Commanding Officer.

"As we were not moving, I left the jeep to move up the column to find out what was wrong. I was not certain that my actions were particularly brave, but it certainly saved my life and provided me with knowledge as to how soldiers can act when they are completely uninformed."

McCoy had no intentions of sitting and wondering what had happened or if a similar fate awaited him. He investigated the scene at once.

"As I moved up the line of vehicles, I discovered that there would be a group of 5-10 vehicles with a huge gap between the lead vehicle and the rest of the column. Each lead vehicle did not have a person in the driver's seat. It wasn't that these drivers had been killed in their vehicle, for they had apparently abandoned their vehicles. My mission became a task of finding drivers to get that portion of the column moving.

"In one case, I found 10-15 men huddled in the rear of a truck as if the canvas top would provide protection from the rapidly increasing enemy fire. I asked them if anyone could drive and one soldier admitted he could, but didn't have a driver's license."

McCoy did not have time to worry about minor protocols like who was licensed to drive and who was not. There were no traffic cops around to check, even though many people considered the Korean War a "police action," as President Truman labeled it. He discarded the rule book.

"I broke normal military procedure in order to get the column moving. I estimate that 10 percent of the vehicles in that column were without drivers and were blocking the road at a time when rapid movement would have placed them a long way down the road to Hoengsong and safety."

Canadian troops found a similar scene in mid-February involving

African-American American troops. In a way, their discovery was a testament to Harry Truman's 1948 Executive Order to integrate the United States' armed forces. It gave soldiers of all races, religion, and ethnic backgrounds equal opportunities to serve their country.

On July 26, 1948, President Truman, the nation's 33rd president, signed Executive Order 9981. The order read in part:

It is hereby declared to be the policy of the President that there shall be equality of treatment and opportunity for all persons in the armed services without regard to race, color, religion or national origin. This policy shall be put into effect as rapidly as possible, having due regard to the time required to effectuate any necessary changes without impairing efficiency or morale.

Compared to some of Truman's momentous decisions after he attained his office following President Franklin D. Roosevelt's April 12, 1941 death, Executive Order 9981 was fairly innocuous. Like his others, though, it turned out to be significantly propitious. Even though his order was not carried out fully by early 1951, it provided one dubious benefit: equal opportunities to die ignominious deaths, regardless of race, religion, or gender.

Michael Czuboka, a member of the Canadian "Princess Patricia" Regiment, was appalled at the scene he and his comrades encountered in mid-February. It was unsettling for even the most hardened troops. These Canadians were relative neophytes when it came to combat. Thus, the sight literally sickened them, just as the scenes encountered by veterans like Frankville and McCoy affected them adversely.

Czuboka recalled the scene with remarkable clarity:

"In the middle of February 1951, our battalion was loaded onto trucks and half-tracks at Miryang in preparation for our move to the front, at that time about 200 kilometers (120 miles) to the north," he said. "I remember the cloudy skies, snow-covered valleys and mountains, icy and winding roads and the bitter sub-zero cold.

"It took us about two days to get from Miryang to the front. Very cold Arctic winds from nearby Siberia often descend down the Korean peninsula, and they certainly came frequently in the winter of 1950-51.

"As we arrived on our half-tracks at the Korean village of Kudun, near the front line, we were suddenly confronted with a scene of horror. I had never seen a dead body until that day, but now something like 68 black and mostly naked American bodies were scattered all around us. They had been bayoneted and shot by the Chinese, and their weapons and clothing had been removed.

"They were frozen solid and looked like black marble statues. Some were magnificent physical specimens, and I remember feeling overwhelmed with pity over their horrible fate."

The Canadians learned later that the dead soldiers had been a black infantry company. Color aside, they had met the same fate as many of their comrades, as Czuboka explained.

"Some had their ring fingers cut off, and their winter clothing, sleeping bags, boots and weapons had been removed. The Chinese coveted American clothing and weapons and took them whenever they could. Apparently these black American soldiers, led by white officers, had posted a single sentry on the previous evening and had not dug slit trenches."

Sadly, what he and his Canadian comrades witnessed was a small part of the picture.

Czuboka reported that although only about 68 bodies were counted on that day, it was subsequently reported that more than 200 had been killed.

"In later years I read a report by the Chinese Communist Forces (CCF) 116th Division that claimed that two companies of the U.S. 23rd Infantry Regiment had been annihilated at dawn on February 14, 1951," he revealed. "Since American infantry companies do hold about 100 soldiers, if two companies were wiped out, 200 dead seems like a reasonable estimate.

"The Chinese had a habit of removing dead bodies, and especially their own," he added.

Czuboka was so shocked by the bloody spectacle that he ate very little for the next several days.

"I knew that we were in a war," he said, "but I was not prepared for such a sudden and violent introduction. I noticed that my three companions on our half-track were also taking it badly. All had turned very pale and silent."

There was at least one bright spot in the discovery; it became a teaching moment for the Canadians. As Czuboka explained:

"Our commanding officer, Lieutenant-Colonel Jim Stone, considered this to be an important lesson for all of us. We would, in future, never be allowed to use sleeping bags in the front line. And needless to say, it became apparent that a strong contingent of sentries was always needed, and especially at dawn, the time when the Chinese preferred to attack."

It was a shame that so many American soldiers had to die to set up that lesson—and who was to blame for the reason behind it?

The question in the minds of veterans like Frankville and McCoy was why so many friendly troops died in and around Hoengsong and were left in place. They were not alone in wondering. Army brass wanted to find out as well. They set up an investigation of the Hoengsong massacre in an attempt to answer the question and apply what they learned to future operations. That was de rigueur after any massacre.

The ultimate answer could be found in two words" "command problems." The intro to the February 1-28, 1951, 38th Infantry Special Report, stamped "Secret," hinted loudly at the cause of the disaster at

Hoengsong. It read:

"In order that the Hoengsong action may be correctly evaluated, it is necessary to understand the command problems that were involved and the large area the 38th Infantry and attached units were spread over when the enemy started his counter-attack 112000 February.

UNIT	COMMANDER	COMPOSITION	LOCATION	MISSION
38th Inf	Col. John G. Coughlin	3rd Bn (-)	SAEMAL	secure road junction at Saemal
Hoengsong SF #21	* Lt Col Keith ** *** ****	Neth det 15th FA Bn A 'Btry 503 FA 1st Bn 38th D Btry 82 AAA	0785	Secure direct supt 8th ROK Div
ST "B"	Lt Kallmeyer *****	L Co., 38th Inf 2nd plt Tk Co 38th INF	0785	direct supt 21st ROK Rgt
2nd Bn 38th	Lt Col. Skeldon		WONJU	secure Wonju (Corps reserve)

* Commanded By: Lt Col den Ouden
**   Capt Jones
***   Lt. Col Keleher
**** Capt Stevens
***** Lt Mace"

The biggest questions, though, were ones that have been asked many times in different situations: what exactly constitutes a massacre, and can any one person be held responsible for one? And, should the name Hoengsong be entered in the annals of massacre history? Does it rise to the level of some of the more famous massacres?

CHAPTER 3

Massacre, Murder, And Mayhem: Never Pleasant Either Way

"We know about every massacre that has taken place close to the present, but the ones in the distant past are like trees falling in the forest with no one to hear them." (Steven Pinker)

LET'S PUT THE Hoengsong massacre in context compared to other historical massacres. However it is defined, massacre is not a word that should be thrown around loosely, although it is. Boston Massacre(s), St. Valentine's Day Massacre, Jonestown Massacre, My Lai Massacre, Malmedy Massacre, Beirut Massacre, Hoengsong Massacre, Saturday Night Massacre ...the word "massacre" is used in many contexts to define a loss in circumstances ranging from sporting events to political firings and battles in war. So-called massacres don't always involve death and mayhem.

Consider the "Saturday Night Massacre" that took place during former U.S. President Richard M. Nixon's tenure. It comprised a series of events on Saturday, October 20, 1973, during the Watergate scandal in the United States. Heads rolled, but not literally, as they sometimes do in military massacres.

Nixon ordered Attorney General Elliot Richardson to fire independent special prosecutor Archibald Cox. Richardson refused and resigned, effective immediately. So Nixon ordered Deputy Attorney General William Ruckelshaus to fire Cox. Ruckelshaus refused, and he resigned. That did not deter Nixon.

The president ordered the third-most-senior official at the Justice Department, Solicitor General Robert Bork, to fire Cox. Bork hesitated, but complied with Nixon's order. Neither the American public nor its political representatives were pleased with the chain of events, which was labeled a "massacre." No one was hurt—at least not physically—and everyone involved survived.

In the long run the fallout was more damaging to Nixon than anyone else, as a new special counsel was appointed on November 1, 1973. Two weeks later a court ruled that the dismissal had been illegal in the first place. The entire affair gave massacres a bad name.

The word massacre, seldom used in a positive vein, is applied occasionally to describe a devastating loss in a sporting contest, e.g., the "Tampa Bay Bucs massacred the Kansas City Chiefs in the 2021 Super Bowl, 31-3." That was hardly a massacre. Unlike in a real massacre, nobody died or got hurt, except for some fans' and players' feelings. The use of "massacre" in this context is completely innocuous.

In reality, the word normally does not evoke pleasant images in people's minds, and it is used indiscriminately. For some strange reason, for example, it is rarely used to describe a maritime disaster, as the cases of the USS Indianapolis and the Lusitania suggest.

(Incidentally, all of the cases presented here are treated in decidedly cursory fashions. The overviews do not touch on the related events in any great detail. Readers are free to pursue the details wherever they can find them—and there are ample sources available to help them in their pursuits.)

A Japanese submarine (I-58) torpedoed Indianapolis at 12:14 a.m. on July 30, 1945. The ship sank in only twelve minutes, carrying about 300 sailors of its 1,196-member crew down with it. (Some records indicate that there were 1,199 crew members, of whom 882 died.) The remaining 900 crew members were left floating in shark-infested waters with no lifeboats and no way to report their plight to Navy units elsewhere. Most of them did not have any food or water.

Almost two-thirds of the sailors who survived the initial explosion died in the water. Of the total crew, only 317 sailors survived the incident. Even though approximately 880 sailors died in the tragedy, it is not generally classified a massacre. Ditto the Lusitania.

On May 7, 1915, during World War I, German submarine U-12 sank the British ocean liner Lusitania off the coast of Kinsale, Ireland. The ship sank within eighteen minutes. Of the 1,959 passengers aboard, 1,198, including 128 Americans, perished. Despite the large loss of civilian life, the incident is not called a massacre. Maritime massacres simply do not occur, at least not according to the definition. They are not even referred to as murders in many cases.

There are differences between murder and massacre when the definitions are considered. We will leave the arguments to the nuances in the definitions to etymologists to debate. In real life, whether we label mass killings as murders or massacres is inconsequential. Both involve mayhem. Murder, massacre, and mayhem: they are all synonymous for purposes of this book—and the label is often determined by who dies and under what circumstances.

The term murder is generally reserved for incidents in which small numbers of people are killed by others. But, what is a "small number"—especially to the victims' loved ones? Seven people died as the result of the St. Valentine's Day "Massacre." That was 911 fewer than at Jonestown and almost 12,000 fewer than at Hoengsong, depending on who is doing the counting. The numbers do not lessen the pain for the people who survive the events—if any—or the grieving family members, relatives, and friends.

Any time people are killed purposely by others their deaths affect those they leave behind. So, if 2,000 people are killed in a single event, their loved ones single out the deaths of the people they knew as a part of a larger event. They want to know how their sons, daughters, fathers, mothers, etc., died and receive instructions about how to retrieve their bodies for proper burials.

Sometimes it is possible to find out how the victims of a murder or massacre died. The victims of the St. Valentine's Day Massacre were shot to death. The vast majority of the people who died at Jonestown used cyanide to kill themselves. Their bodies were retrievable and available for burial.

Neither manner of death nor retrieval of the bodies was entirely possible at Hoengsong for reasons that will be revealed later, although some families have received closure over the years as more remains of the victims of the battle are identified by the DPAA. The manner of death and lack of disposition of the bodies led to feelings of outrage among the first responders to the massacre, and an urge among them to avenge the victims' deaths—which they did.

The "Boston Massacre(s)"

There is no better example about the definition—or lack thereof—of a massacre than the March 5, 1770 "Boston Massacre." The British called it the "Boston Riot." Massacres, like so many other things in life, are in the eyes of the beholder.

Tempers were flaring among British soldiers and American colonists in 1770. The colonists were unhappy with King George III and his treatment of them after he hit them with the Townshend Acts, a series of laws passed by the British Parliament in 1768. The acts made clear that the parliament had the right to tax the colonists without

THE HOENGSONG VALLEY MASSACRE

their consent. The latter demurred. King George sent his soldiers to uphold his belief in taxation without representation.

The colonists and the soldiers did not develop strong bonds. On March 5, 1770, several Bostonians and British soldiers got into a pushing match. It escalated to the point where the soldiers felt threatened. They fired into the crowd, allegedly in "self-defense." They killed three colonists on the spot; two more died later. Eleven more were injured.

The "massacre" is often cited by historians as an opening act of the Revolutionary War, which did not start officially for another six years. And, to demonstrate another use—or misuse—of the word "massacre," there was a second Boston Massacre 202 years later in professional baseball when the New York Yankees beat the Boston Red Sox four games in a row in September by a combined score of 42-9. Nobody died—except for the Red Sox' pennant hopes—in the series, but sportswriters and fans labeled it a massacre nonetheless.

As the old saying goes, "words have meanings." Of course, the context in which they are used affects their meanings in given situations. Losing four baseball games does not constitute a massacre. The number of deaths and the circumstances at Hoengsong does, as will be evidenced later.

St. Valentine's Day Massacre

The Saint Valentine's Day Massacre was relatively minor as far as massacres go. Seven people died on February 14, 1929 when gangsters posing as Chicago police officers gunned down their rivals as part of a prohibition-era conflict.

Allegedly, four members of an organization run by the infamous Al Capone shot six people and an "intern" affiliated with George "Bugs" Moran's work team in a warehouse on Clark Street in Chicago. The crime appalled the citizens of Chicago—and even "upset" Al Capone, who was in Miami at the time, and allegedly knew nothing about the incident.

None of the shooters were ever tried for the murders, and the gang violence and under-the-table liquor sales continued. The "massacre" label was added to the incident because of the romantic nature of the holiday and the need to aggrandize its significance. Again, the definition of "massacre" is in the eyes of the beholder. For example, can an event be labeled a massacre if the victims kill themselves?

Jonestown Massacre

In a bizarre event at Jonestown, Guyana on November 18, 1978, 907 members of the People's Temple, a cult formed by the Reverend Jim Jones, ingested cyanide and died. In all, 918 people perished in and around the community. Naturally, outsiders labeled the suicides a massacre.

Philosophically, there is some question as to whether such an incident can be called a massacre if the victims died at their own hands—especially since some of them were babies who had no choice in the matter. Their parents administered the cyanide to them. Definitions aside, a large number of people died in one place at one time, which members of the press and outsiders depicted as a massacre, since the word has more cachet than "event" or "incident."

The families, friends, and associates of the seven men killed in the St. Valentine's Day incident would most likely agree with the use of the term massacre in the case of the St. Valentine's Day murders, as would those connected to the Jonestown victims. Others, i.e., those unaffected by the shootings, but who had a morbid fascination with them, would too. Disassociated people probably would not care one way or another. After all, depiction more than anything else plays a large part in the definition of massacre.

There was a scene in the fictional 2000 movie *The Patriot* in which British forces during the Revolutionary War locked scores of Americans in a church from the outside and set it ablaze. The scene was not real, but it was based on real events. Real or not, theatergoers cringed in revulsion as they watched the church go up in flames and the people inside died in agony in a fictional massacre. Director Roland Emmerich depicted the burning of the church and people as a heinous massacre. Therefore, it became a massacre in the eyes of the theatergoers.

Genuine massacres dredge up similar reactions, whether they involve civilians or military personnel. There is no one definition of massacre when used to describe a large loss of life. Generally, it suggests that large numbers of people died in a single incident. Certainly, the American military has suffered—and perpetrated—its share of massacres. Some, such as Hoengsong, are well known; some are not.

The military is not always anxious to label a particular action as a massacre or accept anyone else's definition of one, since doing so can lead to embarrassment and doubts about its leadership and efficiency. Nor is it always willing to release details of a gruesome killing of its troops.

American military leaders have at times tried to cover up certain actions that involved large numbers of service members' deaths or massacres they have perpetrated. They have not always been successful. Names like USS Indianapolis, My Lai, and Hoengsong come to mind, although the latter is less well known.

The sinking of Indianapolis is arguably the worst disaster in U.S. Navy history. The ship was on a secret mission to deliver the atomic bomb from San Francisco to Tinian to be dropped later on Japan. The bombing in itself might have been described as a massacre, although it generally wasn't.

Indianapolis had completed its mission and was returning to the naval base at Leyte when the Japanese submarine attacked. Per orders, Captain Charles Butler McVay III was maintaining radio silence, which became unnecessary after the ship sank. All communications were lost aboard Indianapolis after the torpedo struck. That explains in part why it took three days for a Navy patrol aircraft to spot the site of the sinking during a routine patrol on August 2nd.

Navy administrators were not pleased with the outcome of the ship's mission, the fact that 880 sailors died, or that people were pressing it for an explanation as to why Indianapolis sank. To placate critics, the Navy conducted an "investigation" of the incident. The results were questionable.

The Navy awarded Captain McVay a court-martial, despite protests from Admirals Chester Nimitz and Raymond Spruance. Naval authorities in Washington, particularly Secretary of the Navy James Forrestal and Chief of Naval Operations Admiral Ernest King, scheduled a court-martial to begin on December 3, 1945, at the Washington Navy Yard. Subsequently, the Navy found McVay guilty of "hazarding his ship by failing to zigzag."

Even Mochitsura Hashimoto, the commander of the Japanese submarine that torpedoed Indianapolis, found that laughable. He testified that zig-zagging would not have made a difference. The evidence uncovered in the investigation suggested that the navy, not McVay, should have been court-martialed. The navy did not see it that way.

The court-martial board convicted McVay in what was considered by many people to be a circus trial designed to protect the navy's reputation. The conviction—not to mention the court-martial—was unusual. The navy lost more than 370 ships during World War II, and McVay was the only commander singled out for court-martial. He paid a stiff price that ruined his navy career. At least he was not discharged altogether.

The following year, Admiral Nimitz, who had replaced Admiral King as Chief of Naval Operations, requested that Secretary Forrestal remit McVay's sentence and restore him to duty. Forrestal agreed. McVay completed his service at the New Orleans Naval District and retired in 1949 with the rank of Rear Admiral. He, too, became a victim of the Indianapolis sinking in effect when he committed suicide in 1968.

Thirty-two years later, President William Clinton signed legislation that exonerated McVay of blame in the loss of the ship and the deaths of the sailors who perished. Thus, the scapegoat in a massacre that was not referred to as such had his name restored, but too late for him to learn about it. Technically, Captain McVay's conviction remains on his record. The U.S. military is not in the habit of overturning court-martial verdicts. There is not even a process to do so.

The Navy could have avoided all the adverse publicity by treating the incident as what it really was: a misfortunate result of war to which there should have been no individual blame assigned. The same can be said of other "massacres," whether they are labeled such or not.

The British were as embarrassed by the Lusitania's sinking as was the U.S. Navy over the loss of Indianapolis. Captain William Thomas Turner and Captain McVay had a couple things in common: they were forced into ignominy by circumstances beyond their control, they were singled out for blame, and they were exonerated eventually. Exoneration, however, is not synonymous with historical cleansing.

Turner, like McVay, did not go down with his ship. The British Admiralty formed a board of inquiry to ascertain who was to blame for the sinking. There was not a lot of doubt who that person would be. It was Turner.

Critics claim that evidence that would have established Turner's innocence was not introduced at the inquiry. They suggest that was done to protect the Admiralty, which had failed Turner in two major ways: it had loaded large stores of munitions aboard a civilian ship without acknowledging it publicly, and it had withdrawn the Lusitania's warship escort, HMS Juno.

According to some historical accounts, the Admiralty deliberately falsified accounts of the sinking in order to put itself in a positive light. The board charged Turner with failure to zig-zag and accused him of gross negligence and treasonable behavior. They even asserted that he was on the Germans' payroll! At least the U.S. Navy did not go that far to discredit McVay.

The charges against Turner did not stick—but the memory of them did. Even though Cunard gave Turner two more ships to command, Ultonia and Ivernia, the latter of which was torpedoed by a German submarine on January 1, 1917, he could not live down the charges the British Admiralty had leveled against him.

The British government tried to placate Turner by awarding him the coveted O.B.E. (Order of the British Empire) in 1918, but that did not remove the stigma against him. (The O.B.E. is an award granted to British citizens for merit. The motto is "For God and the Empire." There are five levels of the award. Turner received the fourth level in the seniority chain.) He retired and tried to live in seclusion. That did not work.

In 1921 Winston Churchill published a four-volume work of history, *The World Crisis*, in which he included the charges against Turner. Churchill tamed them a bit, but the damage was done. Turner never lived down the charges leveled against him, and he died a bitter man on June 23, 1933.

Over the years his reputation was restored, ever so gradually. But, as in McVay's case, his reputation was damaged beyond repair. As is often the case, somebody has to pay the price for an embarrassing massacre—and it is rarely anybody at a high command level. Enter Lt. William Calley, U.S. Army.

The massacre at My Lai, Vietnam was a real tragedy of war. (People often forget there was another hamlet involved, named My Khe.) Between 347 and 504 civilians, most of them women, children, and elderly people, died in the killings. This incident is a classic example of the thin line between murder and a massacre and what happens when authorities try to cover up a heinous event.

In all probability, had any of the slain people at the hamlets been enemy combatants, the killings would not have been labeled a massacre, because some of the victims were soldiers trying to defend themselves. The killings would have been justifiable under such circumstances. That turned out not to be the case, however. Investigators determined that the killings at My Lai and My Khe were nothing less than murder, ergo a massacre.

On March 16, 1968, battle-tested U.S. Army soldiers of "Charlie" Company, 1st Battalion, 20th Infantry, 11th Infantry Brigade, Americal Division, entered several hamlets to search for enemy soldiers of the 48th Battalion of the NLF (National Front for the Liberation of South Vietnam), who had been operating in the area. The Americans' orders, which may have been unclear, were to find the enemy, wipe them out, burn the houses of the villagers, who may or may not have been Viet Cong sympathizers, kill their livestock, destroy foodstuffs, and close the wells. The purpose of the devastation was to deprive the enemy of materiel they could use to support their operations.

Matters got out of hand quickly when the American soldiers reached the hamlets. They exceeded their orders and went on a murderous rampage. A few members of the unit tried to stop the killings, but to no avail. By the time the soldiers were through they had killed hundreds of villagers. They moved on after the "battle" and continued fighting elsewhere.

Remarkably, the massacre was not made known until November 1969, when an independent investigative journalist named Seymour Hirsh broke the story. Despite several attempts by different people, civilian and military alike, to alert the U.S. Army to what had happened at My Lai and the other hamlets, Army officials dragged their heels on investigating the events. Finally, mounting pressure forced them to conduct an investigation.

At first, the Army claimed that its soldiers had killed 128 Viet Cong and 22 civilians in a significant battle at the hamlets. General William C. Westmoreland, Military Assistance Command, Vietnam (MACV) commander, even congratulated the unit on their outstanding job. (MACV was the designated term for the United States' unified command structure for all of its military forces in South Vietnam during the Vietnam War. General Westmoreland commanded U.S. military operations in Vietnam from 1964–68. He employed a strategy of attrition against the National Liberation Front of South Vietnam and the North Vietnamese Army.) Not all of Westmoreland's fellow Army officers agreed with his assessment.

Different Army officers, e.g., Major Colin Powell and General William R. Peers, conducted separate investigations into the My Lai massacre. None of the findings were particularly damning to the soldiers who had participated in the killings. There were a few soldiers singled out for blame—several of whom were dead by the time the investigations were concluded. Results aside, the Army finally got around to holding a court-martial.

It wasn't until November 17, 1970, almost three years after the massacre occurred, that the Army acted. On that day it charged fourteen officers with suppressing information related to the incident. Among them was Major General Samuel W. Koster, the Americal Division's commanding officer.

The Army dropped most of the charges eventually. Only one officer, Brigade Commander Colonel Oran K. Henderson, who had ordered the attack, actually stood trial on charges, but they were related to the cover-up, not the killings. Either way, he walked free. Henderson was acquitted on December 17, 1971.

Twenty-six other officers and enlisted soldiers faced charges as well. The prosecution used a theory of "command responsibility" to pursue a conviction. One of the defendants, Lieutenant William Calley, was charged with several counts of premeditated murder. The others were charged with related charges. Of those 26 soldiers, only Calley was convicted.

On March 29, 1971, the court-martial board found Calley guilty of premeditated murder for ordering the shootings. He was sentenced to life in prison—or two days, whichever was longer. Two days after the sentence was pronounced, President Richard M. Nixon ordered Calley's release from prison pending appeal of his sentence. Nixon's decision was controversial, but it worked in Calley's behalf. His sentence was modified later. Eventually, he served four and one-half months in a military prison at Fort Benning, Georgia.

Calley alleged during his trial that he was merely following the orders of his commanding officer, Captain Ernest Medina, at My Lai. There was some truth to his defense, although Medina denied giving any such orders. (Command responsibility is the doctrine of hierarchical accountability in cases of war crimes. It was established by the Hague Conventions IV (1907) and X (1907) and applied for the first time by the German Supreme Court in Leipzig in 1921 after World War I. Today, it is known as the Medina Standard.)

Captain Medina was not held blameless in the My Lai massacre. He was tried separately. Like most of his fellow defendants, he was acquitted of all charges, effectively negating the prosecution's theory of "command responsibility." He admitted later that he had suppressed evidence and had lied to Colonel Henderson about the number of civilian deaths.

It took almost forty years for Calley to say publicly that he was sorry for what happened at My Lai. During a speech to the Kiwanis club of Greater Columbus, Georgia, on August 19, 2009, he said, "There is not a day that goes by that I do not feel remorse for what happened that day in My Lai. I feel remorse for the Vietnamese who were killed, for their families, for the American soldiers involved and their families.

MASSACRE, MURDER, AND MAYHEM: NEVER PLEASANT EITHER WAY

I am very sorry."

At least he lived to say he was sorry for his role in a massacre. One of his predecessors, George A. Custer, who was on the receiving end of one, did not.

On June 25-26 1876, Lakota (a branch of the Sioux tribe), Northern Cheyenne, and Arapaho Native Americans teamed up at the Little Bighorn River in eastern Montana to attack elements of the U.S. Seventh Cavalry, including a battalion of nearly 700 troopers led (or misled) by Lieutenant Colonel George Armstrong Custer. (The actual number is reputed to be 647. Historians have debated for years the real numbers of participants on both sides.) The Indians, who called the fighting the Battle of the Greasy Grass, routed the cavalry, wiping out five of Custer's twelve companies.

Contrary to some people's beliefs, the Indian allies did not wipe out Custer's entire battalion. They killed 268 soldiers and scouts and wounded 55 more, compared to 36-136 Native Americans killed and 168 wounded. The U.S. dead included Custer, two of his brothers, Boston and Thomas, nephew Henry Reed, and his brother-in-law, James Calhoun. Not all of the slain troopers were identified after the battle, which is a sad fact about many massacres.

Other 7th Cavalry troops led by General Albert S. Terry reached the battlefield to save what was left of Custer's troops. By the time they discovered the dead troopers, some of the bodies had been mutilated beyond recognition. Others were too badly decomposed to be identified. That is one of the sad outcomes of combat—particularly massacres.

One of the worst things for the families of soldiers killed or missing in action is being unable to find out exactly how their loved ones died—or if they died. There is some solace involved for them in knowing the truth. Massacres often make the truth impossible to determine. That was the case with "Custer's Last Stand"—and Hoengsong.

At Hoengsong, there were too many Chinese for the UN troops to fight effectively. In Montana, there were too many Native Americans for Custer to fend off. Estimates place the number of Native Americans at somewhere between 900 and 1,800—or as many as 2,500. Regardless of the actual figure, Custer was outnumbered. That did not faze him. He did not stop to count the enemy; he just blundered into their trap, and he and his troops paid the price.

Historically, the battle was just one more skirmish in the lengthy wars fought between the U.S. Army and various tribes for control of western lands. Its popularity—if indeed a tragic loss of so many lives can be called "popular"—is due to the public's perception of Custer as a valiant soldier who took on a force far larger than his, but which he believed was inferior in fighting skills. His popularity was one of the reasons there was no serious investigation by the Army after the battle into what wrong.

There was an attempt to initiate an investigation. But, the nation was celebrating its first centennial, and Custer's wife, Elizabeth Bacon Custer, did not help the Army much. She was highly protective of George's reputation and hindered serious attempts at an investigation until she died. Unfortunately for potential investigators, she did not pass away until 1933—57 years after the battle took place. By that time, any evidence that existed on the battlefield was gone.

One of the vagaries of military history is that the Battle of the Little Big Horn was considered a massacre but the worst defeat Native Americans ever inflicted on the U.S. Army was not. On 4 November 1791, a combined force of Miami, Shoshone, Delaware, and Potawatomi Native Americans killed about 600 U.S soldiers led by Revolutionary War hero General Arthur St. Clair at the Battle of the Wabash in the Northwest Territory. The battle is generally known as St. Clair's Defeat, rather than a massacre.

As a practical matter, the Army accepted Custer's loss as an inevitable outcome of war, and the nation assigned the "massacre" to history under "romantic defeats" to save his reputation as a dashing, courageous military leader. Realistically, that was not the case.

In truth, Custer was a rather arrogant leader who refused to listen to scouts and fellow officers' advice and engaged in a battle he could not win, to the detriment of his troops. Such are the makings of massacres, not all of which can be prevented.

German SS combat troops of Kampfgruppe Peiper, (part of the 1st SS Panzer Division), murdered 84 American troops at Malmedy, Belgium on December 17, 1944, during the Battle of the Bulge. (Actually, these killings occurred at Baugnez, but there were so many similar murders in the region that they are all lumped under the name Malmedy, which was a center of operations in the area.) The number of slain Americans did not approximate those at Custer's Last Stand or aboard Indianapolis. The news of the massacre created at least equal the outrage.

It wasn't long after the massacre occurred that almost every newspaper and radio station in the United States publicized the story of the German atrocity. It was, after all, the worst mass killing of U.S. troops in Europe since 1941, when President Franklin D. Roosevelt declared war on Germany. It paled in comparison to the number of people killed in various "camps" by the Germans throughout the war or at Katyn Forest in 1940 when Russian secret police murdered approximately 22,000 Polish military officers, police officers, and intelligentsia. But, these 84 soldiers were Americans, which raised the ire of the people back home.

The atrocity was due in part to Hitler's foreboding about the outcome of the war. He ordered his commanders to offer no quarter to enemy combatants or Belgian citizens as they tried to stop the allies from reaching Germany. It was his way of demonstrating that the Germans were no longer the "nice guys." The lesson did not have its desired effect.

During the afternoon of December 17th, German troops trapped a convoy of about thirty vehicles containing members of the American 285th Field Artillery Observation Battalion (FAOB) and other units. They were en route to St. Vith to join the 7th Armored Division. German tankers opened fire on the convoy, and immobilized its first and last vehicles, a tactic the Chinese used successfully at Hoengsong. That brought the convoy to a halt; the lightly armed Americans (compared to the tanks and tankers) surrendered.

The prisoners were taken to an open field, where they joined other Americans who had been captured earlier. There were about 130 prisoners all together. According to eyewitnesses, German SS troops using machine guns began shooting the prisoners without provocation. Germans claimed later that some of the prisoners started the firing by using hidden weapons or that others tried to escape. The evidence refuted their claims.

Some Americans managed to escape the immediate scene and hid in a café at a nearby crossroad. The Germans discovered them, lit the building on fire (a la the church in *The Patriot*), and shot the Americans who tried to escape. A few prisoners tried to play dead, but Germans walked among the bodies and shot anyone who looked to be alive. A month later, investigators found a total of **88** Americans with head wounds inflicted by gunfire.

Forty-three fortunate prisoners managed to escape and reached Malmedy, which was in American hands at the time. They reported the incident. Rumors started spreading among the other American troops that the Germans were executing prisoners indiscriminately. At least one American unit commander issued orders to shoot any German prisoners in retaliation.

Since the site of the massacre was in "no man's land," investigators were unable to reach it until January 14, 1945. They were still finding bodies as late as April 15th. The evidence suggested that the slain Americans were victims of deliberate murders. Worse, there were

MASSACRE, MURDER, AND MAYHEM: NEVER PLEASANT EITHER WAY

stories of other murders perpetrated on soldiers and citizens alike in the area. American commanders determined to find the Germans responsible—which they did.

In May and June 1946, a Tribunal tried more than seventy German commanders and soldiers for the murders at Malmedy and the surrounding area. The court pronounced 43 death sentences and 22 life sentences. Eight other men were sentenced to shorter prison sentences.

None of the death sentences were carried out. Eventually, most of the sentences were commuted, and all the prisoners were released by December 1956, almost six years after the next massacres of American troops occurred at Hoengsong and Chaun-ni and 27 years before the killings at Beirut, Lebanon.

The Beirut massacre occurred on October 23, 1983 when terrorists drove bomb-laden trucks into the U.S. Marine and French barracks during a Lebanese civil war. The coordinated attacks killed 241 American service members: 220 Marines, 18 sailors, and 3 soldiers. Another sixty Americans were wounded.

The French did not suffer as badly numbers wise: 58 paratroopers were killed and 15 were wounded. There were six civilians killed in the blasts as well. The combined losses were devastating to the units involved, and embarrassing to the countries whose military forces were the targets.

The troops were in Lebanon as part of a multinational peacekeeping force stationed there after Israel's invasion of the country in 1982 and the ensuing withdrawal of the Palestine Liberation Organization (PLO). The attack had its intended effect on the multinational force. Its ground troops were withdrawn from Beirut after the explosions. The Marines were moved offshore, and six months after the bombing all multinational troops were gone from Lebanon.

There was a half-hearted attempt on the Americans' part to get to the bottom of the situation. President Reagan proposed retaliatory attacks on some of the alleged perpetrators, but Secretary of Defense Casper Weinberger talked him out of them. A U.S. grand jury indicted a senior member of a Lebanese terrorist group, Hezbollah, but he was never apprehended. Ironically, he died in a car bombing in Syria on February 12, 2008.

Reagan appointed a military commission to determine why the bombing occurred without any resistance. One of their findings involved an old chestnut in investigations of massacres: the military chain of command broke down. The commissioners determined that if the guards had been armed, they might have been able to stop the bombers from driving into the barracks. Likewise, if there had been something stronger than barbed wire in place to stop the trucks the disaster could have been averted.

Families of some of the victims filed civil suits against Iran, which many Americans believed were behind the bombings. The Iranian government denied any involvement, and the U.S. government never determined who was at fault. Gradually, the issue faded away, and another massacre went into history books as a footnote to world events.

The same thing happened to the subjects of this book, the thousands of allied soldiers who died, were captured, are still missing in action, or who survived the February 11-13, 1951 debacle at Hoengsong, South Korea.

CHAPTER 4

Setting Up The Story

> *"It appears that it is as necessary to provide soldiers with defensive arms of every kind as to instruct them in the use of offensive ones. For it is certain a man will fight with greater courage and confidence when he finds himself properly armed for defense."* (Vecetius: Military Institutions of the Romans)

THERE WERE TEN distinct phases of the Korean War, which reflected the back-and-forth swings in the early stages of the conflict. The first three were the UN Defensive (June 27-Sept. 15, 1950), the UN Offensive (Sept. 15-Nov. 2, 1950), and the Communist Forces Offensive (Nov. 3, 1950-Jan. 24, 1951). The Battle at Hoengsong was part of the fourth phase: the first United Nations (UN) counteroffensive.

Operation Roundup

At the end of 1950 communist troops launched a major offensive near Seoul, concentrating on crossing the Imjin River, north of the city. They posed a big enough threat to the UN troops that General Ridgway feared they would surround his position. On January 3, 1951, to everyone's surprise, he ordered UN troops to evacuate Seoul. The Chinese, who were as surprised as anyone else, entered the city and used it as a jumping off point for operations to the south.

Communist troops were particularly active as they moved east towards the mountainous central region of Korea, and then headed south through the mountains on a line through Hongchon (where they set up a base), Hoengsong, and Wonju. Their goal was to reach a position behind the U.S. I Corps and IX Corps, from which they could attack the highway and railroad between Hongch'on and the port of Pusan, the UN's main north-south supply route. Their offensive was made easier when large numbers of ROK (Republic of Korea) units withdrew.

In order to thwart the enemy's plans, UN commanders implemented a series of military operations designed to locate and deter the communists. One of them, Operation Roundup, led to the Hoengsong Massacre.

Operation Roundup, which began on February 5th, was designed to envelop the town of Hongchon to trap the enemy forces operating south of it. It involved the ROK 3rd, 5th, and 8th Divisions and the ROK III Corps, which were assigned to carry out a pincer movement to capture Hongchon. The 38th Regiment of the U.S. Army's 2nd Division, reinforced by the Netherlands Detachment, would provide infantry and artillery support after a few days.

At the outset, the regiment limited its activities to close-in patrolling to prevent any possibility of engaging in fights with the 8th ROK Division. Commanders were afraid the Americans would improperly identify the members of the 8th ROK Division as enemy troops as they moved through the 38th's zone and open fire. Misidentifying ROK troops had been a problem for UN troops before, and would continue to be for a while.

The operation began smoothly. Allied units progressed six to twelve miles west, north, and northwest of the strategically important town of Hoengsong. The town was located near the road center of Wonju, where the U.S. Army 2nd Division and its allies maintained a supply and communications center. Control of the roads in the area was vital, since there were so few of them.

ROK troops did not meet any resistance until February 6th as they moved north. For all intents and purposes, they might as well have been operating independently, since coordination among them was limited. The ROK 5th Division, moving on the right, could not keep up with its 8th Division partner to the west, even though the 8th was not moving with any great haste. The ROK III Corps could not keep up the pace either. Worse, the inclusion of so many ROK units left a gaping hole in the U.S. X Corps' right flank.

By the 8th of February, North Korean troops were attacking the U.S. X Corps' exposed right flank. They were doing what communist forces did best: probing for weak spots along UN units' flanks. When they found them—as they invariably did—they directed their troops through the gaps and attacked from behind.

UN commanders, aware of the enemy's strategy, assigned the ROK 5th Division to take up blocking positions along X Corps' exposed flank, which removed it from the pincer movement. That left the ROK 3rd Division to attack Hongchon from the east, while the ROK 8th Division moved to the west. On February 9th, UN commanders, exercising their penchant for moving troops around for reasons that were not always apparent, attached the ROK 3rd Division to the X Corps for operational control and ordered it to move by truck to an assembly area immediately northwest of Hoengsong. The division's orders were to report to the assembly area no later than 8 a.m. on February 11th— and be prepared for immediate tactical employment.

The movements were made between February 8-11, a timeframe that turned out to be the proverbial calm before the storm. It may have been relatively calm, but many units were incurring a small, but steady, number of casualties as Operations Roundup and Thunderbolt overlapped. In a sign of things to come, 22 men from the 9th Infantry Regiment were KIA on February while attacking and securing Hill 444 in the area of Soju. These ongoing, relatively small losses by different units at the time were about to change with the opening salvos of the Battle of Hoengsong.

Starting on February 12th and lasting two days, the CCF, reeling from losses in the first half of the month, launched a major counter-attack in the area north of Wonju. The Hoengsong Valley was enveloped quickly in this attack, swallowing up entire American units from the 2nd Infantry Division in the process.

The 3rd ROK Division played an integral part during the Hoengsong ambush. According to LtCol Rollins S. Emmerick, if it weren't for one battalion of the 3rd ROK Division the entire 2,400-member force might have been annihilated. Perhaps that explains why one newspaper report a month after the battle said the "American casualties were relatively light" at Hoengsong.

Emmerick, a United States Military Advisory Group to the Republic of Korea Military Advisory Group (KMAG) advisor to the division, said that one battalion of the 18th regiment fought its way over the mountains flanking the road on which the ambushed force was traveling.

"It would have been a lot worse if it hadn't been for those ROKs," he said. "They went to the rescue and pushed up both sides of the road. They kept the Chinese from sending in reinforcements and killed off just about all of the attacking force."

He opined that the ROKs never got the credit they deserved for the action. "It was one of the bravest feats of the war, but because of the heavy fighting at the time and right after the ambush the word never got out," Emmerick explained. Their valiant service did not end there.

He recalled that after the 3rd ROK Division threw a protective arm around the GIs caught in the ambush they pulled back into the lines and held on to the Wonju front between the U.S. 2d Division on the left and the U.S. Marines 1st Division on the right. The 3rd ROK Division was responsible for a line that extended 8,000 yards. The Americans were no doubt happy to have at least one reliable ROK unit there.

As the ROK divisions headed north, they and the U.S. Army X Corps met with more serious resistance. The signs of a significant enemy build-up were becoming more and more obvious to UN commanders, which portended to have an adverse effect on Operation Roundup. But, they had a safety valve positioned around Hoengsong, between Wonju and Hongchon: the 38th Regiment of the U.S. Army's 2nd Division and its Netherlands attachment.

Early in February 1951 the 38th Regiment, comprising three battalions and the Netherlands Battalion (aka the Dutch), occupied high ground in the vicinity of Hoengsong. Their mission was to secure the area from enemy incursions and support Operation Roundup. The assignment was difficult at best. However, Army commanders' decisions made it almost impossible to carry out when they separated the three U.S. battalions and removed them from regimental control.

First, they moved the 2nd Bn. to Wonju, fourteen miles south of Hoengsong, and put it in reserve. The 1st Bn. and Company L of the 3rd Bn. were assigned to support the Republic of Korea (ROK) 8th Division. That left the remainder of the 3rd Bn. to stay with the Dutch battalion. Then the Army moved it to Saemal, about four miles north of Hoengsong, because the 8th ROK Division seemed to lack aggressiveness during its initial maneuverings.

Clark L. Ruffner, the Commanding General of the 2d Division, advised LtCol John Keith, the 38th RCT (Regimental Combat Team) commander, to prepare his 3d Bn. for possible commitment in the Saemal area to support and energize the ROK 8th Division. He cautioned Keith not to move unless the ROK 8th Division failed to advance or got bogged down. That division had shown early signs of hesitancy.

The 8th ROK Division ran into trouble shortly after launching its attack. The U.S. Army's 2nd Div. HQ received reports early in the operation about attacks by a Chinese division. KMAG officials denied the legitimacy of the reports. In fact, they said, the reports had been exaggerated greatly.

That inconsistent intelligence information put the UN commanders at a disadvantage, which had been a problem for them since the onset of the war. The lack of reliable intelligence and poor communications became a significant problem for all the UN units operating in the Hoengsong area between February 11th and 13th.

2nd Div. artillery then reported that a ROK unit had stampeded when some 9th Inf. tanks fired into a small enemy patrol group to their rear. The reports of ROK troop skittishness were not auspicious. What was not exaggerated was the knowledge that a large number of enemy patrols were conducting continuous recon operations in the Hongchon–Hoengsong axis. The question in many UN commanders' minds was what would happen when the ROK troops confronted heavy concentrations of enemy troops, as they inevitably would.

So, the decision to reposition the 2nd Bn., 38th Regt. was based on sound reasoning. But, it left the Dutch to hold Hoengsong alone. That turned out to be fortuitous for the 38th Regt., even if was not planned to be. Overall, though, the shifting of battalions turned out to be a critical command error. The ROK divisions did not coordinate their operations effectively due to a salient lack of communications with one another.

Because the ROK division commanders did not have clear ideas of their separate areas of responsibility, they left their individual flanks exposed. Enemy commanders took full advantage of the ROKs' tactical lapse. It gave them an unobstructed avenue of approach for counter-attacks, which they launched with full and deadly fury.

Fury and problems galore

On the night of February 11th, the communists launched their massive counter-attacks, which quickly turned into a rout that the UN forces could not stop. They withdrew southeast, back toward Hoengsong. The 1st and 3rd Battalions engaged in a desperate fight for survival, aided somewhat by the ROK troops that had initiated the original offensive and significantly by the Dutch battalion that stood fast at Hoengsong—but without the critical artillery and air support they needed to facilitate their withdrawal.

A select list of the significant problems the withdrawing troops encountered included:

- The refusal of the Commanding General of the 8th ROK Division to approve defensive artillery fires for the 1st and 3rd Battalion personnel in the ROK sector
- The inability of the ROK officers to rally their disorganized troops once the enemy counter-attack began
- The lack of reinforcements for beleaguered U.S. troops due to the unwillingness of the ROK soldiers to stay and fight
- Enemy soldiers infiltrated the fleeing ROK troops and gained easy access to friendly positions as a result
- The absence of clear identification insignia among ROK soldiers to differentiate them from their Chinese and North Korean enemies
- The encumbrance of vehicles utilized by the UN troops to transport personnel, weapons, and supplies. They became hindrances, rather than assets.
- The necessity of sticking to the only north-south road available between Hongchon and Hoengsong due to the need for vehicles and tanks
- The roadblocks established by the enemy all along the road, which had to be eliminated one by one as the friendly forces withdrew

- The lack of reserves available to UN commanders, other than the members of battalion headquarters units and extraneous personnel, who had to be organized and committed on the fly
- The loss of large numbers of intelligence specialists in both regiments during the withdrawal, and a dearth of trained people to replace them
- The unavailability of air support, reserved for the ROK 8th Division, which was for all intents and purposes nonfunctional as the withdrawal began

Despite these impediments, survivors of the UN units reached Wonju on February 13th, battered beyond belief, and still hardly out of danger. There were more battles and casualties to come following what can only be described as the massacre at Hoengsong.

CHAPTER 5

The 36 Stratagems

"If you have equal or inferior skills, you must use strategy to succeed." The basis of 36 Stratagems

"EVER MORE RUMORS come in about the encircled Americans, they shall have been massacred by the hundreds," Elie Van Schilt wrote. "It is indeed a valley of the dead, they are entrapped like rats in a trap. Now the Chinese have occupied the mountains on both flanks. The ROK divisions do nothing, retreat while leaving all their material behind."

How did that happen?

To understand what happened at Hoengsong and why it happened, it helps to understand the 36 stratagems the North Korean and Chinese troops applied early in the war. (Readers who do not care to connect the dots are encouraged to skip forward a chapter to the start of the battle, which was something the actual participants were not eager to do.) Their strategies and tactics were for the most part unconventional for the UN troops, to say the least.

To be fair, it must be noted that the communists violated their own stratagems at times. Both the North Koreans and Chinese overextended their supply lines occasionally, which allowed UN forces to regroup and inflict serious damage on them. And the Chinese, who were highly effective at holding the high ground, especially at Chosin, came down occasionally to fight UN troops on roads and open territory or attack in the daylight hours and suffered significant losses as a result.

On the bright side, UN leaders adapted some of the communist tactics and strategies to their advantage as the war progressed. For instance, the U.S. Marines learned early in the war to leave the roads and take the high ground, which put a crimp in Chinese operations. Until the allied forces adapted to or applied some of the 36 steps the communists held a decided edge in the fighting.

Some UN military leaders had been exposed to the 36 stratagems during the fighting in the Pacific during WWII and to a lesser extent during the civil war between the Chinese communists and nationalists between 1945 and 1950. Most of them, however, had no experience with them. That posed a problem for UN troops in the first year of the war, even though the warfighting philosophy employed by the Chinese and North Koreans was nothing new. It was almost 300 years old, in fact, at the time the war in Korea began in June 1950.

About three centuries ago an unknown writer compiled 36 military stratagems named The Secret Art of War (not to be confused with Sun Tzu's definitive classic on warfare, The Art of War). They have been attributed at different times to Sun Tzu from the Spring and Autumn Period of China or Zhuge Liang of the Three Kingdoms period. Historians do not believe that either of them is the true author.

The prevailing view is that the Thirty-Six Stratagems may have originated in both written and oral history, with many different versions compiled by different authors throughout Chinese history. The source of the ideas contained is relatively unimportant. What was important at the outset of the Korean War was that the North Koreans and Chinese applied them effectively.

The Secret Art of War is divided into six sections, each containing six stratagems:

A. When in a superior position

B. For confrontation

C. For attack

D. For confused situations

E. For gaining ground

F. For desperate situations

Each section is broken down below. The interpretations are by no means exact or meant to be taken literally. Even the Chinese and North Koreans used different words to describe the strategies. Regardless of the phrasing they used during the Korean War, their individual goals were the same: confuse and destroy the UN troops by using eastern-style military tactics with which the westerners were unfamiliar.

Their approach worked at first, and the UN troops paid a terrible price as they were tortured, executed, and treated harshly as prisoners of war (POWs), especially in the first few months of the fighting, when the North Koreans were going it alone. The Chinese were a little less brutal when they entered the war, ostensibly in October 1950, although evidence suggests they were actually in theater well before that. It was just that Generals MacArthur and Almond and other senior U.S. Army leaders refused to believe it, despite significant intelligence reports to the contrary.

The "Hoengsong Valley Massacre" was the culmination of the 36 Stratagems approach. Later, many Chinese troops paid with their own lives—although that was not widely publicized—for their brutality and "indiscretions" at Hoengsong.

In all probability, many of the Chinese troops had no idea of what the stratagems were. They simply followed orders, as good soldiers do. We have the advantage of hindsight and can see how at least some of the stratagems were applied at the massacre site. Let's take a look at them.

A. Stratagems when in a superior position

1. Sneak across the ocean in broad daylight:

   - Create a front that eventually becomes imbued with an atmosphere or impression of familiarity, within which the strategist may maneuver unseen while all eyes are trained to see obvious familiarities.
   - Combat application: Hiding your motion in motion. Example: light hopping in sparring can hide your attack.

2. Surround one state to save another.

   - When a strong group is about to take over a weaker group, a third party can "have its cake and eat it too," gaining a good reputation by attacking the aggressor in apparent behalf of the defender, and also eventually absorb the weakened defender to boot, without incurring the same opprobrium that would be leveled at outright aggression.
   - Combat application: Protecting a loved one or friend.

3. Borrow a sword to attack another, i.e., kill somebody by using another person's knife

   - When one side in a conflict is weakening, it may draw its own friends into battle, thus delivering a blow to its enemy while conserving its own strength.
   - Combat application: Literally disarm the attacker and use their weapon.

THE 36 STRATAGEMS

4. Face the weary enemy in a condition of ease.

    - You force others to expend energy while you preserve yours. You tire opponents out by sending them on wild goose chases, or by making them come to you from far away while you stand your ground.
    - Combat application: Stay out of your attackers' range and make them expend energy on useless attacks.

5. Plunge into a fire to pull off a robbery, i.e., loot a burning house

    - You use others' troubles as opportunities to gain something for yourself.
    - Combat application: Take advantage of your attackers' disadvantages, e.g., if the sun, rain, wind gets in their eyes, they become distracted by other conditions, etc.

6. Feint east, strike west.

    - You spread misleading information about your intentions, or make false suggestions, in order to induce the opponent to concentrate his defenses on one front and thereby leave another front vulnerable to attack.
    - Combat application: Feint, fake. In sparring, fake a low kick and follow with a high strike when your attacker lowers their defense.

B. Stratagems for confrontation

7. Make something from nothing.

    - You create a false idea in the mind of the opponent, and fix it in his mind as a reality. This means that you convey the impression that you have what you do not, so you may appear formidable to obtain a security that you had not enjoyed before.

- Combat application: Use ruses to plant ideas in the enemies' minds that lead them to believe you have something that can be used to your advantage.

8. Cross the territory via a hidden path.

- Pretend to travel along one path while secretly going along another.
- Combat application: Fake left, go right

9. Watch the fire from the opposite bank of the river, i.e., act unconcerned.

- Watch calmly when enemies experience internal troubles, and wait for them to destroy themselves.
- Combat application: Take advantage of any environmental distractions or misfortunes your attacker may suffer.

10. Hide a sword in a smile.

- Ingratiate yourself with enemies, inducing them to trust you. Once you acquire their confidence, you can move against them clandestinely.
- Combat application: Don't let your enemy know that you are about to attack.

11. One tree falls for another.

- Individuals may have to make sacrifices in order for the group to achieve a greater goal.
- Combat application: Create a false opening to lure attackers into a trap.

12. Steal a sheep as you pass by.

   - Take advantage of opportunities, however small, and avail yourself of any profit, however slight. This comes from the story of a destitute traveler walking on a road. As he went along, he came across a flock of sheep; making his way through them, when he emerged from their midst he had a sheep with him. He behaved so calmly and naturally, as it he had been leading his own sheep to market all along, that the shepherd never noticed him. (Lead away a sheep in passing)
   - Combat application: Hide your attack in a natural, unthreatening motion.

C. Stratagems for attack

   13. Beat the grass and frighten away the snake.

   - When opponents are reserved and unfathomable, create some sort of a diversion to see how they will react.
   - Combat application: Test your opponents' reactions with hand strikes, low kicks, verbal attacks, etc. Try to "push their buttons" to see how they react.

   14. Borrow a corpse to bring back a spirit.

   - Don't use what everyone else is using. Rather, use what others aren't using, e.g., find uses for things that had previously been ignored or considered useless.
   - Combat application: Improvise a weapon from a natural object.

   15. Train a tiger to leave the mountains.

   - Don't go into the heart of a powerful enemy's territory.

Induce the enemy to come out of its stronghold.
- Combat application: Lure your enemy by creating a false opening.

16. Let the enemy leave in order to catch him.

- When you want to take prisoners, let them roam freely for a while. Fleeing enemies may turn and strike ferociously if pursued too diligently. Conversely, if they are allowed to run freely, they scatter and lose their energy. At that point, they can be captured without further violence.
- Combat application: Control your attackers' motion, cutting off his options and forcing them into a place you want them to be.

17. Toss out a brick to attract a gem.

- Present something of superficial or apparent worth to induce another party to produce something of real worth.
- Combat application: Bait your attacker with a false opening.

18. Catch the leader first in order to capture all his followers.

- When confronted with significant opposition, take aim at its central leadership.
- Combat application: Eliminate the leader or the most feared of a group and generally the followers will become disorganized.

D. Stratagems for confused situations

19. Remove the firewood from under the pot.

- When you cannot defeat an enemy in a head-on confrontation, you can win by undermining his resources and morale

by taking drastic measures to strike at the source of a problem.
- Combat application: Use the environment. For example, if you are on higher ground, draw the enemy up there—but don't look down on him.

20. Stir up the waters to catch fish.

- Use confusion to your advantage and to take what you want.
- Combat application: Fight with the sun, wind, etc., at your back so the elements are in the enemy's eyes and faces. Use horns, bugles, drums, and other instruments to throw the enemy off guard and then take advantage of the distractions.

21. A gold crab molts its shell.

- When a crab or other creature molts or changes its exterior, its changed appearance confuses the enemy. It's as if the original creature has escaped. The change creates false external appearances, but the inside remains the same and can continue to create new and confusing strategies.
- Combat application: Maintain an element of surprise. While the enemy is looking for the before-change creature, the new one can create havoc.

22. Lock the gates to catch the thieves.

- You can trap invaders by not letting them get away. In so doing, you prevent them from returning to their bases with anything they took from you. But, if they do escape, don't chase them. If you do, you will fall prey to the enemy's plot to wear you down.
- Combat application: Step on your enemy's foot, trap their

hands, etc. Anything to slow them down.

23. Make allies at a distance, attack nearby.

- When you are more vulnerable to those close by than you are to those far away, you can defend yourself by keeping those around you off balance. Meanwhile, inhibit their field of maneuver by creating a wide circle of alliances around them.
- Combat application: Concentrate on the immediate threat, and handle the others later when the opportunity is more propitious.

24. "Borrow" the right of way to attack the enemy, i.e., obtain permission to cross another country or occupied territory to get at him.

- Forge neutral alliances and then secure the temporary use of the ally's facilities to attack a mutual enemy. After a successful attack, you then continue to use the ally's facilities to continue operations against the enemy—or even use them against the party from whom you borrowed them.
- Combat application: Use one enemy against the other. Move when fighting so they constantly cross each other and get in one another's way. Use one enemy's weapon against the other to create confusion.

Stratagems for gaining ground

25. Replace the beams and pillars with rotten timber

- Try to recruit top talent from among allies.
- Combat application: Use negotiations and undermine the enemy's confidence. Attack the legs to get at the entire body.

26. Point at one to scold another.

    - Criticize the enemy indirectly. Get your point across without confrontation, e.g., chastise one enemy leader through another.
    - Combat application: Blame somebody else for a disaster, e.g., collateral damage, and swear that you will take care of the people affected as a way to solicit friends and allies—even if you have no intention of making good on your promise.

27. Feign foolishness.

    - Pretend to be stupid and ignorant, but avoid talking loosely.
    - Combat application: Fake injury, sickness, stupidity, etc., to fool the enemy.

28. Let them climb the roof, then take away the ladder.

    - Maneuver enemies into places and situations from which they cannot extract themselves by luring them into what appears to be advantages and opportunities for them.
    - Combat application: Use any trick available to let the enemy enter a trap and then spring it. For example, let them through the door and then lock it behind them.

29. Make false flowers bloom on a tree.

    - Deceive the enemy by creating showy displays that are nothing but decoys.
    - Combat application: Destroy the enemy's confidence with a demonstration of skill and materiel, albeit it mostly deceptive. Build wooden tanks, march the same troops round and round, etc., to give the appearance of a large, well-trained Army.

30. Turn the guest into the host.

- Let the enemy believe he has taken over the fighting.
- Combat application: Use your enemy's energy against them. Let him attack, and fall back a little. Then, when pushed and he has expended his energy, push back hard.

Stratagems for desperate situations

31. Scheme with beauties.

- Use women's charms to seduce and influence key figures in an enemy's organization.
- Combat application: Use something attractive to the attacker, such as money, a reward, scantily clad women etc., to divert the enemy's attention. When they turn their attention to the decoy, attack.

32. Use the empty castle ploy, e.g., create the illusion of an empty city with open gates—but with troops waiting in ambush to pounce.

- Foster the illusion that you are weaker than you appear. If you do this successfully, the enemy may defeat himself by one of three responses to your supposed weakness: he may become overly complacent; he may become arrogant and aggressive; or he may assume you are setting up an ambush and retreat to avoid it. In the first or second instances, the enemy may react with too much confidence, thus leading to his destruction.
- Combat application: When weak appear strong, when strong appear weak. Don't let the enemy know your true condition. Lure him by pretending to be weak or discourage him by appearing strong.

THE 36 STRATAGEMS

33. Scheme with double agents to sow discord in the enemy's camp.

    - Compromise other organizations by enticing their members to work for you.
    - Combat application: In an attack situation, attack first in a rapid, aggressive, and unpredictable manner to confuse the enemy.

34. Scheme with self-inflicted wounds to lure the enemy.

    - Inflict minor injury on yourself to gain the enemy's trust. This technique is used primarily for undercover agents. By using it you make yourself look like a victim of your own people in order to win the sympathy and confidence of enemies.
    - Combat application: Pretend to be injured, sick, or slowed down—and then attack.

35. Scheme by using various, interlocking stratagems.

    - Don't use force against a more powerful enemy, and don't concentrate all your resources on only one strategy. Implement different strategies simultaneously in one grand scheme.
    - Combat application: Remain aware and active in your total environment, and use every trick you can to throw your enemy off balance.

36. Know when to hold 'em and when to fold 'em. Sometimes the best strategy is to retreat.

    - When overwhelmed, don't fight. If it is advisable, surrender (complete defeat), compromise (a partial defeat), or flee (not a defeat, and gives you another chance to win at a later date).
    - Combat application: Run, if the situation dictates it!

THE HOENGSONG VALLEY MASSACRE

It was the failure of some UN commanders to recognize the significance and employment of the 36 stratagems outlined above that contributed to the debacle at Hoengsong. They simply failed to apply some of the lessons learned from earlier tactics, strategies, and atrocities utilized by the North Koreans earlier in the war. If they had done so, they might have avoided the massacre at Hoengsong and saved the lives of thousands of UN troops.

Worse, incredibly, they did not apply the lessons learned immediately after Hoengsong. There was another massacre—on a much smaller scale—at Chaun-ni just three months later. Once again, members of Dog/7 Marines were the first to discover it.

On May 22, 1951, D/7 Marines discovered the remains of a massacre alongside the road near Chaun-ni. Fred Frankville, who had also been among the first on the scene at Hoengsong, wrote:

"I have seen a list of over 300 dead soldiers who were killed on May 18 1951 in Chauni–ni. This shows me the Americans were bunched up with no room to maneuver and defend themselves. The same thing happened north of Hoengsong, where Dog/7 Marines found mostly 2nd Division troops massacred along Road 24.

"This carnage was blamed on South Korean forces who failed to protect the Americans. The sad part is that the Army top brass did not learn any lessons from what happed at Hoengsong on February 12-14 1951. And the carnage was repeated at Chauni-ni on May 18, 1951, when South Korean forces assigned to defend the Americans just ran away.

Where was the outrage for this failure of command?"

The outrage Frankville asked about was there, just as it was at Hoengsong. It's just that the U.S. Army was loath to share the information about Hoengsong with the American public. The reasons are clear based on the following account of the massacre at Hoengsong.

CHAPTER 6

Hiding Hordes Around Hoengsong

"Sicily demonstrated the many limitations of interservice and inter-allied cooperation, ones that foreshadowed problems that the allies would encounter in Italy." Douglas Porch

HISTORIAN DOUGLAS PORCH was speaking specifically about conditions in World War II when he mentioned the inherent problems in inter-service and inter-allied cooperation. But, he could well have extended his idea to Korea.

Problems for the U.S. military with its allies and cooperation were nothing new. They went back to the American Revolutionary War, when foreign officers such as the Marquis de Lafayette sided with the colonists, but had a hard time conveying their thoughts, ideas, and orders because they did not speak English fluently or appreciate American tactics. Some of those same problems existed during ensuing wars, up to and including Korea. Those problems, on the U.S. side at least, were caused in part by the failure of American military commanders to pay attention to history.

Applying lessons learned has never been a military strongpoint. Even though commanders produce after action reports that include lessons learned, both the reports and the lessons are often ignored. That was the case in Korea, where hubris afflicted some leaders who believed they could ignore the lessons of history and dictate events based on their own ideas of what would work best in certain situations. That was all too often a recipe for leadership disaster.

Many of the American officers who served in Korea were veterans of WWII, so it must have occurred to them that a road-bound Army was asking for trouble against an enemy that traveled lightly and took the high ground, as the communist armies did throughout the Korean War. They only had to look back three months. MacArthur and Almond, anyone?

The Chinese armies at the Chosin Reservoir, unencumbered by motorized vehicles, had raised havoc with the allied troops because of their ability to hold the high ground. (They had horses, camels, and other modes of transportation, but they did not clog up the roads.) The allied troops broke out of the Chinese trap eventually, but at a high cost. And, because they had thousands of vehicles with them, they had to stick to the one road out while the Chinese poured fire down on them from the hills above.

Had commanding officers studied more closely or paid attention to the history of the World War II battle for Sicily, which some experts considered the turning point of the war, and applied the lessons learned, they would have recognized that rugged, mountainous terrain could cancel one of a modern-day Army's biggest advantages: a highly mechanized, technologically advanced force —especially one that relies on roads.

There was one primary road into and out of Hoengsong, Route 29, which ran north-south. Another north-south road, Route 24, ran a few miles to the west. They were connected by the east-west Rt. 2, which connected with Rt. 29 at Samael. Route 29 was bordered by steep hills, where the Chinese XIII Army Group waited in large numbers—and practically undetected.

They created traffic bottlenecks at various points along the road that posed major problems for the retreating UN forces and led to disaster. There were no detours around Hoengsong for the allied troops, especially for the ones dependent on motor vehicles. The enemy took advantage of the limited road system in Korea throughout the war, especially at Hoengsong.

Derwin Lester's experiences in the Hoengsong area demonstrate that the U.S. Army leaders in the area were familiar with its geographical and topological pitfalls and potential trouble spots. He was drafted in September 1950, given four weeks of basic training, and shipped to Korea. He arrived at Inchon in December of that year, where he got an early taste of Army life in country.

As soon as they arrived at Inchon, Lester and his comrades were transported by truck to Seoul, where they were loaded onto a train and moved to somewhere that the crew was in no hurry to get wherever it was going. They lived in box cars for four days, where they got a feeling for the war. The cars' windows had been shot out, and they received very little food.

As Lester described his experience, the box cars didn't exactly have all the comforts of home. There was a barrel to burn wood and coal for heat, and a hole in the floor for a toilet. Soldiers used their duffel bags to sleep on. There wasn't much food. That was a common theme in Lester's experiences in Korea.

Finally, they were shipped north on trucks to Munsan. There, Lester joined the mortar platoon of M Co., 38th Inf. Regt., 2nd Inf. Div. as a replacement. The division had just returned from North Korea, where they had fought the Chinese in the western mountains and incurred heavy casualties. The unit needed every new man it could get.

The North Koreans and Chinese were moving south, and M Co. moved to the Chungju region, arriving around 15 December 1950. The members still had very little food and water available, since logistics were not keeping up with troop build-ups. The company moved into Hoengsong to conduct a blocking action. That place would become a thorn in Lester's side.

The troops slept outside in the cold with no shelter. Christmas came and went. On 6 January 1951 M Co. moved back by foot to Wonju, with nothing to eat. The next night the communists launched an assault. That was when Derwin Lester earned his Combat Infantry Badge (CIB).

The CIB was awarded to infantrymen and Special Forces soldiers at the rank of Colonel and below who participated in ground combat any time after 6 December 1941 as members of either an infantry, Ranger, or Special Forces unit of brigade size or smaller. Everyone who served at Hoengsong in February 1951 earned a CIB, which was small consolation for those who were killed or taken prisoner there.

Life at Wonju was hard. The communists were attacking everywhere. Army troops had to set an ammunition train and all the homes in Wonju on fire to eliminate places where the enemy could hide. From 12 January to 9 February the 38th Regt. was in constant combat, in temperatures as low as -30°. Soldiers fought and slept in a foot of snow—and still with very little to eat. The conditions were brutal, but nothing like what they would face on 12-13 February.

As the Chinese and North Koreans massed their troops around Hoengsong, friendly intelligence sources and observation pilots (OPs) had failed to recognize the size of their build-up. The allies knew that small enemy groups were working in the area, but they overlooked the larger units to which they were attached. That allowed the enemy to construct a road block between Hoengsong and the combined 1st and 3rd Battalions of the 38th Regiment, 2nd Division. The road block was approximately three miles long—and devastatingly clever.

The gauntlet was manned by an estimated one enemy battalion armed with automatic weapons and mortars. Once the ROK and American troops started passing through the road block, the enemy kept careful track of their whereabouts by marking the front of their positions by shooting red star flares in the air. There was simply nowhere to go for the allied troops to escape the withering fire poured on them from all directions.

Perhaps the enemy troops could have been prevented from establishing the road block had the UN command been more diligent in its analysis of data supplied by patrols and the enemies' movements. But, they were not, and the omission cost the allied forces at Hoengsong dearly, as did the intelligence community's failure to assess exactly—or approximately—how many enemy troops they were facing, just as it had done at Chosin.

After tabulating OP reports and battalion estimates of known enemy groups, it was estimated that three enemy divisions confronted friendly forces in the Hoengsong-Wonju axis. By contrast, the allies had only two battalions of infantry, the Netherlands Detachment, whose activities around Hoengsong will be detailed in a separate chapter, one battalion of 105 Artillery, and one battalion of 155 Artillery to confront the enemy.

The North Korean Army enjoyed a great deal of success against its South Korean and U.S. foes early in the war. Approximately 90,000 North Korean troops, supported by hundreds of tanks, including numerous Russian-made T-34s, launched a massive ground campaign against its poorly armed neighbor to the south on 25 June 1950 (June 24th in the U.S.). They attacked over the 38th Parallel, the arbitrary dividing line between North Korea and South Korea that had been established after WWII.

The U.S. rushed poorly trained, ill-equipped troops from Japan to Korea as quickly as it could to aid its South Korean allies. They were essentially sacrificial lambs. The North Koreans rolled over them as well. Then, on 15 September 1950 the U.S. Marine Corps' 1st Division (the only division it had at the time) made a daring amphibious landing at Inchon. That turned the tide, so to speak.

The Marines and elements of the U.S. and ROK armies began to slowly but surely push the North Koreans back over the 38th Parallel—and beyond. They pushed so far, in fact, that the North Koreans were in danger of losing the war. Enter the Chinese.

The Chinese were not willing to see their North Korean allies lose the war. They let it be known that if the UN troops pushed too far north and threatened China then they would enter the war on the North Koreans' side. U.S. Army commanding officers Generals Douglas MacArthur and Edward ("Ned") Almond did not believe them. Nor did they believe that the Chinese were building up their forces along the Yalu River, the border between China and North Korea.

Yet, the Chinese managed to transfer approximately 150,000 of their soldiers into North Korea undetected. Well, they were detected, but U.S. military leaders denied that they were there, even after friendly troops captured some of them and turned them over to commanders for interrogation. They would repeat that mistake at Hoengsong four months later.

The Chinese troops, wearing sneakers and light uniforms, waited until the Yalu froze over and crossed at night. Then they hid in the mountains and railroad tunnels by day and moved after sunset. They traveled lightly, carrying their food and supplies with them. What they could not carry they hauled on the backs of horses and camels. Later speculation was that they probably could have stood up en masse and waved at MacArthur and Almond, who would still have denied their existence. But, the generals could not deny it for long.

1st Lt. Bill Funchess, a Platoon Leader with "C" Company, 19th Infantry, 24th Division, was captured 4 November 1950 and released alone on 6 September 1953. He had the unique opportunity to see up close and personal some of the tricks the Chinese used to avoid detection. He described his ordeal just before being captured:

"Sgt. Hartwell Champaign and I saw naked Chinese soldiers crossing the river at dawn on 4 November, 1950, holding their clothing and weapons above water to keep them dry, even though there was a bridge nearby. When I advised Battalion headquarters I was promptly told, "There are no Chinese troops in North Korea." Two hours later, however, I was hit by machine gun fire, my platoon was overrun by hundreds of Chinese, and I was a prisoner of war.

"On the two-week nighttime march to the POW camp, I had opportunities to observe some of the methods Chinese troops used to avoid detection. The Chinese used light-weight, easy-to-carry weapons and equipment. This enabled them to travel through mountainous areas at night while avoiding roads, bridges, and open areas. In contrast, our heavier, superior weapons and equipment caused our Army to become road-bound and easy to detect.

"I saw no mess trucks traveling with the Chinese Army. Neither did I see any bulky C-rations. Each soldier carried rice or grain in a cloth tube about the size of a bicycle tire, tied at both ends, and slung over his shoulder. Several of their cooks carried 6-foot sticks on their shoulders with a lightweight cooking pot on each end.

"When it came time to eat, each pot was set on several stones, partially filled with water or snow, and a fire was built underneath. Each soldier untied one end of his rice tube, and the cook pinched off a certain amount of grain from the tube and let it fall into the pot to be cooked. There was no need for mess vehicles.

"On the march northward, I observed a unique method the Chinese used to warn of incoming aircraft. On occasion, sentries positioned on mountain tops would suddenly shout, "Hungo! Hungo!" Other sentries would immediately repeat the warning shout, giving their troops time to either hide or "freeze." Usually, within seconds, I would either hear or see the incoming U.S. plane. The system was primitive but effective."

Dolores Nieves, a member of the U.S. Army 65th Infantry Regiment, which was composed primarily of Puerto Rican troops, aka the "Bourinqueneers," a derivation of the word Borinquen, used by Puerto Rico's original inhabitants, the Taino Indians, noted that North Korean and Chinese soldiers sometimes camouflaged themselves as gravestones in cemeteries. (The regiment was also known as Los Diablos de le Montana, or Devils of the Mountain, for their ability to throw the enemies' grenades back at them before they exploded.) They placed crosses on themselves, moved from place to place, and lay on the ground.

As Nieves revealed, one minute the American soldiers would not see an enemy nearby. The next time they looked, there would be one right beside them. That was unsettling for the friendly troops, and one more enemy trick they had to get used to.

In late November 1950 Chinese troops trapped elements of the U.S. Army 7th Division and U.S. Marine Corps 1st Division, which combined to form X Corps, the U.S. Eighth Army, ROK units, and other UN troops in the mountains of North Korea and almost wiped them out. It was no trick for the Chinese, then, to hide an estimated three divisions around Hoengsong and once again decimate UN troops.

Even Eighth Army commander Matthew Ridgway was fooled by the Chinese and their ability to mask large-scale movements. In mid-January 1951 he took a recon ride in a plane piloted by Fifth Air Force commander Earle Partridge. They flew for two hours over a seemingly empty expanse of land marred only by a few isolated huts and occasional footprints.

Ridgway inferred that the footprints were made by Chinese troops who were traveling by night and sleeping in the huts by day, according to their usual modus operandi. He determined from what he saw that the Chinese were few and far between and not much of a threat. That jibed with Dutch intelligence reports published a couple weeks later.

There was some scouting and recon activity conducted by UN troops around Hoengsong, and there was a series of mini-battles between UN and enemy troops. The Dutch, who would play a significant role in the battles around Hoengsong and pay a terrible price for their effort, conducted periodic patrols from their defensive positions around the town between February 5th and 11th.

The Dutch sent out one patrol a day, mostly to the west and southwest, but reported limited contact with the enemy. They took a few North Korean soldiers as prisoners, but there was no reason to believe that any enemy force was present in large numbers, despite evidence to the contrary. Wrong!

CHAPTER 7

The Hoengsong Shuffle

"The Korean War has also shown quite clearly that in a major conflict manpower is as important as horsepower." (Aly Khan)

THE MEMBERS OF the 38th Regiment may have wondered early in February 1951 if they were involved in a game of musical chairs, or even what century they were in, What they knew for certain was that the regiment was in for trouble. According to the 38th Infantry Regiment's February 1951 Command Report, "On the 10th of February, AOP continued to report the enemy massing at DS 820555. Included in these sightings was an estimated 1,200 horses."

Horses? In 20th century warfare? Regardless of the animals' presence near the battleground, 38th Regimental battalions and companies were assigned and reassigned to different locations in and around Hoengsong and placed under different commands, all in conjunction with Operation Roundup and changing enemy threats.

At the beginning of the month, while the 38th Regiment was intact and positioned around Wonju, the troops occupied themselves with establishing defensive positions and conducting patrols to the north designed to keep tabs on the enemy. One patrol in particular determined without a doubt that there were well-trained enemy troops in the vicinity—and in large numbers.

On February 1st, the 3rd Bn. sent one company-sized patrol northwest, where it encountered a large enemy group near a lake. The two forces engaged in a firefight during which the Americans called in artillery and air support. The strike killed an estimated 63 enemy soldiers. Not only did the patrol verify that there were large enemy forces in the area, but that they were well disciplined and tactically clever.

Patrol members reported that when the artillery and air strikes were in progress, the enemy troops would take cover in their fox holes. When the fire stopped, they would step out and resume the firefight with deadly effect. That was a common-sense lesson learned for the American troops: well dug-in troops had a better chance of survival under fire than those who chose to remain unprotected.

The next day the revolving troop assignments began. The regiment received orders from the 2d Division to secure the high ground just north of Hoengsong. One battalion would be deployed west of the town to set up a blocking position. The 1st and 3rd Battalions traveled to Hoengsong in the company of ROK units scheduled to participate in their first offensive operation of 1951, named Roundup. They reached the town at about 11:30 that night. The 2nd Battalion, minus F Co., did not arrive until 5 a.m. on the 3rd. It was assigned positions to the north and east of Hoengsong. F Co. remained just north of Wonju to protect the town. No sooner had the regiment reached Hoengsong than the division changed the plan.

Division ordered the 2nd Bn. to return to its original positions north of Wonju. The 3rd Bn then occupied the positions vacated by the 2nd Bn. Then, the division created SF21, which removed the 1st Bn from American control, although it would still be supplied by the 38th Regiment. Henceforth, SF 21's mission would be to provide close-in security for 15th FA Bn, which was supporting the ROK 8th Division. The revolving doors kept spinning.

L Co. and the 3rd Platoon of the 38th RCT Tank Company were also removed from the regiment's control and assigned to the ROK 8th Division as Support Team Baker. All the maneuvering left a gaping hole in the defense of Hoengsong. The Netherlands Detachment was ordered to take up defensive positions north of the town to relieve the 1st Bn., i.e., SF 21. The replacement was completed on the afternoon of February 5th, at which time the 1st Bn moved to an assembly area about 2,000 yards south of the town.

That night the regiment was ordered to conduct a reconnaissance operation to locate a site for a possible "blocking position" for one battalion near Samael, where Routes 2 and 29 merged. That proved to be a wise decision as subsequent events proved. Then came the final weakening of the regiment; C Battery of the 38th FA Bn was detached and placed in general support.

The two sides engaged in a sparring contest over the next few days that gave the UN commanders pause to worry. They saw an increasing number of enemy troops in the area that led to a growing number of skirmishes. That did not bode well for the participants in Operation Roundup, especially the 38th Regiment and its components, which became scattered to the wind.

Support Team (ST) Baker left the regiment at 7:30 a.m. February 6th in compliance with the 8th ROK Commander's directive. By noon it had arrived at Saemal. Intelligence reports indicated that the enemy was using the village of Changmal, near Wonju, as a headquarters. The U.S. Army's 1st Ranger Company was attached temporarily to the 38th Regiment and dispatched to Changmal to burn the village and inflict as many casualties as possible on the troops there. The company, attached to the 2nd Division, was ideally suited for the mission, which ultimately did not achieve its goal, to the detriment of ST Baker.

The 1st Rangers specialized in counter-infiltration force, conducting defensive patrols, and burning vacant buildings to stem the Chinese advance. In the winter of 1951 they were used as forward observers and snipers and to conduct frequent long-range patrols. The division used the rangers as a scouting force during the February counter-offensive.

At Changmal, the company killed an estimated 50-100 enemy soldiers, destroyed 20 enemy rifles, and captured 5 machine guns and 9 burp guns, at a cost of 2 wounded Rangers. They did not adversely affect the enemy's resiliency, though, as ST Baker and the entire regiment would soon find out.

While the Rangers attacked Changmal to disrupt the Chinese, the 38th Regiment continued to move troops around. The division relocated the 3rd Bn to Saemal to relieve the ROK 21st Regiment, which was preparing to attack northward.

The battalion arrived at Saemal on February 6th. Once again the repositioning left a gap in the Hoengsong sector. To compensate, the 38th Regiment's right boundary was moved approximately 3,000 yards to the west, and a new player stepped in to help. The 187th Airborne Regiment moved some of its troops into the gap created by the 38th Regiment's swing.

Once again the Netherlands Detachment was called on to fill a hole. It pivoted from the west of Hoengsong to the northeast to protect the 38th's new flank. The 38th Regiment's I&R Platoon (Intelligence & Reconnaissance) assumed responsibility for the left flank by patrolling continuously in the area.

The 1st Bn, in its role as part of SF 21, moved up Route 29 to the vicinity of Chadong on February 7th. ST Baker was also on the move. The next day it reported that it was in a fight with an estimated 200 enemy near Changmal. The two-hour exchange involved primarily small arms and friendly tank fire. Once it ended, L Co., minus one platoon, withdrew to an assembly area in the vicinity. The platoon that remained behind dispersed the enemy, then rejoined the company. ST Baker lost one member killed in action and another one wounded. The number of enemy casualties was not determined.

On February 9th the Chinese demonstrated another one of their flairs for trickery. A regimental tank commander reported that they were transmitting on the same frequency as one of his platoons, using the call sign "K." It was a sign that the enemy was growing bolder. Moreover, they were growing in numbers.

Intelligence reports noted that the enemy was massing in the central Korea area between Hongchon and Hoengsong. Air strikes were called in against the enemy gathering on February 10th. Friendly planes strafed and napalmed the soldiers and their horses at approximately 6 p.m. All the available artillery in the area joined the attack. As a grand finale, B-26 bombers attacked the area at 8 p.m., 8:30 p.m., and midnight—and again at 3:30 a.m. on February 11th.

There was one more move on February 10th that affected the 38th Regiment. The 38th FA Bn., with the exception of C Battery, was removed from regimental control and assigned to the 9th Infantry Regiment. The revamped 38th Regiment was about to enter a three-day period that would test it severely—and practically decimate its ranks, thanks in large part to the collapse of the ROK units spearheading the offensive. That was not uncommon for the ROKs, who made up a relatively inexperienced Army.

CHAPTER 8

ROK Army History: Anything But Spectacular

"At 120250 12 February, the 1st Bn,. 38th RCT, reported that the 21st ROK Regiment had collapsed and were now withdrawing through the 1st Bn. area...Friendly casualties were now mounting, for the enemy was placing accurate mortar fire in and around the perimeter." (38th Infantry Regiment Command Report, February 1951)

IN ALL FAIRNESS, the ROK Army did not have a great deal of experience in warfare prior to the North Korean invasion of South Korea. Many of the "soldiers" were teenagers—some not even that—who had literally been dragged off city streets and impressed into the Army. They were neither well trained, well-armed, nor keen on going to war. As a result, ROK units' performance in combat was, to say the least, uneven. That was one of the most significant causes for the Hoengsong massacre.

Japan had ruled Korea for forty years, which meant the Koreans had no need for a military of their own. That ended on August 15, 1945, when the country gained its independence as a result of Japan's capitulation in WWII. But, independence for Korea did not mean unity.

There existed a divided Korea.

The 38th Parallel separated North Korea (the Democratic People's Republic of Korea) from South Korea (the Republic of Korea). According to the terms of Japan's surrender, Russia controlled the northern half of the divided country; the United States had nominal responsibility for the south. The differences between the two Koreas were stark.

Ironically, North Korea was the more advanced of the two sections immediately after WWII. It was home to a communist form of government. The Soviets had installed Kim Il-Sung as head of the Provisional People's Committee in 1945. Russia and China, its allies, furnished North Korea's military with training and equipment. South Korea was more democratic, but neither a true democracy nor a republic.

The individual leaders, Syngman Rhee in the south and Kim Il-Sung in the north, wanted to unite the two Koreas, but under different forms of government. Rhee did not want a dictatorship such as the one in North Korea. Il-Sung did not want a democracy, which was anathema to a communist form of government. Neither leader was afraid to go to war to unite the country under his favored form of government. Il-Sung beat Rhee to the punch. His military forces outnumbered and out armed his southern neighbors.

While the Russians were arming the North Koreans with modern equipment such as T-34 tanks and MiG fighter planes, the South Koreans were short-changed by the U.S., its key ally. The U.S. government was unwilling to supply the Republic of Korea with up-to-date weapons, training, etc., for fear that Rhee would launch an attack on the north in an effort to reunite the two entities under his terms. The two sides were at an impasse by mid-1950.

William Borer saw firsthand the conditions under which the ROK "Army" was operating in its formative days. He arrived in Korea for the first time in September 1946 and was assigned to the 20th Inf.

Regt., at Kwanju, South Korea. His duty station at Camp Sykes was just down the road from the South Korean Constabulary camp, the forerunner to their Army. He saw them drilling daily.

"Unlike their northern neighbors, who were supplied with tanks, artillery, heavy weapons and even fighter aircraft, the South Korean Constabulary was given only captured Japanese small arms," Borer recalls. "The largest piece of equipment I ever saw them with was an old 37mm Anti-Tank Gun from WWII, which was as useless then as it was during WWII against even the lightest tank in our enemy's arsenal."

He said that no one was surprised when North Korea attacked the south, or that the South Korean Army collapsed. "They had nothing more than Bolt action rifles and 60mm mortars to use against the T-34 tanks and infantry armed with automatic weapons," Borer said. "A good friend of mine who was assigned to KMAG at the outbreak told me they did not even have 81mm mortars in all their units."

He concluded that if Truman had given them the weapons to defend themselves, early on, when they asked for them, "I believe the north would never have attacked. And, if they did, the outcome would have been quite different."

In reality, Truman did not arm or supply the U.S. troops properly, let alone the South Koreans. As Borer explained:

"Another thing which I believe led to North Korea's attack was Truman allowing our presence in South Korea to deteriorate to the level it did. Believe me, I was there.

"We were so low in strength that we had lieutenants pulling duty as Private of the Guard. We had no time for training. All we did was pull guard duty seven days a week, nonstop, week after week, until we finally rotated back to the U.S.

"We got no supplies. We ate "C" rations three times a day, which were delivered to us at our guard posts. We had some soldiers who went barefoot because Supply couldn't get them a pair of shoes. I have photos of one friend of mine, shoeless!

"We had two divisions in South Korea, the 6th in the south and the 7th in the north. If those divisions were kept supplied like MacArthur's 1st Cavalry Division in Japan, and if they were not pulled out of Korea, the story would have been much different."

Borer offered one more reason why the decks were stacked against the South Korean Army. "Lastly, if Truman did not make a speech to the United Nations and say to the world that South Korea was not in the United States' sphere of influence, the war would never have taken place. When Truman made that statement, he unknowingly gave Stalin the 'go ahead' to attack South Korea. And the rest is history."

Despite the odds against success, the South Koreans worked hard to provide their own defense.

The heart of the South Korean Army in the late 1940s comprised Koreans who had gained military services abroad. They realized that the newly independent republic needed an Army of its own based on Korea's painful historic experiences of the past. Consequently, they established a process to build their armed forces, with the assistance of the U.S.

The U.S. military government stepped in, dissolved the group of South Koreans trying to create a defense force, and formed a military corps of 25,000 soldiers. It was more of a police force than an Army. The government's first move was to create the Military English Academy on December 5, 1945 to train cadets for the defense force. The first class comprised young men who gained military experiences in Japan, Manchuria, and China.

A total of 110 cadets completed their Basic English education, after which they were commissioned as officers. These young men founded the National Defense Force in Taenung, Kyunggi Province on January

15, 1946. That same month the U.S. Army assigned 18 lieutenants from its 40th Infantry Division to organize 8 Korea Constabulary Regiments, one for each South Korean province. Their role was to act as a police force.

Eventually the regiments grew from 2,000 men in April 1946 to 50,000 in March 1948, the year they were incorporated into the Republic of Korea (ROK) Army. The U.S. created a Provisional Military Advisory Group (PMAG) to train and advise the new armed forces. The 100 U.S. advisors in Korea at the time were reassigned to PMAG, which evolved into KMAG. It was known officially as the 8668th Army Unit, under the command of the U.S. Eighth Army. On December 28, 1950 it was redesignated as the 8202nd Army Unit—just in time for the Hoengsong Massacre.

The South Korean Army was slow to grow. The 1st Division was formed on May 12, 1945. The next division formed was the Capital Division, on June 20, 1948. It was created from the Capital Security Command. It included the 1st Cavalry Regiment, which was equipped with 24 M8 and M20 armored cars plus 12 M3 halftracks. The division became part of I Corps after the first fall of Seoul.

Four years to the day after the 1st Division was formed, the Army added four more divisions, the 2nd, 3rd, 5th, and 6th. (There was no 4th.) The 7th Division and 8th Divisions were formed on June 10 and June 20, 1949 respectively. Those seven divisions composed the South Korean Army when 200,000 North Korean troops poured over the 38th Parallel to attack on June 25, 1950.

On that date the ROK Army comprised 8 divisions and 98,000 soldiers, many of whom were actually North Koreans. An unknown number of them infiltrated into the ROK forces for two primary reasons: to plant communism and initiate riots by using a variety of propaganda and schemes. They inadvertently helped the South Koreans gain some military experience in the process. Two examples will suffice.

One of the North Koreans' favorite activities was causing riots such as the one that began on Je-ju Island, off the southern coast of South Korea, on April 3, 1948. The riots were the culmination of significant political differences.

There was no love lost between the residents of the island and the South Korean government. On March 1, 1947, some of the island's residents commemorated the Korean struggle against Japanese rule and denounced the South Korean Constitutional Assembly election scheduled for May 10, 1948. Their objection was based on the belief that the U.S. military government, under the guise of the UN, was trying to create a separate southern regime under the leadership of Syngman Rhee.

The South Korean government assigned police officers from the Korean peninsula to the island. (Remember, the constabulary was the South Korean Army at the time.) Rather than diffuse the situation, they fired on a crowd of protesters and killed six Jeju residents. As a result, there was extensive rioting that lasted off and on until 1954. The rioting led to between 14,000 and 30,000 deaths of people who were killed in fighting among various factions on the island or executed.

The South Korean Army perpetrated what was considered by the islanders to be a brutal suppression of the rebellion. Its tactics caused many deaths, destroyed numerous villages on the island, and led to more rebellions on the Korean mainland. The suppression was so bad that several hundred members of the South Korean 11th Constabulary Regiment mutinied, which led to isolated incidents of fighting up until September 21, 1954. The ROK Army had gained some experience, but it paid a heavy price in damaged public relations as a result.

Déjà vu At Yeosu

The South Korean Army attracted similar scorn and gained added experience a few months later in an October 19, 1948 incident related to the Je-ju riots. The incident, known as the Yeosu–Suncheon Rebellion, or the Yeo-Sun incident, occurred in Yeosu, Suncheon, and surrounding towns. Once again communists, spurred in part by the events at Je-ju, led an uprising against the South Korean government. Many of the ROK soldiers in Yeosu declined to suppress the rioting. In fact, they seized weapons and took control of the town.

The soldiers' rebellion emboldened the town's residents, who paraded through the streets waving red flags. They restored the town people's committee, then "tried" and executed numerous policemen, municipal officials, and landlords. The rebelling soldiers caught the fever. Their numbers grew to between 2,000 and 3,000. They massacred families who supported the South Korean government and Christian youths. Their action invited a government reprisal.

The South Korean government waited a week before stepping in. It dispatched troops to the town. They quickly overwhelmed the rebels with the aid of U.S. forces. American commanders planned and directed the military operations. U.S. military advisors accompanied all ROK units, and U.S. aircraft were used to transport troops.

The South Korean Truth and Reconciliation Commission, which was established on December 1, 2005, reviewed the incident and determined that the government forces had killed between 439 and 2,000 area civilians. (Many of the victims were never found, which accounted for the discrepancy.) Once again, the ROK troops had gained experience in putting down insurrections and working with their U.S. counterparts.

The Je-ju and Yeosu incidents were not large scale in scope. But, combined with other similar situations, they gave some ROK troops at least a taste of combat. The string of incidents led the ROK Army to establish a Battle Command and execute the missions to repress the riots. It also concentrated on uncovering the communist infiltrators in its ranks, which it did with a modicum of success.

Army officials arrested 1,300 communists between October 1948 and the onset of the Korean War. Unfortunately, the North Korean infiltrators were gaining experience as well, which played a part in the communists' ability to get behind UN lines around Wonju and Hoengsong.

Before June 1950 North Korean guerrillas entered South Korea through the East Sea and Taebaek Mountains. Once they gained access, they created as much confusion as possible in rear areas. The North Koreans were forcing military confrontations all along the 38th Parallel prior to June 25, 1950. ROK soldiers operated sweeps continually to stop them. But, the cat-and-mouse games ended the day the North Koreans crossed the 38th Parallel into South Korea. From that point on, ROK troops gained experience in abundance.

The First Is First

The ROK 1st Division was the first South Korean unit to try to stem the tide of North Koreans on June 25, 1950. They were unable to stop or even slow down the enemy hordes. It took only three days for the North Koreans to capture Seoul. The ROK 1st Division did not have any significant success in combat until mid-August, when it combined with elements of the U.S. 23rd and 27th Infantry Regiments to successfully defend the Naktong (Pusan) Perimeter in the Battle of the Bowling Alley, west of Taegu.

A little more than a month later, on September 27th, U.S. and ROK forces recaptured Seoul. From that point on additional ROK units got involved more heavily in the fighting. The ROK I Corps crossed the 38th Parallel on October 1st and moved up the east coast. (I Corps, created on July 24, 1950, just before the Battle of Pusan Perimeter, consisted of the ROK 8th and Capital Divisions. The ROK II Corps was created the same day.) In another week the two ROK II Corps infantry divisions, the 1st and 6th, crossed the 38th Parallel in the central part of the country.

On October 10th, the ROK I Corps captured the major port of Wonsan. That opened the door for the 1st Marine Division to land there on October 26th, by which time ROK forces had reached the Yalu River at Chosin.

As the Marines landed in Wonsan, the Chinese entered the war. They confronted ROK forces for the first time on October 25th. From that point on ROK forces engaged in a series of skirmishes with enemy forces as the UN and communist foes punched and counterpunched. The UN used that time to build up its forces until early 1951, when it launched its first true offensive of the war, with ROK divisions in the vanguard.

Not all the South Korean troops who participated in the war were members of ROK divisions. Thousands of them served with other units, due in part to a lack of numbers in U.S. forces. As of July 17th, all ROK ground forces were placed under the command of U.S. Army General Walton H. Walker, according to President Rhee's wishes.

The U.S. was scrambling early in the war to find enough troops to fill its ranks. The U.S. Eighth Army in particular was understaffed. General MacArthur alleviated the shortage somewhat by assigning to it 8,600 South Korean recruits, known as KATUSAs (Korean Augmentation to the United States Army). A ROK Marine Corps regiment was attached to the U.S. 1st Marine Division. Many of these "augmentees" served with the UN X Corps, which landed at Inchon on September 15, 1950 and worked its way north, where it was attacked and severely impacted by communist forces in November.

One of X Corps' problems was a lack of reinforcements. The ROK 17th Regiment, which was reassigned from the Eighth Army to the X Corps, was the only source of reinforcements available for the landing at Inchon. After the successful landing, the troops moved on to Seoul, which was recaptured with the valuable assistance of the ROK 17th Regiment.

That battle was costly for X Corps—and the ROKs attached. The Corps suffered about 3,500 casualties, including 166 KATUSAs. ROK troops were not only participating in the war to save their country, but they were paying a heavy cost for the privilege.

ROK troops performed well in the battle of the Pusan Perimeter in mid-September. The ROK 6th Division encountered the North Korean 8th Division in the mountainous region of the ROK II Corps. The fighting was hard, but the ROK troops inflicted about 4,000 casualties on their North Korean enemies, and eliminated their 8th Division as a combat unit. As the North Korean survivors fled north, the ROK 6th Division stayed on their tails and advanced toward Uihung.

To the east the ROK 8th Division confronted the North Korean 15th Division which, like its 8th Division counterpart, was all but annihilated. Units of the ROK Capital Division, operating in the ROK I Corps sector, fought in the streets of An'gang-ni and elsewhere. They were facing stubborn resistance as they engaged with the North Korean 12th Division near Kigye. The North Koreans put up heavy resistance as they withdrew northward to the mountains. They may have fought stubbornly, but they were being forced northward regardless. Kigye fell to the ROKs on September 22nd.

On September 17th, Capital Division troops linked up with forces of the ROK 7th Division, which was advancing eastward from the ROK II Corps sector. Their meeting was important. It closed a gap between the two corps that had lasted for two weeks.

Meanwhile, the ROK 3rd Division was engaged in a difficult battle against the North Korean 5th Division in the harbor village of P'ohang-dong. The ROKs captured the village on the morning of September 20th. Their aggressive attacks forced the North Koreans to retreat in a chaotic fashion toward Yongdok. The ROK divisions were earning a reputation as proficient fighters as 1950 came to a close. Unfortunately, they ran into a buzz saw in October as the Chinese entered the war.

On September 27, 1950 General MacArthur received permission from the Joint Chiefs to cross the 38th Parallel. The goal was to destroy North Korea's military forces. The mission failed, due to the Chinese military's entrance into the war. The ROK Army paid a fearful price for what turned out to be a botched command decision.

Between October 1st and the end of the year several ROK divisions engaged enemy troops in North Korea. At the end of September UN troops congregated to begin their push north. The ROK 1st Division joined I Corps near Kaesong, just below the 38th Parallel. The ROK II Corps, comprising the 6th, 7th, and 8th Divisions, massed between Ch'unch'on and Uijongbu in central Korea. The ROK I Corps, comprising the Capital and 3d Divisions, moved between Yongp'o and Chumunjin-up, on the east coast.

Six ROK divisions prepared for the drive to the Yalu River. The Chinese had warned UN troops to stay out of North Korea or face the consequences. MacArthur did not listen. The UN forces suffered the severe consequences the Chinese promised for his mistake.

While these forces prepared to attack northward, X Corps elements boarded ships at Inchon and Pusan for an amphibious landing at Wonsan, a major port on North Korea's east coast, 110 miles above the 38th Parallel.

The first ROK Division to move across the 38th Parallel was the 3rd. It crossed the line and moved up the east coast. The ROK Capital Division followed. They combined to capture the port of Wonsan on October 10th, before the X Corps got there. The UN troops pushed farther into North Korea.

On October 14th ROK 1st Division troops entered the North Korean capital of P'yongyang. The next day they captured the strongly fortified administrative center in the middle of the city with little opposition. It seemed like any organized North Korean resistance had evaporated. The Eighth Army established its headquarters in the city, which was a slap in the face to the North Koreans. The UN troops were 160 miles north of Seoul, 130 miles into North Korea, and getting closer to the Yalu River.

The ROK II Corps, with the ROK 1st Division, advanced towards the Yalu while the ROK 8th Division to the east arrived at Tokch'on, forty miles north of P'yongyang. The ROK 6th Division raced unopposed up the Ch'ongch'on River valley to Huich'on, where it arrived on October 23rd. As it passed through Onjong during the night of October 24th, its 7th Regiment turned north toward Ch'osan, fifty miles away on the Yalu River. A patrol from the Regiment entered Ch'osan the next morning and witnessed a welcome sight: North Koreans crossing a narrow floating footbridge across the Yalu into China. Their enthusiasm would not last long.

UN forces were poised to chase all the North Koreans across the Yalu. The Chinese had a surprise for them. The first to feel their wrath was the 3rd Battalion, 2nd Regiment, ROK 6th Division. As the battalion reached a point 8 miles west of Onjong, 50 miles from the Yalu, members saw a small force of North Koreans. At least they thought the troops were North Koreans. They were actually Chinese troops setting up a trap, into which the battalion stumbled. The Chinese troops destroyed the 3d Battalion and knocked it out of the war.

The next evening the ROK 6th Division command ordered its 7th Regiment to withdraw south. The regiment waited for an air drop of badly need supplies before it could move. It received the supplies on October 28th and headed south. The next day it ran into a buzz saw: a Chinese roadblock about twenty miles south of Kojang.

Another omen surfaced on Halloween Day, which turned out to be more of a trick than a treat for ROK troops. Chinese troops initiated attacks on the ROK 8th Division's 16th Regiment that day near its boundary with the ROK 1st Division. At the same time the Chinese pushed the ROK 7th Division back to the vicinity of Won-ni. The attacks created havoc among the ROK II Corps' ranks.

The Corps pivoted east, which created a gap between its left flank and the U.S. I Corps. The Chinese quickly took advantage of the move and launched a series of attacks that all but crippled the ROK II Corps, which was forced to retreat south of the Ch'ongch'on River. It took up a position on the U.S. I Corps' open right flank.

The Chinese seemed to be everywhere. On the west side of North Korea they were attacking the ROK 1st Division, which was spread out on the road from the Ch'ongch'on River to Unsan. The division was lulled into a false sense of security.

Its 15th Regiment passed untouched through Yongbyon en route to Unsan with elements of Co. D, 6th Medium Tank Bn. in the lead. Just before 11 a.m. the tanks approached a bridge 1-1/2 mile northeast of Yongbyon. As they arrived, enemy mortar fire destroyed the bridge. ROK soldiers estimated that there were 300 Chinese troops in the hills just north of Unsan.

The second unit in the 1st Division's order of march was the ROK 12th Regiment, which turned west when it arrived at Unsan. It participated in a skirmish with Chinese troops just outside the town. The Chinese engaged in a series of attacks on the ROK 1st Division as it proceeded south on October 26th, but backed off the next day.

As the ROK 1st Division headed south, the U.S. Eighth Army passed through its lines at Unsan to attack the enemy near the Yalu River. As it did, the ROK 1st Division redeployed to positions northeast, east, and southeast of Unsan. The ROK 15th Regiment, which was deployed east of the U.S. 8th Cavalry, across the Samt'an River, was involved in a life-and-death struggle to hold its position.

The month of November arrived, but it had no impact on the Chinese strategy of establishing a stranglehold on UN troops around Unsan. The Chinese troops pressed their attack north of the town on the afternoon of November 1st. They exploited a gap between the 8th Cavalry's left flank and the ROK 15th Regiment and destroyed the regiment. By midnight on November 1st, the ROK 15th Regiment ceased to exists as a combat unit. That was one more serious blow to the ROK Army and the UN's effort to end the war by defeating the North Koreans in their own backyard.

ROK troops continued to fight, die, disappear, and incur wounds as the initial Chinese attacks continued. Some of them were involved in the Battle of the Chosin Reservoir in late November-early December 1950, which resulted in a total of 37,500 casualties. (Overall, South Korean casualties during the war included 570,947 killed in action, 950,073 wounded in action, 84,715 captured, and 460,428 missing in action.) The losses did not faze the ROK troops, however.

As 1951 approached, many of them had become seasoned combat veterans. They were destined to play a pivotal role in the UN offensive in the first quarter of the year, including the operation around Hoengsong—which was not their finest hour, despite all the combat experience they had gained earlier.

CHAPTER 9

February 11th: Springing The Trap

"I proudly served in the United States Army during the Korean War as an artillery operations specialist in the all-black 503rd Field Artillery Battalion in the Second Infantry Division." (Charles B. Rangel, former U.S. Congressman)

OPERATION ROUNDUP ENDED on February 11th. The communists moved immediately to regain their losses by utilizing their one great advantage in the war: numbers. Their goal was twofold: to control the road from Hoengsong to Wonju and crumple the Allies' entire 155-mile front across Korea. They did not succeed.

The Chinese 66th Army lay in wait along Route 29, whence one division headed south to attack allied forces. One division of the Chinese 40th Army and one division from the Chinese 39th Army were in place along Route 24. These two divisions launched their attack from the southeast in the vicinity of Hongchon and Chip'yong-ni. Their target was the ROK 8th Division, supported directly by the U.S. Army's Support Force (SF) 21, which sustained the brunt of attacks starting late on the night of February 11th.

SF 21, formed on February 4, 1951 in accordance with the U.S. Army's Second Division Operation Order 22, comprised units of the division. They included the 15th Field Artillery (FA) Bn., commanded by Col John W. Keith, Jr., who doubled as the SF commander, the 503rd FA Bn., commanded by Captain Jones, the 1st Battalion, 38th Inf., commanded by LtCol William P. Keleher, and "D" Battery, 82nd AAA (Antiaircraft Artillery, Automatic Weapons) Battalion.

SF 21's primary mission was to provide artillery support to the 21st Regiment of the 8th ROK Division. The 1st Bn., 38th Inf., its attached units, and Battery D were responsible for providing perimeter defense for the field artillery units.

At the same time, Operation Order 22 created Support Force 22. Both SFs were to provide the artillery support to the 8th ROK Division. SF 22 consisted of one battery of the 37th Field Artillery Battalion, a section of the 82d AAA Bn., and a rifle company of the 23d Infantry. All the component units were to be designated by the commanding officer of the 23d RCT.

The ensuing Operation Order 23 directed the establishment of Support Teams A and B. ST A would be organized by the 9th RCT, with Company K and the 3d Platoon of its Tank Company. ST B included Co. L of the 38th Infantry and the 3d Platoon of its Tank Company. Each of these teams was to be subdivided into smaller teams capable of independent action.

The support teams were to act under the operational control of the commanding general of the 8th ROK Division. That did not work out well as Operation Roundup progressed. As it turned out, the support teams needed support. And the support force and the troops who came to their aid got caught in the melee and had to join the retreat.

There wasn't much activity along the 2nd Division's front on February 11th. At 11 a.m. the 1st Bn was still operating as an integral part of SF 21 a few miles north of Hoengsong on Rt 29, in the vicinity of

Changbong-ni. At 3 p.m. ST Baker was continuing its support of the 8th ROK Division's advance. But neither unit was involved in any heavy action. The general inactivity in the vicinity did not lull any of the UN commanders into false senses of security.

The Eighth Army was gearing up for a heavy enemy attack along the entire front. Its command notified X Corps that the 8th ROK Division's forward progress was halted, at least temporarily. Instead, it would remain in position, and there would no movement north or west by friendly forces unless it was cleared by the Eighth Army command. There was a good reason for the order to halt in position. Late in the day, the route of withdrawal had been cut behind the ROK 10th and 16th Regiments. They weren't the only ROK regiments in trouble.

Enemy activity began to increase toward nightfall. The first signs of trouble at Hoengsong occurred at 8:30 p.m. that night near Hill 930, when the Chinese launched a furious attack on the 21st ROK Regiment, which was trying to clear them off the hill. Hill 930 was the farthest point north the support force had reached up to that point—and it did not remain there long.

The enemy attacks quickly became more widespread along the entire line. The ROK units began to disintegrate early. Worse, they lost contact with their support force. The 38th Infantry reported shortly after the enemy attacks began that there was increasing evidence of a ROK collapse. The Support Team fell back to positions behind the 3rd Bn., bringing wounded soldiers with it.

The 1st Bn., part of SF 21, lost contact with the 8th ROK Division. That was a bad sign, since it was under 8th ROK Division control. The battalion was not involved in much action on the night of the 11th, but it needed some guidance on what to do since it was now essentially a "free agent."

Actually, there was no more ROK 8th Division. It had disintegrated. The division had been attacked by four enemy divisions and had lost over

8,000 men. The wheels were in motion for a pending firestorm. That is how Derwin Lester remembered it: "Sometime in the early morning of February 12th, South Korean soldiers were running through our gun positions to get away from attacking Chinese and North Korean soldiers attacking our front lines. Four Chinese divisions had already wiped out over 8,000 South Korean soldiers."

Confusion reigned. The Americans stayed and fought throughout the night. As daylight approached, they realized that they were surrounded, out in the open, and directly in the line of enemy fire.

As Lester explained, "Shortly after daylight every man was ordered to shoulder a weapon, becoming a rifleman. We were surrounded by the enemy. My squad leader, a lieutenant, was shot almost immediately and had to be carried back for aid. After that we didn't have a squad leader, and since most of the men were from Headquarters Company, and I was from a mortar company, none of us had any real training to be a rifleman."

That was a problem all across the friendly troops' lines. Leadership had all but vanished, and individual soldiers were too busy fighting for their lives early in the battle to worry about strategy and tactics. Lester, a relatively new soldier, took some initiative. Chaos was the order of the day, as he continued.

"We were right out in the open line of fire, so I decided we should move back to our foxholes, a few hundred feet back. Shortly after we got into them, I decided it was my turn to watch for enemy that might be throwing hand grenades. I raised up and immediately a bullet slammed into my shoulder area."

Theoretically, Lester was out of the battle. But, like so many of his wounded comrades, he could not stop to worry about his wound. He wanted to survive, and the only way to do that was to fight his way out of trouble. He recalled:

"A medic quickly came and put a bandage on the wound. I was then told to get into one of the trucks trying to get through the ambush. I looked into the back of a truck that was pulling a 105 Howitzer. There was no room on it because there were so many wounded soldiers aboard. I went to the front, and the driver said I could get in.

"The truck started to move through the road block the Chinese had established. There was fighting everywhere. It was like the 4th of July, with fireworks coming right at us. No man could experience more fear than I was feeling.

"Later, I learned that only 11 trucks made it out of the ambush; 120 trucks carrying wounded soldiers did not. The eleven trucks that did get out headed for regimental headquarters, south of Wonju. They made it sometime during the night."

It wasn't until the next day that Lester received more advanced first aid. He was by no means alone, he recounted.

"It was now February 13th and I headed for help. There was a tent with a stove in it and soldiers were sleeping on cots. I lay down by the stove and went to sleep. In the morning I went to the door of the tent and exited into the sunlight.

"I was feeling and looking lost when a lieutenant saw me and took me to a first aid station. Medics put me on a stretcher and covered me with blankets. All too soon everyone that could walk was ordered to get on a truck. Very soon the truck was filled with men, all standing.

"The floor of the truck was steel, and there was no room to move our feet. My feet became so cold that later my toe nails came off. I had never experienced such cold."

At least Lester was alive. That was more than could be said for almost 12,000 of his comrades who perished at Hoengsong. And, he could still travel.

"The truck took us to a train that would head for Pusan, Korea," he continued. "From the train they put us on a hospital ship in Pusan Harbor. There I got my first bath in 2-1/2 months."

Lester was unprepared for what he saw aboard the ship.

"There was a soldier that was paralyzed from the neck down, so I fed him his meals. Another soldier had his hands and arms burned so badly we put liquid on them to keep them moist. There were wounded soldiers still bleeding and getting blood transfusions while waiting for surgery. The smell of death was everywhere."

Doctors assessed Lester's wound and determined that it would take a long time to heal, so they put him on a cargo plane headed to Japan. His reward for his heroics at Hoengsong, as it was for so many of the survivors, was a return to duty. On 10 April 1951 he returned to Korea via ship. Three days later he arrived back with his old unit, but he did not see anyone he knew.

"Could they all be dead?" he wondered. He thought that the bullet that hit him probably saved his life—for the time being.

Lester spent the next few months in combat. Ironically, he got to fight in another "massacre," this time with the winning side. In mid-May he participated in the battle at Soyang, during which the UN troops held their lines and killed about 5,000 Chinese troops. He was in constant combat between May 17th and May 20th, with no sleep. Once again he survived. Two months later, he went home, with only memories of Hoengsong. He was one of the lucky ones who lived to have memories. Those who did recall them vividly. Many never forgot them.

CHAPTER 10

Time On Your Hands

"The object of war is not to die for your country, but to make the other bastard die for his." (General George S. Patton)

THERE IS NO doubt that the besieged soldiers at Hoengsong fought hard. Their philosophy was simple, and in accordance with General George Patton's paraphrased philosophy: "If I am going to die I am going to take as many communists with me as I can." That was epitomized in two lines from the Recommendation for Reward for Heroism produced for Master Sergeant Jimmie Holloway's Bronze Star award: "Repeated attacks by enemy forces were thrown back with enemy losses very heavy. [Holloway's] actions saved the lives of many men in his units and other nearby units."

Holloway was a hero; he encouraged many of his comrades to follow his lead and make the communists pay for what turned out to be for them a pyrrhic victory.

NOTE: All times cited throughout this account are approximate, as are some of the details of the incidents portrayed. Different report writers indicated different times for events and saw and heard things differently. That is understandable. They did not have time to glance at their wristwatches or survey their surroundings in great detail as events unfolded—and several of their watches ended up in Chinese hands anyway. The Chinese soldiers prized wristwatches as souvenirs.

Oscar Cortez, a member of Battery A, 15th FA Bn., was one of the soldiers whose watch was checked. "I was one of the lucky ones to come out of that massacre alive," he said. "I was captured on February 13th, 1951. Before our battery moved up names were picked to go to R&R to Japan. Two guys were lucky."

February 12th was a nightmare for Cortez and his battery mates. "After moving up, our 105s were pointed almost straight up," Cortez recalled. "That night we got hit. I can still hear the sound of Chinese bugles. We couldn't move out because of darkness and we were pinned down. At daybreak we moved out. We received rifle and machine gun fire along the way."

Cortez remembers trying to repel the Chinese. "We made a stand along the way," he said. "We were firing point blank at the Chinese but they kept coming. We exhausted all our ammo, even the color smoke rounds."

Just how bravely that stand in which Cortez was involved is epitomized in the story of Master Sergeant Jimmie Holloway. When the battery bogged down under the withering fire coming their way from the large numbers of enemy troops, Holloway stepped forward to exhibit exemplary leadership.

Even though he was under heavy fire himself, he directed the defense and retrograde (backward) action of Battery A. As they fought, the battery changed locations. When Holloway learned that one wounded soldier had not been evacuated from the area just vacated, he dashed approximately 150 yards across open, fire-swept terrain to rescue him. Later, as the battalion moved back, it encountered a roadblock where it received vicious enemy fire. Once again, Holloway distinguished himself.

During the fighting, a mortar burst ignited one of the ammunition trucks. Holloway ignored a withering barrage of fire aimed at him and directed the removal of the ammunition from the burning vehicle. Then, he helped push it off the road.

The enemy fire increased in volume and intensity, which forced the battalion into hastily constructed defensive positions. Once again Holloway raced through devastating fire. This time his goal was to uncouple a Howitzer from a truck. Next, he delivered protective fire on a hill to enable a company of infantry to effect a withdrawal. But he was not through yet.

The battery's executive officer was wounded in the action, which rendered him unable to respond to a call for artillery fire. Holloway rushed forward to an exposed vantage point which was undergoing a heavy enemy mortar attack. He ignored the incoming mortar rounds, even though they were falling only fifteen feet away. Coolly, Holloway directed deadly accurate artillery fire into the enemy positions.

The attack on the battery continued as it received orders to secure commanding terrain and establish defensive positions for the night. That involved sending out a combat patrol, for which Holloway volunteered to act as point, arguably the most dangerous position in any patrol, whether it be front or rear. He and the patrol began moving up the high ground toward the enemy. That was the last anybody saw of Master Sergeant Jimmie Holloway. But, no one had time to reflect on his disappearance. Cortez and the rest of Battery A were too intent on saving their own lives.

As it turned out, the Chinese captured Holloway that same day. He reportedly died in captivity on or about 12 May 1951. He was unaccounted for after the war—and still is—and is presumed to have died or been killed while in captivity.

Cortez remembered vividly when he was captured:

"My section chief, Sgt. Barrett, was wounded on the leg. We left quite a few dead friends behind and we moved out again. Along the way we stopped and we were to join the infantry in trying to get out. That was easier said than done.

"The word came that all wounded were to get back to the convoy, and since I was helping Sgt. Barrett I went back to our truck. All this was at night and we started moving out once more. We hadn't had any sleep for almost forty hours and we fell asleep in the back of the truck.

"When I woke up I called for the driver and Sgt. Barrett. When no one answered I figured they were slumped over in the cab. I reached in but couldn't feel anyone. I grabbed my carbine and jumped from the truck. There were a lot of people on the side of the road. Since it was dark I couldn't recognize anyone, so I called out quietly for Sgt. Barrett.

"Everyone was looking at me and someone fired a shot at me, so I opened fire. I felt something hit me on my stomach and realized it was a grenade. I ran to the other side of the road and hit the ground when the grenade went off.

"I heard a tank firing out front, so I started crawling towards the sound of the tank. I crawled about thirty yards. Then it ceased firing. I crawled under a truck to see and hear what was happening.

"All of a sudden I was pulled out from under the truck. I left my weapon under the truck and I played dead. I was checked if I had a wrist watch. I was stepped on a lot and then someone turned my face up. The first thing I thought about was what POW (prisoner of war) life would be like.

"I opened my eyes and was told to get up. The next thing I thought was about the two guys who went on RR to Japan.

"I was taken to the rear and joined other GIs. Later that night we started moving toward the front. We passed a lot of dead GIs. They were half naked and with no boots. The road was covered with bodies."

Cortez said that he knew of only two or three other GIs who survived that battle. He was one of the lucky ones, even though he spent the rest of the war in North Korean prison camps. At least he lived to tell the tale. So did Forward Observer 1st Lt. Wilbur R. Webster, a member of the 82nd FA Bn.

Webster's involvement with the Hoengsong battle began on the night of February 11th. He recalled setting up the Battery Commander's (BC) Scope outside the Battery D Command Post. The scope was one of the most important pieces of equipment used by Forward Observers (FOs). It was a special set of binoculars that helped the FO calculate coordinates and call fire missions. The binoculars had a twin-lens viewing scope, usually of ten power, with a reticule for adjusting fire. The lenses were designed so the FO's head could be several inches below them. They were perfect to give Webster and his comrades a view of what was transpiring on the hill.

At about 10 p.m. Webster was sleeping in the Motor Maintenance tent. A guard woke him to tell him there was a steady column of people marching down the road. Webster confirmed what the guard had told him, but he could not tell whether they were ROKs or Chinese. He guessed that they were the latter, which did not bode well for his troops.

Webster hurried to the Battery CP, where he learned that the 8th ROK Division had been overrun by a large Chinese attack, and that the Support Force Commander was trying to get permission to withdraw. He had, in fact, issued orders for "march order" (the order in which assigned units or personnel move out) in anticipation of the authorization.

Oddly enough, even though the column of troops marching down the road continued unabated, there was no gunfire being exchanged. That was not unusual where the Chinese were involved. Each of their units had a definite mission in any battle, so some of them bypassed friendly units without returning fire. They would even ignore them while heading off in another direction, intent upon their assigned mission. That was one more sign of Chinese unpredictability.

At one point, two U.S. Army tanks, which had been part of a road block north of the SF artillery position, passed by the artillery position, apparently heading to the rear. They were using the same road as the troops Webster believed were Chinese, yet no one was firing—at least not at that point.

At approximately 11:30 p.m. the preparation for withdrawal was about complete. Webster was ordered to take an M-16, a WWII-vintage half-track vehicle carrying a Quad 50 caliber gun mount, and move out ahead of the column to scout the road. Above all, he was told, report back frequently about any enemy activity he encountered.

The M-16 was towing a 1-ton trailer loaded with .50 caliber ammo. The crew comprised the squad leader, a gunner, two cannoneers, and the driver. The recon started well. They went about a mile without being fired on or observing any enemy activity. That was as far as they got.

Webster and his group reached a spot where the road narrowed. There was a steep bank on the left. On the right there was a sheer drop of about twelve feet into a dry stream bed. It was a perfect place for an ambush, and the Chinese were adroit at taking advantage of such spots.

Topography and the Chinese worked hand-in-hand in Korea. There was not a lot of natural terrain in the Hoengsong area that was suitable for building smooth roads. The one on which Webster was traveling had been cut out of a hill, which accounted for the steep bank on the left. But, much to Webster's consternation, the bank on one side of the road and the drop on the other were the least of his problems.

"Just as we arrived at this point we saw two U.S. Army tanks blocking the road in front of us," he recalled. "The driver stopped the M-16 just short of hitting the rear most tank. We immediately came under heavy enemy small arms and hand grenade fire from the hill to the left."

That was when all hell broke loose. February 11th turned into February 12th, but the nightmare Webster and his comrades encountered spanned both dates.

The Chinese had established an effective road block at the turn of the road. The Quad-50 gunner attempted to aim his weapon on the road block, but a Chinese soldier tossed a concussion grenade into the open bay of the vehicle next to the turret. That disabled the M-16. The driver could not go forward because of the tanks blocking the road. And he could not back up because of the trailer attached to the M-16. The crew bailed out.

Five bullets went through Webster's clothing as he and his comrades did the prudent thing and dived over the bank and into the dry stream bed. For some reason the Chinese did not fire at them as they moved. They were patient. The Chinese knew they could bide their time gathering prisoners, whose options of places to flee were limited.

"We assembled in the stream bed and I told the men to follow me," Webster recounted. "I knew the road made a right turn just in front of the tanks and crossed a bridge. I started to cross the stream bed and the little valley in the direction of the road. For some reason the men did not follow me. I don't know if they didn't hear me in all the noise, or if they saw something I had not seen." Whatever the reason, Webster was on his own.

He traveled about fifty yards before looking back. He saw enemy soldiers moving in front of him, so he hit the ground and lay still for a few minutes. Once they passed he stood up and started moving again. This time the enemy did not let him pass.

A Chinese soldier appeared in front of Webster and fired one shot at him from only fifteen feet away. The muzzle flash blinded Webster, and the shot hit him in the leg. He fell to the ground, certain that his life was over. His bullet-shattered leg was numb, and he could not move it.

"I lay very still and started trying to move my leg," Webster said. "After a few minutes the numbness started to go away and I found I could move my leg and bend my knee. By feel, I found I had been shot through the knee, the bullet having entered from the front on the inside of the knee and exiting the back of the knee in the middle of the bend. The wound was very small and was probably from a .25 caliber WW II Japanese rifle."

Apparently, the Chinese were like the Americans and South Koreans in that respect: they were both using weapons from WWII that were outdated, but still lethal in their use.

"I suppose I lay where I had been shot for about fifteen minutes, massaging my knee and working to get the feeling back," Webster continued. "When I felt I was ready to travel I got up from the ground, took a couple of steps and was immediately surrounded by Chinese soldiers."

The soldiers searched Webster, took his weapon, and told him to lie down in the road ditch between the tanks and the hill. There were several other American prisoners there, and more joined the group as the battle raged throughout the night. The battle of Hoengsong was over for Webster and his fellow prisoners, but it had just begun for thousands of other struggling allied forces.

The question was who was better off: those who were killed at Hoengsong or those who were captured, sent to communist prison camps, and died after long periods of brutal treatment? There is no real answer, but the next chapter leaves room for wonder.

CHAPTER 11

Held After Hoengsong

"Many thousands of men vanished or became POWs in the Korean War, and the death rate for that war's prisoners was the highest in American history. Additionally, many of those who survived captivity were known to have been held back by the North Koreans during the prisoner exchanges in 1953." (Paul Riley)

THE CHINESE FORCES that pressed southward in the early spring of 1951 captured U.S. warfighters at Hoengsong in February, South Chorwon and Kumhwa in April, and in the mountains east of Chunchon in May. Virtually all those POWs were herded gradually north and west to large holding camps near Suan, North Korea. From there, some went to specialized interrogation camps at Pak's Palace and Pike's Peak. But most staged north through Kangdong, to arrive at Camp 1 or Camp 5, later that year. Carl Ramsey Burgess was among them.

Burgess's experience in a prison camp after Hoengsong is an example of the military equivalent of "out of the frying pan and into the fire." (See Appendix D for a description of prison life in Camp #5.) Burgess, like so many other U.S. warfighters in Korea, was a veteran of WWII.

He enlisted in the Army on December 17, 1942. He was assigned to the 82nd Field Artillery in the South Pacific Theater of Operation. Carl was discharged after completing his service on February 18, 1946. He then joined a local Army reserve unit to continue his career.

In July 1950, at the age of 28, he was recalled to active service for the Korean War. Burgess reported to Fort Hood, TX for a brief refresher orientation and training procedure before being shipped out to Korea. He was assigned to the 9th Infantry Regiment, 2nd Division in Korea as a Staff Sergeant and was soon promoted to Sergeant First Class. He landed in Korea in late August 1950 and went straight to the front lines.

On February 13, 1951, Carl and members of his unit were captured or killed in a bloody battle with Chinese soldiers. His unit was caught off guard in their make-shift shelter. They did not have proper weapons to defend themselves or their position. They were in a horseshoe tactical arrangement that was not effective in their particular situation.

The Chinese closed in on the unit in large numbers. The foes engaged in hand-to-hand combat. During this fight attack Carl incurred a bayonet wound to the right knee and leg before being captured. At the beginning of the struggle there were 76 men in Carl's unit; only 6 of them remained after the attack.

There were approximately 787 American prisoners captured and rounded up for a trip to North Korea, which was similar to the "Bataan death march." During the first 3 to 4 days they were marched in lines with their hands tied behind their backs and were gouged frequently in the back with bayonets to keep them moving and awake. Upon his release Carl had unbelievable scars on his back from the many bayonet thrusts he received during that march.

The prisoners traveled only at night and on cloudy days. During sunny days they were herded under pine trees and bushes to avoid being seen or found. They traveled approximately 750 miles in about 3 months. The prisoners who survived got to their forced destination on the Yalu River on May 19, 1951. Only about 285 of the original group completed the trip.

Of this group of primarily American prisoners, all of them suffered from horrific treatment. Over 60 percent of them died and were discarded along the trail during the march. On the trip to the Yalu River they ate everything from weeds and turnips to soy bean balls. Occasionally, they got a little dog or horse meat. They were glad to get any food.

They stopped on their journey at a camp referred to as "bean camp" by the prisoners (which was an old mining camp), where they were given soy bean balls to eat. They stayed at this location about three weeks. Many of the prisoners died from starvation, injuries, infections from bayonet stab wounds, intestinal and kidney problems, or total exhaustion while there.

After arriving at the final camp they had to go on "wood gathering detail." Each prisoner was required to complete a daily round trip of approximately 14 miles to the mountains to cut wood and carry almost 80 pounds tied to their backs on the return to the camp area.

Carl had a swollen, injured, infected leg. Out of sympathy for an "old man," as other prisoners called him, because he was a 28-year-old and a WWII veteran, younger prisoners helped him carry the load and survive. The wood was used primarily to prepare food for the Chinese and North Korean soldiers and for them to use for heat.

Sometimes the POWs stayed in huts made with mud and straw. Mostly, though, they stayed outside with no shelter, lying on the ground with little protection in the winter.

Unrelenting interrogation of prisoners was an everyday occurrence. The higher the rank the more times a prisoner was interrogated. The prisoners were punished if they did not tell the enemy what they wanted to know. One of many dreaded punishments was isolation for thirteen days in a tunnel.

During the daytime, the prisoners were required to take "brain-washing" classes showing the benefits and value of communism. The classes lasted several hours each day. The prisoners went without baths, clean clothing, and other necessary sanitary needs on a regular basis. They wore tennis-type shoes, shabby shirts and pants, and endured some days of high and low temperatures, which were reported to be below minus 40 degrees at times.

They basically received only one meal a day. Carl indicated that he often thought about the advice he got from his dad and mother, William and Mary Martha Burgess, of Yellow Creek Community, near Dickson, TN, about eating black-eyed peas as a child, which he did not like. They told him to eat the peas and that the day might come when he would be happy to get them. He thought that the time had come for him in North Korea, and he would now appreciate black-eyed peas. Overall, the diet was bad, and extremely limited for prisoners. However, it was similar to the food that the peasant population had to eat, with fewer restrictions in quantity.

Carl was confined for most of his 33 months as a prisoner of war in WI Con Camp No. 4 on the Yalu River. After a cease fire was agreed upon and signed with an effective date of July 27, 1953, the prisoners were told that they were being moved to another camp. Their names were called in groups on different days. One night Carl's name was called from the list, along with those of other prisoners. They were loaded onto trucks and hauled approximately 10-12 miles to a barn-like structure in which they were locked for the night.

The prisoners had not heard any news and did not know where or why they were being moved. The next morning, they were given about a half cup of soy bean and millet ball to eat. A man from Denmark, with the Red Cross, came and told the prisoners they were going to be released from prison at 9 a.m. that morning. They were loaded on trucks and crossed the 38th Parallel into South Korea.

After arriving in South Korea on September 1, 1953. Senator Nolen from California helped Carl, by then a physically, mentally weakened, damaged soldier, get off the truck and onto friendly soil. At the time of Carl's release from prison, he weighed 78 pounds, which was down from his normal 180 pounds. On the ship home, Carl and all the others were drilled and interrogated by the FBI to determine if they had accepted communism.

They landed in California and Carl flew to Fort Meade, MD, where he stayed in a hospital for ten days. He regained some weight and got back up to 117 pounds. He was granted a 20-day leave to go home, after which he returned to the hospital for surgery on his leg, which required hospitalization for about 45 days.

Finally, on November 28, 1953, Carl was honorably released from military service as a former POW, permanently handicapped and disabled for life. He, like so many of his fellow POWs who survived years of incarceration, would never forget Hoengsong. Some of the military commanders responsible for their leadership failure there, albeit indirectly, wished that he would.

Burgess survived his ordeal. Others did not. Some lingered for months or longer in the notorious camps. One POW, who preferred to remain anonymous, described his experience in less than pleasant terms in an essay titled "One Of The Few To Survive That Horrible Day:"

"I was captured at Hoengsong with a Sergeant from the tank corps and a South Korean. Not too long after, I was included in an Associated Press photo that was taken by the Chinese. The photo depicted several of us who were taken prisoner, including Lt. Colonel Keith, who was leading the group.

"We were all rounded up in a few days and sent north to the Yalu. I reported Keith missing. I saw him fall so many times, which is not surprising, since he was wounded in several places. After a day or two, I didn't see him anymore. I checked the POW missing list when I got home. Sure enough, his name was on it.

"I see that picture in my mind every day. The reason I got it was because my mother wrote to the Associated Press and asked if they had any pictures of missing military personnel. She was worried since I had been missing for ten months.

"They sent her a package of fifty photos, told her to keep any in which I appeared, and asked her to return the rest. She recognized me in one photo. When I got home she showed me the picture, which sent me back 2-1/2 years in time. Needless to say, I was stunned. The Marines who have described the massacre are the first and only people in that war who saw what I did.

"After the war, I could never get any info on the Hoengsong Massacre, and I gave up talking about it to people. All they talk about was Chip'yong-ni. In fact, I never talked too much about anything related to my Korean experience, since I knew so little about everything. That's because I was there only a short time before I was captured-and I was one of the few guys who survived that horrible day."

NOTE: There is some question as to whether Keith was killed or captured at Hoengsong. He is not included in any DPAA lists.

The family of North Carolinian George LeTell Rights had no idea that he was even a POW. George, like so many other soldiers, had reenlisted in the Army to serve in the Korean War. He was attached to the 2nd Army Division as a member of the 15th Artillery Battalion, which was overrun at Hoengsong.

The family learned that he was missing through a January 1954 telegram from the Army, which included a formal "statement of death" to his mother and father. That's when they learned that George had been captured by the communists and sent north to a POW camp, where he died of malnutrition. As best as they could determine George died in March or April 1951 in the Bean Camp. He was left behind with 100 or so prisoners who were too sick to endure another forced march to a new camp. His father tried to learn as much as possible about George's final days.

He wrote letters to men who were in the same POW camps and visited some who had known George. Most of what he learned was horrifying. He heard gruesome stories about soldiers who froze to death, died of starvation, and/or who were too sick to move while lying in abject filth and the brutal cold. The family had to live until 2015 with what they had learned. That was when George's remains were identified by DPAA and they were able to get closure. Similar stories abound.

Army Sergeant First Class Jack Daniel Lawver, who was captured on February 13, 1951, lasted almost four months in a POW camp. He experienced what was called "a critical situation" that resulted in his death on May 30, 1951. (Some sources post has date of death as June 30, 1951.) He was a member of Battery B, 15th Field Artillery Battalion, 2nd Infantry Division.

Army Corporal George A. Perreault suffered a similar fate, although all physical sightings of him disappeared after the initial stages of the battle. On February 5, 1951, Perreault was a part of Support Force 21 and assigned to Headquarters Battery, 15th Field Artillery Battalion, 2nd Infantry Division, which was supporting Republic of Korean Army (ROKA) attacks against units of the Chinese People's Volunteer Forces (CPVF) in the area known as the Central Corridor in South Korea.

On the evening of February 11, the CPVF launched a massive counterattack against the ROKA regiment. The regiment withdrew, leaving American units to fight alone at Changbong-ni, until they were forced to withdraw too. After enduring a sustained enemy attack, the Support Force abandoned Hoengsong and moved toward Wonju. Perreault never reported to Wonju and he was reported missing in action on February 13, 1951.

A list provided by opposing forces on December 26, 1951 stated that Perreault died as a prisoner of war, though the information could not be confirmed. Additionally, no returning American prisoners of war could provide any information on him. Based on the lack of information of his status, the U.S. Army declared him deceased as of January 18, 1954.

Such stories about Hoengsong continue today to appear in various places as more remains are identified. Even people who may have never heard about the battle are exposed to stories about it. The story of the Hoengsong massacre will not go away.

In November 2016 U.S. Army Private First Class William W. Cowan's remains were returned to his family at Columbus, Ohio. The ceremony provided closure for them, but left many more families in limbo regarding their missing warfighters. Cowan's story was unique. He did not have to be at Hoengsong. It was only through his persistence that he was in the Army at all.

Originally Cowan tried to enlist in the U.S. Navy. He was turned down because of unspecified medical issues. He spent months after the navy's rejection visiting a doctor. Consequently, he was able to enlist in the Army in August 1950. He shipped out to Korea in December that same year and was assigned to Company M, Third Battalion, 38th Infantry Regiment, Second Infantry Division. On February 12, 1951 his unit was attacking a road block set up by the Chinese near Hoengsong. Subsequently, Cowan was reported as missing in action.

Eventually he was determined to have been a prisoner of war at a work camp. Other prisoners reported that several months after Cowan entered the camp, he died, likely from malnutrition. His remains were identified by DPAA in June 2016. He became one more reminder of the horrendous Hoengsong massacre, which will remain in the public's eye due to stories like those of Burgess, Sawver, Perreault, and Cowan, who keep the legacy alive.

CHAPTER 12

Run, ROKs, Run

"Time and the retreating Reds have fully disclosed one of the bitterest stories of the Korean War—the battling march three weeks ago of half an American regiment through 'Massacre Valley.'" (John Randolph)

IRONICALLY, THE U.S. Army's 38th Regiment, serving with the 2nd Infantry Division, was nicknamed "The Rock of the Marne." Yet, the ROKS with whom they fought at Hoengsong did not put any stock in that special designation. Not many of them stood like rocks—or even pebbles—in the face of the Chinese hordes.

(As a matter of historical interest, the U.S. Army 3rd Infantry Division was also known as "Rock of the Marne." IN WWI the 3rd Division had four infantry regiments: 4th, 7th, 30th, and 38th. On 15 July 1918, at the Marne River, the 30th and 38th received the brunt of the German attack. The 38th claimed the name "Rock of the Marne" and U.S. Grant McAlexander, the Regimental CO, was also called the Rock of the Marne. As it was a divisional fight, the Division also received the Rock of the Marne moniker.

In 1940, the Army went four regiments to three, losing the 4th and 38th and gaining the 15th. The 2nd Infantry Division added the 38th Regiment, which served with it in WWII and Korea.)

The ROKs broke quickly at Hoengsong when attacked, turning what had started as an offensive operation into a defensive struggle. That was not a surprise to some American commanders, many of whom did not have a high opinion of the ROK troops to begin with, as Col James W. Edwards, who commanded the 2d Battalion, 23d Regiment opined:

"The Chinese Divisions, which had been streaming east for days, hit the ROK III Corps on the morning of 11 February 1951. How many of them hit the three ROK Divisions will never be known. The three ROK Divisions, as usual, disintegrated like chaff before a wind. The newsmen called them the "volatile" ROKS, and that is a good description.

"A Battalion Commander of the 38th Infantry told [me] that the 8th ROK Division, which was supposed to be one of the best divisions, came down on the road through his Battalion like a herd of wild cattle in a stampede. Most of them were at a dead run and had thrown away their weapons.

"The U. S. officers of the 38th Infantry tried to stop them, but the one way that they could have been stopped would have been to use the communist method of setting up machineguns and firing into them. The United States Army just couldn't use this method against their allies.

"The general opinion of all officers of the Infantry Regiments of the 2d Division was that the ROKS were only good for running to the rear and for cluttering up the supply roads with their speeding vehicles. Operation Roundup had turned into a stampede as far as the ROKs were concerned. The ROKs in their stampede had failed to even notify their supporting U. S. Artillery Battalions they were pulling out. The Chinese overran many of these Artillery Battalions and killed most of their personnel."

At first there was no reason for the Americans to believe that trouble lay ahead. The ROK units had been on the move all day and were making steady progress in their drive to push the Chinese out of the area. They had advanced 7 or 8 miles since Operation Roundup began officially. The Chinese offered varying levels of opposition, but not enough to hinder the ROKs' advance. And, SF 21 had played a major role in the advance by supplying artillery support—with no opposition.

Battery D personnel looking through the BC scope saw the ROK infantry on the hill just north of Changbong-ni. They were engaged in hand-to-hand combat with enemy troops. As darkness approached, the Chinese withdrew, so the ROKs dug in for the night, which they knew from experience would be uncomfortable. The days at the time were mostly sunny and warm, which created very muddy and wet conditions. But, once daylight disappeared, the temperature plummeted close to zero. As the Chinese had proved at the Battle of the Chosin Reservoir, the frigid conditions were ideal for their activities.

The Chinese 198th Division, 66th Army struck the first blow when it attacked the 21st Regiment head on. Then, some of the 198th's troops swung around to the west between the 21st and the ROK 10th Regiment. Simultaneously, the 120th Division, 40th Army attacked the ROK 10th Regiment and the Chinese 117th Division, 39th Army flowed through the 16th Regiment's left flank.

The ROK troops broke and ran almost immediately. The retreat included Support Team (ST) Baker, which consisted of Company "L," 3rd Bn., 38th Infantry, and one platoon from Tank Company, 38th Infantry. (Generally, one tank platoon includes four tanks.) Company "L" had been detached from 3rd Bn., 38th Inf. Regt., which was in a defensive position near the town of Saemal. The battalion would play a critical role in the overall battle as it progressed. ST Baker withdrew to SF 21's perimeter, where it arrived at 10 p.m. The withdrawal quickly became a full-blown retreat.

Word of the initial attacks reached ROK 8th Division's headquarters

(HQ) in Hoengsong soon after they began. Division commander Brigadier General Choi Yong Hee ordered the 21st Regiment to make a short withdrawal, which was redundant, since they were already in full flight. He also instructed Support Team B, an armored group, to move back down Route 29 and join SF 21 at Ch'angbong-ni.

While all the maneuvering was going on, part of the Chinese 198th Division units that had moved around the 21st Regiment raced down both sides of Route 29, past the American position at Ch'angbong-ni, and blocked the road near a bridge three miles farther south.

Around 11:30 p.m. Keith notified the 1st Bn., 38th Inf. Regt. that the 21st ROK Regiment was withdrawing. That was bad news for SF 21. So, Major John Blackwell, the 1st Bn., 38th Inf.'s S-3 (training officer), asked the 21st Regiment's commanding officers and its KMAG officer to halt the withdrawal until SF 21 was ready to move out.

Simultaneously, Keith, following the chain of command, got in touch with General Loyal M. Haynes, the 2d ID's artillery commander. Keith asked Haynes to contact the 8th ROK Division's commanding officer to request that his troops stand and fight at least long enough to allow SF 21 to withdraw. That was like asking the ocean to stop the tides.

As American troops had learned earlier in the war, once the ROK troops started "bugging out" there was no stopping them. SF 21 was on its own as the ROK soldiers continued their chaotic withdrawal. They had good reason to flee. There were Chinese everywhere.

The Chinese 120th Division sent additional forces through the ROK 10th Regiment. Some of them turned behind both the 10th and 16th; others moved southeast toward the mountain road leading west from Route 29. Those troops overran the CPs of the 10th and 16th Regiments around midnight and cut off the ROK 20th and 50th Field Artillery Battalions and Support Team A (ST A). Worse, they set up strong blocking forces between the support units and Route 29.

Meanwhile, the Chinese 117th Division launched a strong frontal attack on the ROK 16th Regiment and penetrated its left flank. The 117th had enough troops to divert some personnel eastward on the mountain road, directly toward Hoengsong. The friendly forces were in total disarray as midnight approached.

CHAPTER 13

February 12, 1951: Caught In A Crossfire

"Here the dreamless dead would lie, leached to bone by the passing seasons, and waiting, as all the dead would wait, for doomsday's horn." Rick Atkinson, referring to the dead Americans at the ill-fated battle of the Rapido in Italy, January 1943. (The Day of Battle, p. 350)

THE FRIENDLY TROOPS did not realize just how much trouble they were in as February 12 arrived. They started to get an inkling shortly after the witching hour. Carroll D. Harrod, assigned to the 49th FA Bn. of the U.S. Army 7th Division, was among those who gauged immediately the predicament the friendly troops were in.

The 49th FA Bn. was providing general artillery support to the ROK 5th Division with reinforcing fires from a six-gun battery of the 31st FA Bn. (155mm Howitzers) of the U.S. 7th Division. Like so many support units, the 49th got enmeshed in the Hoengsong debacle.

Harrod was at the 49th's CP at 1 a.m. on February 12th when the eerie sound of bugles echoing across the frozen rice paddies awakened him. "I knew immediately we were in serious trouble," he said.

A guard told Harrod to get everyone up and ready to move out. Heavy small arms fire had already broken out around the ROK Regiment CP. When the 49th troops tried to load up and get their jeeps moving, they came under heavy small arms fire and hand grenade attack. Their contingent of about fifteen officers and men were badly outnumbered. Their position was quickly overrun by the attacking Chinese.

Harrod did the best he could to stop the enemy. He suffered a serious injury in the process. As he recalled:

"While I was firing at the shadowy figures of our Chinese attackers with my .45 pistol, I received a grenade fragment in the left shoulder, which felt like a bolt of electricity when it entered, and which resulted in complete loss of movement and feeling in my left shoulder, arm, wrist, and hand," he reported. "One of the Forward Observers had received a serious grenade wound in the head area and was unconscious. Another Forward Observer had received fragments in the hand and arm, and several of the enlisted men had received slight wounds."

The Chinese took them all prisoner, as Harrod explained.

"After our position was overrun we were placed under guard and moved into a Korean hut, along with about fifty South Korean prisoners. As the forward elements of the Chinese attack moved south, things calmed down, except for more prisoners being brought in periodically. From the other prisoners being brought in we could tell this had been an attack along a broad front and many positions had been overrun.

"By nightfall of 12 February, the realization that we were prisoners of the communist forces had sunk in, and it was hard for us not to be depressed, especially those of us suffering wounds. Additional prisoners kept being brought in, with the ratio being about two ROK troops for every one US troop.

"We were given no food that night and kept warm simply because of the number of bodies crammed into that Korean hut. The Chinese had brought in our wounded FO, and he was in pretty bad shape with his head wound. My wounded shoulder remained completely numb from the shoulder blade to the tip of my left hand, but there wasn't much pain from the wound itself."

The real pain would come later as he endured the long trek to a North Korean prison camp, along with numerous other POWs. Ironically, one of his comrades on the trip was Wilbur R. Webster.

At 12:30 a.m. members of K Co., 3rd Bn., 38th Inf. noted small arms and mortar fire to their front. The company was not under attack at that point, however, and may not have known there was a battle going on since they were not in the direct line of fire. Communications between and among friendly units were almost nonexistent at that point, which simply added to the surprises the enemy forces had at the moment.

The Chinese had a major advantage in the early hours of the battle, and they pressed it fully. As the ROK 8th Division began to fall back after midnight, the Chinese 66th Army commander expanded his advance below Hongchon.

He sent his 197th Division south five miles east of Route 29 against the ROK 3d Division. Chinese infiltrators west of Route 29 and along the road initiated heavy frontal assaults against the 23rd Regiment's command post. Next, they attacked a battalion of the 22nd Regiment. Their goal was to catch them in a trap. But, before they could spring it, the two ROK regiments withdrew to a defensive position about three miles northeast of Hoengsong.

By 1 a.m. communications were out between ROK 8th Division headquarters and all three of its regiments, which were withdrawing without a clue about where they were going. They were trapped. The Chinese were all around them.

The withdrawal started in an orderly manner, but broke down quickly as commanders lost communications with one another and control over their troops. To make matters worse, none of the ROK commanders knew which direction to move. The Chinese blocked them in every direction. The ROK units were fighting blind—if they were fighting at all.

It was not long before unit integration broke down. Units became separated and divided—and most of them were surrounded by hordes of Chinese troops no matter which way they went. In no time individual troops bolted and the withdrawal became every man for himself. Some of the affected troops were Americans.

Cool headed officers tried their best to rally the troops and restore order. Around 1:30 a.m., troops, some of them wounded, from K Co., 9th Inf. entered the K Co. 38th Inf. area. The newcomers were members of a task force attached to the 16th ROK Regt., 8th ROK Division, which was engaged with the enemy.

One of the wounded soldiers was Captain Jones, the CO of K Co., 9th Inf. Jones told LtCol Harold Maxiner, the 3rd Bn.'s commander, that the enemy had overrun the 16th ROK Regiment and had mauled his company in the process. He had lost most of his company, and he had no idea where they were located. After he delivered his report, the slightly wounded Jones was removed to the Battalion Aid station.

The troops grew increasingly edgy as the night progressed. Meanwhile, elements of the 8th ROK Division were in full retreat. Troops of its 10th and 16th Regiments were rushing south past the 3rd Bn. HQ with no apparent interest in stopping there. Maxiner seized the initiative. He realized that he had to stop the stampede. But, he had a thorny problem: he did not have any command control over the ROK troops. That did not deter him from trying to stop them.

Around 2 a.m. Maxiner ordered that a check point be set up at the Y junction on the road near Saemal to detain passing ROK and American troops until he could figure out what was going on. The location was a logical collection point for all the retreating friendly troops, since their escape routes were limited and they had to go through the junction. He assigned every soldier he could to a position on the defensive perimeter, although his intention was to turn the ROK stragglers over to their KMAG officers at some point.

Assuming defensive positions was acceptable to the American troops, who were comforted somewhat by the presence of friendly comrades. The ROKs were less than interested in participating. That was Maxiner's main problem at the moment: no one seemed to know who—if anyone—was in charge of them.

Stragglers were everywhere. Fleeing troops of the 21st Regiment straggled into SF 21's perimeter at Ch'angbong-ni about 1:15 a.m. LtCol William P. Keleher, who was in charge of 1st Battalion, 38th Infantry, Keith's infantry protection, and his officers were doing their best to stop the retreating ROK soldiers and place them on the American perimeter. That, as Maxiner had discovered, was fruitless. The ROK troops just kept on their merry way to what they hoped was safety, wherever that might be, as Keith tried to re-establish order.

He informed Brig. Gen. Loyal M. Haynes, the 2d Division artillery commander, about the ROK units' withdrawal and sought permission to join them. He wanted to move about three miles to a position he had occupied previously, just above the 3d Battalion, 38th Infantry at the junction of Route 29 and the mountain road leading west. He also requested that Haynes ask the ROK 8th Division commander to stop the 21st Regiment's withdrawal until Keith got SF 21 and ST B ready to move out. Haynes tried, with no success.

He contacted General Choi, who informed Haynes that he had lost contact with the 21st Regiment. He added that he believed the 21st was not in full flight. Rather, he said, it was completing the short withdrawal he had called for earlier. Consequently, Choi didn't do anything to help Haynes or Keith. Moreover, Haynes was reluctant to okay

Keith's withdrawal without clearing the move first with General Clark L. Ruffner. Ruffner passed the buck; he told Haynes to check with the X Corps artillery commander.

Haynes forwarded Keith's request to General Ruffner, who instructed him to check with X Corps. There, Haynes talked to Colonel William P. Ennis, Jr., the Corps' artillery commander, around 1:30 a.m. Ennis bounced the request to Colonel William J. McCaffrey of the Corps' Chief of Staff's office. McCaffrey advised General Almond directly about Keith's request.

Almond approved the withdrawal, which was passed back through the same chain in reverse. All in all, it took ninety minutes for Keith's request to be approved—an eternity to a troop commander under attack on virtually all sides. Even then there was some confusion about where he was going to move.

As so often happens with a message that is funneled through multiple people, it got muddled along the way. By the time Keith's request reached Almond, it had gotten a bit altered, at least as far as the general was concerned. He thought that SF 21 wanted to withdraw to Hoengsong, not to a position near the 3d Battalion, 38th Infantry.

Keith had not just been twiddling his thumbs while he waited. Nor were the Chinese. They kept spreading their attacks. At 2:20 a.m. members of "K" Company saw a large number of Chinese troops to their front near Chowon-ni. They were certain about the nationality, because their comrades in the 9th Infantry Regiment had informed them earlier that the enemy force was Chinese.

About 300 Chinese troops from the 197th Division raced southwest toward Ch'angbong-ni. Around 2:30 a.m., they struck Company A, 38th Infantry, which was holding the northeast sector of SF 21's perimeter. The company stood its ground initially, but the Chinese kept them under fire.

CHAPTER 14

Diddling, Dawdling, And Dying

"The main effort was against X Corps' ROK divisions north of Hoengsong. The Chinese attack, dramatically announced with bugle calls and drum beating, penetrated the ROK line and forced the South Koreans into a ragged withdrawal to the southeast via snow-covered passes in the rugged mountains. The ROK units, particularly the 8th Division, were badly battered in the process, creating large holes in the UN defenses." (The Korean War: Restoring the Balance)

WHILE KEITH BIDED his time, he began to put his artillery units in march order. He had plenty of time as commanders bounced his request from pillar to post—most of which were under attack by the omnipresent Chinese by that time. Finally, at about 2:45 a.m., Keith received permission to withdraw, but to exactly where was not clear. At the same time 3rd Bn, 38th Infantry requested artillery fire on a located Chinese assembly area near Chowon-ni. Fifteen minutes later, the 1st Bn, 38th Regt. notified their counterparts at 3rd Bn that they were withdrawing to Kaktam-ni—the same positions they had occupied the previous day. Everyone was in motion.

The bureaucracy began. A division officer, Major Reginald E. Ivory, told 3rd Bn that it would have to clear its request for artillery through KMAG, 8th ROK Division. That would be a bit difficult to obtain, since the KMAG officers were retreating with their ROK charges. The battalion responded quickly by telling Ivory that bugles were blowing and that ROK troops who had fallen back to the 3rd Bn perimeter had positively stated that the area was occupied by Chinese, and that the artillery fire was essential. Ivory passed on the request.

A half hour later Ivory called 3rd Bn to tell them that KMAG would not give clearance to fire. The battalion contact informed Ivory that 3rd Bn had already blanketed the area with 81mm mortars and 75mm Recoilless Rifles, and that it needed artillery support at once. It was still not forthcoming. At 4 a.m. Ivory notified 3rd Bn that they still could not get clearance because they had information that a ROK engineer battalion was supposed to pass through the 3rd Bn., attacking west toward Chowon-ni.

Battalion told Ivory that the ROK engineer battalion supposedly in the area had taken up positions on the 3rd Battalion perimeter, that they were not attacking, and that it was safe to fire. Nevertheless Division Artillery and KMAG diddled and dawdled—while soldiers died. It wasn't until 6:27 a.m. that Division Artillery finally obtained clearance to fire. Meanwhile, the Chinese were taking their time rounding up stranded U.S. troops and preparing to ship them to prison camps.

The aforementioned Wilbur Webster had been one of the men on the M-16 who was taken prisoner early in the battle the night before. In hindsight, the fact that his M-16 and the two tanks were blocking a critical road for the Chinese was a blessing in disguise. The enemy couldn't maneuver past the allied vehicles blocking the road without a great deal of effort. As early morning on the 12th arrived they were still trying to ease the road block and boldly asked stranded U.S. troops to help them. The delay gave the friendly leaders a little more time to rally their forces.

After daylight the Chinese began a systematic search for friendly troops that were in hiding, some of whom had spent a terrifying night trying to avoid capture. One of them was Pfc. Floyd of the 503rd FA Bn.

Floyd was hiding in the trailer of the M-16 that Webster had been assigned to the night before. The Chinese did not find him until after daylight. The light gave them the opportunity to find stragglers from the earlier battle. When they looked in the trailer they found Floyd. He was sent to join the group of prisoners that included Webster and Harrod.

Finding Floyd was a triumph for the Chinese. But they still had a problem. The M-16 and other vehicles were blocking the road. The Chinese approached the group of prisoners and asked if any of them knew how to drive the vehicles that needed to be moved. There was no great rush to volunteer. The Chinese did not press the issue. They still had a war to fight and a battle to win. Maxiner and his fellow leaders were doing all they could to make sure that desired victory didn't happen.

Maxiner was still trying to corral the stragglers passing through his checkpoint at Saemal and set up a defensive line, using all the able-bodied troops he could muster. This was a case where, as the Scottish poet Robert Burns suggested in his ode "To a mouse," the "best laid schemes o' Mice an' Men often go astray, An' lea'e us nought but grief an' pain, For promis'd joy!" The emphasis for the allied troops was on the grief and pain.

Around 2 a.m., Keith ordered SF 21 to withdraw to the positions they had occupied on the night of 10 February, although they did not actually start moving until between 3 and 4 a.m. Even then, their progress was slow, and lasted for only an hour.

Simultaneously, Keleher ordered ST Baker to dispatch two of its four tanks and two infantry squads to secure the bridge three miles south of there, just above their new position. They had the added protection of some retreating South Korean troops who had just joined the group. Keleher's goal was to facilitate the friendly units' withdrawal.

He was not aware that the Chinese had beaten him to the bridge.

The commanders were buoyed by a promise from the 38th Inf. Regt. that it was prepared to give supporting fire with 4.2 mortars and artillery upon request, and that it had asked for air. (Supporting air strikes were controlled by 38th Infantry Tactical Air Control Party, aka TACP.)

The Commanding Officer, lst Bn., was instructed to keep regimental headquarters informed of progress southward because these supporting fires were being brought down on observed targets south and southeast of his position. But, according to the regimental command report, no requests for additional supporting fires were received. As noted previously, artillery support was minimal and may not have been available anyway.

At 6:43 a.m., an estimated company of enemy troops attacked the 3rd Bn with small arms fire. They attacked from the west along the east-west road. A short while later another group of enemy soldiers attacked from the south. The fights did not last long. After skirmishing with the 3rd Bn, the enemy bypassed them and continued south to join other elements of their force. It was almost as if the enemy was playing with the friendly troops.

The 3rd Bn formed a perimeter defense to counter the large enemy build-up to the south.

At 7 a.m. an estimated platoon of enemy troops struck the 38th Regimental CP in Hoengsong, but the Netherlands Detachment and the 8th ROK Division CP group turned them back. Apparently, the attacking platoon comprised the lead elements of the enemy which had bypassed the 3rd Bn. a short while earlier. While that group attacked the Regimental CP, another enemy force on the regiment's right delivered heavy fire into its defenses, but was unable to penetrate their positions.

Friendly commanders were reeling from all the enemy attacks.

Unfortunately, intelligence was scarce for them. They were practically fighting blind. Keleher had no way of knowing that the Chinese had not only blocked Route 29 near the bridge, but that they had established roadblocks above and below the crossing. One of those blocks was in the new area in which Keith intended to set up operations.

The Chinese did not waste a moment in attacking Keleher's security force. No sooner had Keleher's force started south than Chinese machine gunners overlooking Route 29 from the east disrupted their movement. The infantry and the South Koreans stayed close to the tanks for protection, which was not the best place to be. They had only traveled one mile when something exploded under the second tank.

Platoon leader 2d Lt. William M. Mace jumped out of the tank's turret to check the damage. Fortunately, there was none. The tank continued down the road—without Mace. Chinese machine gun fire prevented him from getting back inside his tank. Then, a grenade tossed by a Chinese soldier in a ditch on the east side of the knocked him off his tank.

Miraculously, neither the machine gun rounds nor the grenade wounded him. He was unwounded and undaunted—but tankless. The two tanks kept on going; none of their crew members realized that Mace was missing. He may have been better off than the crew members anyway.

The tanks rumbled down the road to put some distance between themselves and the Chinese who were harassing them as they traveled. Unfortunately, they were moving so fast they left the infantry behind. Mace, now an infantryman, the two infantry squads, and some of the South Koreans moved to the right side of the road to escape the Chinese fire coming from the left side. They were successful initially.

Mace's group waited until daylight to start drifting south in the hopes of finding the 3rd Bn., 38th Inf. They encountered Chinese all along the route. As they did, the troops scattered. Many of them were killed or captured in a series of skirmishes with the enemy. But Mace and a few other survivors joined the 3rd Bn. around 9:30 a.m. As harrowing as their night had been, they fared better than the tanks they had been accompanying.

As the first tank approached the bridge, an enemy rocket or hand grenade blinded the driver, who lost control of his vehicle. The tank ran off the road and overturned. As the second tank tried to pass it, a Chinese round struck its engine compartment and disabled the vehicle. It rolled over on the opposite side of the road from the first tank. Neither one reached the bridge.

The crews from both tanks ran west into the hills, then turned south toward the protection of the 3d Battalion, 38th Infantry. It did not matter which direction they ran; there were Chinese everywhere, and the situation went from bad to worse quickly for the friendly forces.

The failure of the bridge securing force did not deter Keith from starting his withdrawal, nor did the determined Chinese—at least not at first. At 2:30 a.m., Chinese small arms fire started raining on SF 21's perimeter. The firing increased for the next half hour. By 3 a.m. "A" Company encountered a heavy attack by an estimated 300 enemy. The timing was bad for SF 21, whose troops were loading their equipment and organizing their vehicles for the anticipated move to Haktam-ni. Continuing that process and fighting the Chinese was beyond their multi-tasking capabilities at the time.

Chinese mortar crews blasted SF 21's perimeter with shells and heavy small arms and machine gun fire from the heights east of Route 29. Even though the harassment disrupted any semblance of organization that SF 21 troops had, they doggedly continued their withdrawal. One significant Chinese attack was particularly devastating.

As Keith's main column stretched out on the road, the leading artillery unit, Battery A of the 503d Field Artillery Battalion, was placing its guns in column. Suddenly, a group of Chinese soldiers rushed onto the road from the east and captured the battery commander, first sergeant, and several artillerymen, including Robert C. Chandler, the battery commander's driver. (Chandler, like so many soldiers captured at Hoengsong, died in captivity. His date of death is listed as somewhere around 31 March 1951.)

They melted back into the hills with the POWs as Chinese gunners saturated vehicles in the road with devastating effects. The gunners damaged many of the vehicles and killed or wounded several of their drivers. Keith's withdrawal was doomed to failure. In truth, it never got started fully because of Chinese infiltration and interdiction. Exactly what happened to their unit was a mystery to Keleher.

The colonel wrote later, "To the best of my knowledge, five of the 155mm Howitzers never left their position at 0758. Why they didn't is not known by me. When I last saw their position they had several guns in march order and activity indicated they were preparing the rest of the Battery for march order.

"The 15th FA Battalion had already march ordered and were on the road. "A" Battery, 503rd FA Battalion had plenty of time and were supposed to move out first. My "A" Company fought the rear guard action and when they reached the 503rd area, the battery was in march order but completely abandoned."

By 4 a.m. the Chinese had stopped Keith's column in its tracks. The friendly forces opted to stay in place and fight. Infantry and artillery troops at the head of the column faced east along the road and returned fire. Company A, to the north, originally assigned as the rear guard, turned to face northwest, north, and northeast. The Chinese skirmished with Company A, but that was about all they could do. The other two tanks of ST B and the rear guard troops kept the Chinese from stopping the column completely.

The constant attacks made the 38th Inf.'s positions untenable. Earlier, around 3 a.m., the 1st Bn. 38th Inf. had informed the 3rd Bn. that it had received orders to withdraw to Haktam-ni, where they had been on 10 February 1951. Unfortunately, all the units moving around were doing so without any artillery support, especially those that relied on the 503rd Field Artillery Bn.

All requests for artillery were put on hold, as Division Artillery informed everyone that they could not provide support without permission from the 8th ROK Division, which was not forthcoming. There wasn't much in the way of artillery anyway, and what was available did not contribute much.

The only artillery available in the Hoengsong area at the beginning of the withdrawal, with the exception of that with Support Force #21, was one Battery of 155s (Impact Charlie) and one Battery of 105s (Impair Charlie). The 105s, minus Charlie Btry., had been moved to another sector on 9-10 February. During the height of the battle on February 12th, at 11:15 a.m., Impact Charlie and Impair Charlie, minus two guns, were ordered to the rear for some inexplicable reason. The two guns left behind, which remained in position until 10:15 p.m., composed the only artillery capable of delivering fire into the road block area.

All artillery, regardless of where it was positioned, was coordinated or controlled by Division Artillery. And, there were two key elements lacking for effective artillery support, one for Division Artillery and the other for the 1st Bn., 38th Infantry.

Division artillery could not distinguish at times between friendly and enemy forces, South Korean versus Chinese, which was a problem that would surface time and time again for the combatants at Hoengsong in particular and Korea in general. As the 1 March 1951 artillery command report noted, "The use of supporting fire of all kinds was severely curtailed because of the difficulty of identification. Groups of friendly troops were dispersed over the entire area and were passing through the lines of the Netherlands Detachment at frequent intervals throughout the day and night."

CHAPTER 15

Too Many Ribbons, Too Few FOs— And A Lack Of Intelligence

"We retreated for 9 miles and the Koreans just walked up the road like a parade, with machine gun bullets flying at them like rice." Pfc. Edgar Layman Green, 15th Field Artillery Battalion, 2nd Inf Division, killed in action on 13 Feb.1951 at Hoengsong, in a letter home.

ONE OF THE problems UN personnel had in the first few months of the war was how to distinguish ROK troops from their Chinese and North Korean brethren and civilians who cluttered the roads even in the midst of battles. Refugees roamed freely throughout battle areas, hindering operations and making it necessary for friendly forces to establish numerous checkpoints. The need to staff these checkpoints took soldiers away from their fighting units, which reduced their fire power. In some cases refugees were apprehended carrying contraband for the enemy, e.g., small mirrors, which investigation revealed were used to transmit signals.

The UN troops' inability to make the distinction at times between ROK and enemy troops put them in danger. The Chinese and North

Koreans took full advantage of the dilemma by donning ROK uniforms to trick UN troops, create confusion, and increase allied casualty rates. Moreover, they adapted to allied attempts to resolve the problem.

Early in the war, ROK troops were outfitted in uniforms that were exactly like—or similar to—those worn by the Americans. That was no problem for the enemy. They simply stole American uniforms or stripped them from POWs or dead soldiers. (Wearing the enemy's uniforms was not unusual for the Chinese. U.S. Marines reported long after the Hoengsong fiasco was over that they captured or killed Chinese soldiers wearing U.S. Army 2nd Inf. Div. uniforms.) The UN countered with ribbons attached to ROK soldiers' uniforms. That created a new set of problems. The enemy adapted the idea as well.

The ribbons were hardly visible on the ROK uniforms. They could not be seen once the soldiers got 30-40 yards away from their comrades. The difficulty in recognizing friend from foe became a major problem in the battle around Hoengsong, as did the lack of forward observers (FOs), the soldiers who directed and reported back on artillery fire.

During the fighting around Hoengsong on the 11th and 12th of February the 1st and 3rd Battalions, 38th Regiment shared a significant—and lethal—similarity: they both lost most of their intelligence personnel. They were not easily replaceable. They performed valuable assignments, e.g. map and compass reading, patroling, and outpost operations. Losing soldiers with these skills definitely hampered the UN forces at Hoengsong.

The Army had not cross-trained many of its soldiers to step in when intelligence personnel were lost, and there was no time during the action battle to train replacements. As a result, the battalions were fighting with the proverbial one hand tied behind their backs. Keeping track of enemy movements was difficult for UN commanders in the best of times. Once they lost their intelligence specialists at Hoengsong, it was virtually impossible. The lack of intelligence personnel was not the only reason that some UN forces performed so poorly during the battle, but it was a prime contributor.

The lack of FOs, sometimes called OPs, was also detrimental to the UN forces. FOs often worked in teams in Korea. A team normally consisted of an officer and two enlisted men. The officer was the team leader. One enlisted man was the radio operator and the other was the recon sergeant. Artillery support for the 1st Bn.'s movement to the 3rd Bn perimeter to the vicinity of Samael was obtained from Air OPs and by relaying requests through 3rd Bn, 38th Infantry.

The lack of FOs notwithstanding, the 38th Regiment received some artillery support. Post-battle command reports noted that the 15th Field Artillery Battalion dropped trails (long boxed or pipe extensions to Howitzers and guns used to tow and help anchor the weapon to the ground to absorb recoil) and delivered some direct fire during the withdrawal south. Just how much is not known, though, since those same reports reveal that battalion journals were lost at the roadblock, and the few entries below that survived really do not provide much information:

Following are all entries relating to artillery support extracted from the S-3 Journal 38th Infantry for period 120001 to 122400 February.

From	To	No	Time	
Ivory		12	0245	Have just alerted artillery w/ Support Force 21 to withdraw to positions occupied yesterday. S
1st Bn		13	0250	Support Force §21 falling back to positions held as of 11 Feb. S
Blue		28	0525	Request permission to fire arty on high ground vicinity 076523 Ans/ will ok with KMAG

Blue	29	0627	Permission granted to fire arty vicinity 076523 s
C Btry 82nd AAA	36	0658	Send one section of AA to cover approaches to H-town from NW
38FA	44	0850	"L" plane arrived - overhead - preparing to observe 0351 grid Sq.
Air OP	57	0925	Large Grp in vic 0934-94 and hit it. est 25 to 50 casualties. Grid Sq 0446. 0445 est 4-500 on road hdng S, Ans/Rqsting Air Rad. G-3
Air OP	59	0936	Rqst arty on Village on reverse Slope of hill at 093494
Air Op	60	0936	Firing arty at 093494 now Rad
Air Op	62	1015	Bringing fire on many scattered forces at 0246.
Air OP	76	1250	En dug - in at 054LJ.S3 top of hill; bringing arty on them.

The fact that the gun crews dropped trails suggested that they planned to stay in place for a while. As soon as the 15th FA Bn arrived in the 3rd Bn perimeter, around 10:30 a.m., guns were placed into firing position and registered to the south, east, and west. (Registration is the process of firing successive rounds on a known location to obtain corrective data for future firing.) The crews also placed direct fire on targets to the west. Other than those 15th FA Bn guns, about the only support available was mortars, whose worth in combat was limited, as Medal of Honor recipient Sergeant Charles R. Long demonstrated the night of February 12th.

Long, a veteran of World War II who had fought at the Battle of the Bulge, was with Company M, 38th Inf. Regt., which was in a defensive perimeter on Hill 300. Around 3 a.m. the Chinese attacked Company M with a numerically superior force. The company received orders to withdraw, which it started to do immediately. Long, a forward observer for the mortar platoon, opted to stay where he was to provide cover for his retreating comrades by directing mortar fire on the enemy.

He stayed in radio contact with his platoon as he directed accurate mortar fire on the advancing Chinese. Soon, they had him surrounded. Undaunted, Long fired his carbine and threw hand grenades until he was mortally wounded. In his last radio message he stated that he was out of ammunition and called for a 40-round mortar strike near his position. He was surrounded and killed soon after.

Long did not die in vain. He took a personal toll on the advancing Chinese. In fact, his valorous stand stopped the attack long enough to let Company M withdraw, reorganize, counterattack, and regain the hill. He received the Medal of Honor posthumously on February 1, 1952 for his actions at Hill 300.

Doyle Parman, a member of Long's company and a survivor of the battle at Hoengsong, added a few details about Long and his exploits. Parman did not tell his story until 1998, 47 years after the massacre—about the same time the U.S. Army finally released command reports detailing the events of February 11-13, 1951.

"We were in a position on Hill 300, not really a hill, just a small hill. This was near a small village called Saemel. We were behind the main line about three or four miles. Our L Co, the artillery, and ROK troops were up on the MLR. We were there for several days just waiting, not knowing what was to come.

TOO MANY RIBBONS, TOO FEW FOS—AND A LACK OF INTELLIGENCE

"We were getting two meals a day, one about 9 a.m. and the other about 4 p.m. We had our forward observer, Charles Long, out; he was with other mortar FOs.

"Unlike most of the time, our F.O. was not assigned to any rifle company. I was 1st Gunner on one of our Mortars, 81mm. I went on guard about 2:30 a.m. on Feb. 12, 1951. I hadn't been on guard but a few minutes when I heard screaming ROK troops running down the road past us. They had thrown their weapons down. They weren't trained at all.

"Then we started getting fire orders from Charles Long. We fired as fast as we could till daylight. Then we got no more fire orders. We were surrounded then but didn't know it.

"We were on a south hill slope, and the enemy was just over the hill, maybe 200 or 300 yards away. A sergeant from our machine gun platoon decided he would go up and look over the hill. He was shot through the upper thigh, and passed out. We dragged him back down the hill, a short distance....he was white and in shock.

"At that time we weren't firing, because our FO was dead. We had an aid station there, but being surrounded we couldn't get any wounded out.

"A wounded, ill-fated 1st Lt from the artillery got in the foxhole with us and another guy. He was hit in the foot or ankle. He limped, but he could get along. He had been to the aid station, but they had so many worse off than him that they wouldn't take him. After I came home from Korea I found out this lieutenant was from Kansas City, and he had married a girl from my hometown. Sadly, he was captured that night and died in a prison camp in April.

"A helicopter, one like we see on [the television show] M.A.S.H., came in about midday for wounded. Not knowing what he was getting into, the pilot came in at an angle. As he got close enough, the

Chinese burp gun bullets started hitting the long part of the chopper behind the pilot.

"We didn't know it at the time, but our FO had radioed in the early morning that he had used all his carbine rounds and thrown all his grenades. He was completely surrounded when he called for 40 rounds on his own position, killing himself and many enemy.

"Our Company Commander took toilet paper out of his helmet liner and wrote a recommendation for Charles Long to get the Medal of Honor. Since we were surrounded, he sent his request out with the helicopter pilot. He didn't know whether any of us would get out or not. I ordered a book after I got home about the 2nd Div. In it there were the names of those that had received medals and which one. It said Charles Long had been recommended for the Medal of Honor. I never knew until 1991 that he had gotten it posthumously.

"Anyway, we laid low for the rest of the day, till about 4 p.m. Then we started down the road slowly. The enemy was close but didn't bother us till we got down in the valley. They had troops on the hills on both sides and the road was narrow...and of course there were trees on both sides.

"After dark they let loose with everything they had. Me and a friend decided to stay together. (We were told we were on our own.) We would get on one side of the road then the other. It was real dark. All we could see was the sky full of tracer bullets. I think every 5th one was a tracer.

"It was quiet for just a few minutes and a group of us were huddled together in the ditch. Someone, I'll never know who, said, "If you want to live get up and move....if you want to die stay here."

"I told my friend Bill Sherman, "We better move on." I don't know what rank that voice was, but he was right!

"Our side had sent three tanks up there to help get us out. There

TOO MANY RIBBONS, TOO FEW FOS—AND A LACK OF INTELLIGENCE

were GIs clinging to every part of those tanks. Bill and I opted not to try and get on one. We finally came to the river. By that time our side had sent up flares and we could see a little. The temperature was around 15 or 20 degrees F.

"I guess we started across the river. I could see some stones the Koreans had there to walk on, so I decided to walk on them as far as I could. What I didn't know was that the river had been up and went down, leaving ice on them. On the second one I stepped on my feet went out from under me. I went clear under, losing my helmet and an M-1 rifle I had picked up.

"My official weapon was a 45 pistol. The next day I tried to get it out of my holster and it was frozen. I had to thaw it out. I found my helmet, poured the water out, and put it back on. My clothes had frozen instantly, but I wasn't much wetter than the others, because the water was chest high and I am 6 ft tall.

"We got across the river. Our shoepacks were full of water and all of our clothes were frozen by that time. We walked for a while. We were finally picked up by a truck. We got in the back. There were several things in the back. I sat down on something, but I didn't realize what, until we had gone several miles...... it was a dead GI.

"We finally got to Wonju, just before daylight. Our company was there—what was left of it...25 men! Our chow truck brought breakfast up for the company. They had plenty. We hadn't eaten for two nights and a day, so I ate seven eggs and the works.

"There was no reason for this roadblock. It has been and was kept very quiet by the Army. I read an account of a pilot that flew over the area north of Hoengsong the day before and said he had never seen so many Chinese or North Korean troops moving south as there was then.

"Incidentally, a man in our platoon, Joe Carlin, was captured that night.

He spent the rest of the war in a prison camp. He told me over the phone, "The enemy had 700 prisoners and started marching them north the next day. When they got there, only 400 were left. And by the time they were set free, only 100 of the original 700 went home."

"Most of the artillery was captured and all of the boys that fled to the hills were captured the next day or killed."

Parman did not know it at that point, but he was one of the lucky—and the few—soldiers who survived the Hoengsong Massacre.

CHAPTER 16

No Bang For The Buck— Or Any Other Price

"Still shivering and grouped around a stove in a medical clearing station, the men described "swarms of Chinese like fleas pouring out of the mountains around us after the fight started." (American tankers at Hoengsong)

FRIENDLY TROOPS WERE being shuffled all around as commanders tried in vain to stop the Chinese attack. An engineer unit of the 8th ROK Regiment was dispatched to the area to relieve the pressure on the 16th ROK Command Post. But, like so many other directives at the time, it was too little too late. Captain Tate, 3rd Bn.'s S-3 (the officer is in charge of operational planning and training at the battalion and brigade level) informed Division Artillery that the area had already been taken under fire. And, he added, it was a safe bet that the Chinese were holding this area.

At 3:30 a.m., a large group of Chinese soldiers appeared near Chowonni. Maxiner, who recognized the severity of the situation, ordered his artillery liaison officer to request fire on the vicinity in which the Chinese were concentrated. He didn't have any more luck than his counterparts with other units had. The request was forwarded to the 8th ROK Division commander, who was reluctant to give the okay to fire. As a result, Maxiner did not get his requested artillery for several hours, which proved to be too late.

As Maxiner tried in vain to get artillery support, the 1st Bn. attached to SF 21 told the 3rd Bn. Liaison Officer that the 21st ROK Regiment had collapsed. The ROK troops were indeed rushing through SF 21's position, and it was apparent to SF 21's leader that the last thing on their minds was tangling with the Chinese.

Maxiner put two and two together and realized that he and his troops had to do something to stave off annihilation. He ordered "M" Company and "K" Company to fire every mortar, machine gun, and recoilless rifle at their disposal on enemy positions. The concentrated fire was as useless as a peashooter in a firefight.

The Chinese attack spread like wildfire as the night wore on. At 3:30 a.m. Chinese troops on Hill 333 started firing on "I" Company of the 3rd Bn. At the same time, an increasing number of fleeing friendly troops started arriving at the 3rd Bn. CP. They included members of the KMAG 16th ROK Regiment, an officer from the 82 AAA Bn., and an artillery officer attached to SF 21.

The fact that artillery and anti-aircraft personnel were in the crowd was disturbing. If the friendly forces had any hope at all of beating back the communists, they needed artillery support. To their credit, the KMAG officers had no intention of giving up the fight and continuing their flight. They granted Maxiner permission to employ the retreating ROK soldiers when and where he needed them.

Maxiner seized the moment. He ordered the ROKs to hold the line. As they started to assemble, "K" Company notified Maxiner that a ROK engineer unit, possibly the one that was supposed to attack the Chinese in an effort to relieve the pressure on the 16th ROK Regiment, had taken up a defensive position with the right flank platoon of K

Company instead. That displeased Maxiner, and forced him to change his strategy.

Maxiner summoned the commanding officer of the ROK engineer unit so he could explain to him in person where he wanted his troops situated on the perimeter. The ROK officer told Maxiner that the 16th ROK OP had been overrun, so there was no reason for him and his engineers to launch an attack on the Chinese. Maxiner agreed, and ordered the ROK CO to deploy his unit on the perimeter alongside K Company—just where he had been anyway.

Before the ROK CO left, Maxiner made it clear to him that he had to report to his counterpart of "K" Company, 38th Inf. to ensure proper coordination. Maxiner did not want U.S. and ROK troops to engage in a firefight with one another simply because they were unaware of each other's whereabouts. Maxiner had enough confusion to deal with without having to worry about his own troops killing one another.

As the ROK Co left, Maxiner received news from Division Artillery at approximately 4 a.m. that they still could not obtain clearance to fire forward of the 3rd Bn.'s positions. He explained to them that the ROK engineer unit assigned to attack the Chinese in that area had been redeployed. There was no reason he could see why artillery fire could not be placed forward of the 3rd Bn.'s perimeter. His argument fell on the proverbial deaf ears. He could not convince anyone to support him with artillery. Nobody else was having much luck in that respect either.

While Maxiner continued to plead for artillery, SF 21 got on the move again. It stepped off toward Haktam-ni shortly after 4 a.m. in a column of companies. B Company took the lead, followed by "C," Headquarters, "D" and "A," which was responsible for the rear guard action. They did not get very far before a problem that was commonplace for Army units in Korea manifested itself: a major traffic jam.

Keleher saw what was happening at the head of the column and acted decisively. He ordered "C" Company to move up and assist "B" Company. His purpose was to repel the Chinese attack and open up the road to let the column move forward. Companies "B" (on the right) and "C" (on the left) launched their counterattack at 5:45 a.m. Keleher did not wait for permission from TF Commander Keith, who he could not locate, to deploy the troops or order the artillery and AAA into action. He simply took over and carried the fight to the Chinese.

As the column worked itself toward Hoengsong, the leading elements encountered heavy small arms and automatic weapons fire. The incoming fire disabled several of the vehicles and killed the drivers. In a scene that repeated itself far too often in Korea, Chinese troops swarmed around the disabled vehicles and either bayoneted the people in them to death or took them prisoner. Inexplicably, there were a few lucky survivors who the Chinese simply stripped of their valuables and released. Those lucky survivors could thank Chinese unpredictability for their lives.

Precedent suggested that the Chinese were very unpredictable when it came to treating prisoners and dead enemy soldiers. A few months earlier, X Corps Commander General Almond had been circling over North Korea during the battle for the Chosin Reservoir to assess the effectiveness of friendly artillery fire on the Chinese who were trying to cut off friendly troops from reaching Hagaru-ri and safety. As his plane circled the reservoir he noticed about thirty individuals crossing the ice, apparently unmolested by enemy forces.

Later, an American colonel and seven enlisted men suffering from frostbite and various wounds met some U.S. Marines at the edge of the reservoir. They told the Marines that they had been prisoners, but the Chinese had released them inexplicably. They said that the Chinese had not questioned them, fed them, or harmed them in any way. The Chinese even allowed them to find their own rations before letting them go.

Col Paul C. Fritz, a U.S. Air Force pilot involved in evacuating the Marines from Hagaru-ri, at the southern tip of the Chosin Reservoir, told a similar story in his account of the operation as he started flying wounded and dead Marines to safety—right by the Chinese troops who could have stopped them anytime but did not:

"But where was the war? Only a few Marines with weapons at the ready moved about, artillery pieces were emplaced nearby but unattended, and only the sister-services' fighters droning above reminded one that this was real.

"Looking at the mountains nearby, not one Chinese was to be seen, only some crude bunkers piled high with snow. Even so, you knew this had to be the makings of an updated version of the Little Bighorn, though Custer didn't have the cold. However, these casualties had the important advantage of our Pegasus-type "horses"—the difference between entrapment-and-then-what OR freedom-and-medical-help if we could pull of the operation.

"Then I realized the back of my neck felt as if a few thousand pairs of eyes were staring at me, and through rifle sights. Enough of that, let's get cracking! I started to my bird and a young Marine truck driver came up to me...

"After taking off I climbed straight through the narrow valley. Here was the answer to how the Chinese were staying out of sight. Caves pock-marked each ridge, yet not one man could be seen. They could pick us off easily as we climbed past their "front doors." We were as vulnerable as fish in a barrel. Why were they letting us go?"

One Army medic, Dwight Johnson, revealed that the Chinese were sometimes, but not always, considerate when American troops were killed. During the night they would rescue their own wounded troops, but they did not ignore their enemy. The next day, white body bags containing the American dead were laid out in rows in no-man's land for their comrades to recover. The Chinese had stripped the bodies of clothing and possessions. In these rare instances there was no danger for the medics or litter bearers to go out in daylight to pick up the dead.

The Chinese may have had a different sense of mercy than their enemies did, but they were not completely heartless. Yet, at Hoengsong, they showed very little mercy. The Chinese were indeed hard to figure out. As Fritz asked about Hagaru-ri, "Why were they letting us go?" No doubt many soldiers at Hoengsong asked the question in reverse: "Why didn't they let us go?"

Willy Freeman, a member of Co. A, 1st Bn., 38th Regt., had a unique experience that demonstrated the difference between Chinese and North Korean approaches to prisoners. Freeman, like so many of the soldiers in Korea at the beginning of the war, was a WWII veteran called back to active duty. On February 12th the 38th Regiment was dug in north of Hoengsong and protected on the left flank by the South Korean Army 8th Division—or so it thought.

Shortly after midnight, when the Chinese and North Korean divisions overran the South Koreans, the ROK troops' flanks collapsed and Freeman's unit was caught in the rush to withdraw. As Freeman recalled, there was no officer supervision for instructions and no radios for communications. "It was every man for himself," Freeman said.

Freeman joined a group of about 28 soldiers who were withdrawing. They walked past a truck convoy full of soldiers that was stopped. They, too, had been retreating south toward Hoengsong. Freeman did not know at the time why the convoy was stopped. He did not learn until much later that delay was because the drivers had abandoned their trucks and left the soldiers aboard to their fates.

By 8 a.m., Freeman's group of solders, all of whom were wounded by this time, surrendered to the Chinese. Their captors put them in a house for several days. One of the American soldiers, T. J. Martin, was in telecommunications. He saw his Jeep, burned alongside the road.

Martin talked to the captain in charge of the Chinese troops, who spoke perfect English. Martin learned that the captain had been educated at an east coast university in the United States. More importantly, he was very humane.

Martin talked the captain into issuing the group of POWs a "home free" pass. He promised the captain that the Americans would not take up arms against the Chinese again. The Chinese handed the passes to the Americans. On them was written in English, Chinese, and Korean that they were not to be stopped on their way to American lines.

Unfortunately, before they got very far, some North Korean troops stopped them. The North Koreans read the home free passes, tore them up, and marched them north toward the POW camps about 200 miles north, along the Yalu River. As Freeman remembered it, this "Death March" enforced by the North Koreans was a nightmare.

Martin and Freeman were the only two members of their 28-person group who were alive at the end of the march. Freeman spent 900 days as a POW, during which he experienced firsthand the difference between the Chinese and North Korean approaches to the treatment of captives. At least he didn't have to listen to the enemy's noisemakers anymore.

One of the sounds that stand out in Korean War veterans' minds is the noise of bugles (the Dutch called them trumpets). The Chinese made extensive use of them to guide troops and to rattle and confuse the enemy. The noise the bugles made was chilling to friendly troops, to the point that some of them would seek out the buglers and shoot them first, using anything from a single bullet to an artillery round. Marines at the Chosin Reservoir found a clever way to turn the tables on the Chinese buglers via a "Battle of the Bands."

The Marine Band they weren't. But the "musicians" of Weapons/1/1st Marines at the Chosin rivaled any of history's great musical moments in terms of brass -as in audacious, not melodious. Lt. William Masterpool, so the legend goes and grows, equipped his very fine ragtag, not ragtime, Marching and Fighting Music Appreciation Society with toy banjos, saxophones, and other miniature instruments he had his father send over to Korea.

Masterpool's "band" members never quite mastered the kinds of sounds that stir men's souls. After all, they were combat Marines, not musicians, by trade. But they tried, which delighted their fellow Marines and really didn't disturb the peace and quiet of the war that much when their moment of triumph arrived.

One night, as the Chinese signaled their attack with bugles, trumpets, whistles and whatever, Masterpool's Marines, not to be outdone, rallied behind their instruments and-a-one-and-a-two-and-a-three answered with a defiant, "Twinkle, Twinkle, Little Star." That caught the Chinese off guard, as did the French a couple months later at Chip'yong-ni.

During the battle, when the Chinese launched an attack that included the omnipresent bugles, French soldiers cranked up an old hand siren. The noise stopped the Chinese in their tracks. The French soldiers, who were outnumbered by the Chinese, fixed bayonets and ran at the enemy troops, throwing hand grenades as they ran. The Chinese turned and fled. It was a psychological victory for the French, which played a major role in the positive outcome of the battle for the UN troops.

Of course, the Dutch had their own explanation for what sometimes made their French allies so successful. One of their soldiers, Elie van Schilt, wrote about one engagement just before the detachment moved to Hoengsong, in which he included a couple keen insights into Chinese strategy and one about what motivated the French:

"The boys in the positions have to keep moving continuously in order not to freeze. According to the noise the Americans on the left have come under attack. Shortly afterward artillery fire sets in [and] we can observe lights flashing and see where the grenades hit. If it doesn't work there, they surely shall try the French position. If they find a weak point anywhere they point it out by trumpet or by light signals and within no time a great breakthrough takes place there.

"The firing ends now and indeed an hour later you can hear shots from the French side. Now the French have to slaughter the whole bunch, otherwise you can bet your life that it is the Dutchmen's turn in the valley. A while later silhouettes are observed trying to enter the valley, immediately mortar grenades are thrown at them.

"Now the firing at the French position increases and they are mad enough to storm downhill with bayonets. What may have contributed [to this ferocity] is that the French, even on the front, receive their daily wine ration."

Unfortunately, the ROK and American troops at Hoengsong did not have wine—or much else—to stop the Chinese buglers.

The counterattack by Companies "B" and "C" seemed to drive the Chinese into a frenzy. They reacted by increasing the amount of fire from their positions in the hills on the east side of the road. The Chinese had a penchant for seizing the high ground and pouring fire down onto the roads.

The Chinese, who traveled everywhere by foot or on horseback, recognized early in the war that the U.S. Army traveled virtually everywhere in Korea via trucks, what Fred Frankville called "death by truck." (The Chinese had a tougher time fighting U.S. Marines than members of some military units because the Marines shunned the use of trucks for the most part, clambered along hilltops and ridges as much as possible, and fought the enemy on their terms.) As a result, the Chinese developed a strategy of occupying the high ground and disabling or destroying the first and last trucks or tanks in a convoy along narrow roads. From that point on in a battle they had an advantage.

It was much easier to fire downhill into trapped troops than it was for those troops to fight uphill. The Chinese strategy worked time and time again in the early stages of the war. Hoengsong was a prime example of how effective it was for the Chinese—and how devastating it was for friendly troops in terms of human casualties and equipment losses.

Keleher recognized that he had to drive the Chinese off the hills. He ordered his troops to redirect their fire onto them. The sounds of the battle reached a noisy crescendo. Chinese bugle calls were sounding all over the area, almost as if they were employing a large stereo player to confuse the friendly troops. Some of the bugle calls sounded vaguely like the "Taps" and mess calls so familiar to the American soldiers. They were annoying to the allies, to say the least.

One bugler in particular caught the Americans' attention. He was located approximately 200 yards to the east of their position. They located the bugler and silenced him with a 105mm white phosphorous round. Nevertheless, the battle continued.

CHAPTER 17

The Best Defense Is A Good Offense

On a building near the limits of Hongchon was a bit of Communist advice left behind by the retreating Chinese: "Your folks want you back home. To follow us means death." (William Chipman)

"THE BODIES WERE two miles north of a blasted Second Division convoy which the Marines found Saturday. An undisclosed number of dead were found on that battlefield. The men found today were members of the 105th Artillery Battery..."

"While "B" and "C" Companies fought to break through at the front of the column, "A" Company was busy trying to keep the Chinese away from its rear, even though its OPLR (Outpost Line of Resistance) had been overrun. One platoon was surrounded; a second was sustaining heavy casualties. Fortunately, there were two tanks supporting Company "A" that evened up the odds a bit.

The tanks were the only two remaining from Support Team Baker. They were placed at the tail of the column when SF 21 set off for Haktam-ni, which proved to be propitious. They inflicted so many casualties on the enemy that they were the only things that prevented Company "A" from being destroyed. At this time the entire column was under fire, the volume of which was increasing as time went on.

Tankers were essential weapons against the Chinese at Hoengsong. They were also prime targets for Chinese attacks. One crew member, Kenneth Eaton, whose tank did not escape the ambush, remembered the chaos.

"I was a crew member of one of the tanks that did not escape the ambush at Hoengsong. As I recall, the scene was chaotic. Only two tanks in our unit escaped the ambush, the first and last in line.

"One tank commander, who weighed about 110 pounds, jumped out of his tank to remove bodies from the road so his tank would not run over them as it moved quickly out of the ambush. He was moving them relatively easily, which it looked like he could not do under normal circumstances.

"Most of the firing came from the left as we moved—or attempted to move—down the road. When our tank was hit, I managed to get out and moved over to a rice paddy away from the firing. I left the paddy to join a wounded man, but had to return quickly. Eventually, however, I was captured. I managed to escape twice during my time in prison. (I was at the infamous Camp 5.) But, I was captured both times and returned to the camp.

"At any rate, it was a devastating day for all of us."

Eaton's final observation was accurate. "C" Company, in particular, was facing stubborn resistance from the incessant and increasing Chinese small arms and mortar fire. That was due to its position on the east side of the road. "B" Company, on the west side, encountered light and sporadic opposition, but that changed quickly.

"C" Company fought off the Chinese and moved on, sweeping the high ground as it did. Then "B" Company's turn in the barrel arrived. When it reached Hill 335 the Chinese stepped up their attack. Recognizing the adage that the best defense is a good offense, the company attacked the hill, but sustained heavy casualties. One platoon, with the exception of two enlisted men, was completely annihilated.

Officers tried frantically to find drivers to replace the ones who had been killed or captured. More than a dozen vehicles that had been in the forefront of the column were driverless and left parked alongside the road. Finding drivers for them was relatively easy. The difficulty was locating drivers for the prime movers for the 155mm Howitzers. Not too many of the regular troops were cross-trained to haul Howitzers. But the column could not wait. Soldiers pushed the disabled vehicles off the road and the troops continued along it, with what was left of "B" and "C" Companies protecting them.

They did not get far before the Chinese intensified their mortar fire. "C" Company troops moved into the high ground to drive away the mortar crews on the east side of the road. They succeeded, but only temporarily. As soon as they returned to the road the Chinese reoccupied the high ground and resumed their barrage. Astute friendly officers decided to act on their own to extricate their troops from the teeming Chinese forces.

Captain Jones, the commander of ST A, was one of them. He did not wait for anyone's permission to withdraw and fight his way out of trouble. Jones led his troops east over the blocked mountain road toward the 3d Battalion, 38th Infantry—and he did it early.

As soon as Jones saw what was happening around midnight, he started withdrawing his troops. He witnessed the fleeing ROK vehicles, guns, and troops early in the battle and acted at once to fight through the Chinese and join the main body of U.S. forces. His withdrawal was far from easy. Throughout the night the Chinese directed heavy small arms, machine guns, rocket launchers, and mortar fire at his troops. Several of the ST A members were killed and wounded.

As they struggled to reach the 3rd Bn., 38th Inf. lines, much of their equipment was destroyed. The survivors did not reach safety until dawn. In the process, Jones, the tank platoon leader, and five other soldiers were wounded—and nearly 150 troops were missing. ST A may have linked up with the 3rd Bn., 38th Inf., but the fighting was by no means over.

The combat continued as dawn approached. Keith managed to put some artillery pieces back in action and placed direct fire on the ridges to the east. Keleher repositioned two rifle companies on the high ground on each side of the road. The friendly commanders were grasping the importance of taking the high ground.

A few soldiers remained on the road to push disabled vehicles out of the way. Officers rounded up replacements for missing and dead drivers. Slowly but surely Keith's troops moved ahead in the face of stubborn enemy resistance. Progress was measured in feet and yards; at least there was some progress.

Around 6 a.m., Company A moved out of its rear guard position and rejoined the main column. They were not free entirely. Chinese troops pursued them doggedly in a running battle. Just as the company stepped off, its commander, 1st Lt. George W. Gardner, noted something strange in a paddy on the side of the road southwest of his position. He saw three 155-mm. Howitzers attached to their M-5 tractors, a full ammunition truck, and several jeeps and trailers, all unattached.

The guns and equipment belonged to Battery A, 503d Field Artillery Battalion, which had fallen prey to the surprise raid by daring Chinese troops earlier that morning. The rest of the battery had withdrawn with only one tube. The discovery created a quandary for Gardner.

Gardner's executive officer found at least one more Howitzer, still in firing position, in one of the worst places possible: on the road where Mace's two tanks had been disabled earlier. And, one of the disabled vehicles in the tangled mess was the tractor that had been pulling the

Howitzer. It was blocking Gardner's tanks.

The lieutenant did not have anyone trained to drive the tractors, and he didn't have the time or the explosives to destroy the equipment or spike the Howitzers. Worse, the Chinese were attacking him in the artillery position as he pondered his dilemma. Quickly, Gardner ordered some of his troops to push the abandoned Howitzer to the side of the road so the two tanks could pass.

At the same time, others repelled the attacking Chinese by expending the ammunition allocated to the machine guns mounted on the artillery vehicles. But, Gardner was forced to leave the rest of the weapons, artillery ammunition, and vehicles to the Chinese. That was not likely to please the high-ranking commanders, but it was all Gardner could do under the circumstances.

Slowly but surely Keith's troops neared the bridge. As they did the Chinese intensified their fire. Nevertheless, the support force crossed the structure, under fire all the way. They kept pushing along under fire right up to the area just below the crossing where Keith had intended to redeploy.

Keith's force fought its way through what seemed to be a never-ending series of road blocks. The Chinese pressed them from behind every step of the way, making life miserable for Gardner's rear guard in particular. Keith realized that the position at which he had hoped to set up his troops was unsuitable due to Chinese pressure. So, he kept on moving—as did the Chinese.

At 9 a.m. the Dutch reported an estimated battalion of troops traveling northeast on Hill 303. The problem was that the Dutch could not identify them, since they were approximately 1,000 yards to their front. The Dutch had no idea whether they were friendly or hostile. (Later in the day friendly forces learned that the troops were an enemy unit making a flanking movement around Hoengsong.)

Throughout the morning Air OP reported large enemy groups moving south, east, and southeast. One enemy regiment was seen flanking to the west of Hoengsong, which suggested that it was attempting to cut the Wonju-Hoengsong Main Supply Route (MSR). The only friendly forces in this area were the service trains and one battery of field artillery.

Finally, around mid-morning on February 12th, Keith's beleaguered force united with the 3d Battalion, 38th Infantry just a short way down the road from his intended site. Gardner's rear guard reached the 3d Battalion perimeter about 10 a.m. The number of losses along the way was saddening.

Keith did not have the time to do a thorough count, but the number of casualties exceeded 400. Company A had suffered the most. It lost 2 officers and about 110 troops in its rear guard action. And, Keith was incensed to learn about the five 155-mm. Howitzers and one 105-mm. Howitzer that had been left behind.

The fact that Howitzers and other types of equipment were abandoned was not surprising. The communist attack had caught the Americans completely by surprise. In one case Marines encountering the scene in March along with an Army Graves Registration team found 30 bodies around an American artillery position in the village of Saemal, four miles northwest of Hoengsong. They were two miles north of a blasted Second Division convoy.

There were an undisclosed number of dead found on that battlefield. This particular group comprised members of the 105th Artillery Battery. They had set up a position of four Howitzers ringed by machine guns and foxholes for defenders. The bodies revealed a lot about the failure of that fight.

Piles of cases of fired cartridges were heaped beside the foxholes. Next to one there was a belt of unfired 50 caliber cartridges. The soldier lying nearby never had a chance to fire. Apparently, the battalion pulled out when it finally realized it was pitted against overwhelming odds. The troops departed so fast they left two guns in position. Somehow, the Chinese left them in place as well. The guns were recovered after the Marines arrived.

Setting his dismay aside, Keith sent a message to division requesting air strikes on the discarded weapons. He was also upset to learn that his battle for survival was nowhere near its end. (Seven 105mm Howitzers and all of the 155mm Howitzers lost during the Hoengsong battle were recovered in March 1951 by recovery teams operating under the direction of G-4, Logistics.)

The members of the 3rd Battalion had not been sitting on their hands while SF 21 fought its way to them. They had been under Chinese assault from the north and northwest for about five hours. Not surprisingly, Keith's arrival was good news for the 38th Regiment commander, Colonel John G. Coughlin, who was located at Hoengsong. He desperately needed some reinforcements for his tired troops.

Maxiner, acting with his usual decisiveness, deployed his troops around the perimeter of SF 21's new position. He even remembered to clear his orders with Coughlin, even though the colonel did not have any authority over SF 21. Maxiner positioned Keith's artillery and Keleher's infantry along the perimeter to fend off the increasingly stronger Chinese attacks.

If they had had their druthers, Keith and Maxiner would rather have just kept moving down to Hoengsong, which offered a more sensible defensive position. But, X Corps had ordered the 3rd Bn. to hold the Route 29-mountain road junction at all costs—costs which it was sadly paying. Besides, the Chinese were presenting their own impediment to such a move.

Troops of the Chinese 117th Division had moved east below the mountain road and reached Route 29. As Coughlin discovered the hard way, they had blocked the road between Hoengsong and the road junction three miles north.

Division artillery had asked Coughlin to assist SF 21 in getting through the blocks below Ch'angbong-ni in its struggle to reach the 3rd Bn.'s position. He sent the 38th's headquarters security platoon and a platoon from the regimental tank company north out of Hoengsong to comply with the request. They ran into a buzz saw.

The two platoons encountered heavy Chinese opposition only one mile above Hoengsong. They lost a tank and half the infantry, which forced them to withdraw. Coughlin reacted quickly by placing mortar and artillery fire on the Chinese and requesting air support, which did not begin until 10:30 a.m. Coughlin also requested the return of the 2d Battalion from division reserve in Wonju to clear the road. General Ruffner turned down his request. In exchange for his refusal, he expanded Coughlin's command.

The general told Coughlin to be ready to assume control of SF 21 and get it back to Hoengsong. In exchange, Coughlin recommended to Ruffner that the 3d Battalion return to Hoengsong as well when—and if—he received word to withdraw the support force. Ruffner denied that suggestion too.

Coughlin was left scratching his head. Ruffner denied him the use of the 2nd and 3rd Battalions. That meant Coughlin would have to pull SF 21 through the Chinese road block without lending any more assistance than he already had, which wasn't much. He had one more possible source of support: the Netherlands battalion attached to the U.S. Army 2nd Inf. Div., which was deployed along the northern limits of Hoengsong.

CHAPTER 18

The Chinese Were Devious And Daring

"Chinese troops used white flags and handshakes today in an attempt to wipe out United Nations tanks and infantrymen." (Associated Press)

THE COMMUNISTS WERE not above using devious tactics to eliminate their enemies. Allied troops had to be on their guard at all times when they dealt with the Chinese. That lesson was reinforced on more than one occasion at Hoengsong.

On February 12 Chinese troops used white flags and handshakes in an attempt to wipe out some U.S. tanks and infantrymen who were on a contact patrol about a mile and a half north of Hoengsong. The infantrymen, accompanied by tanks, encountered a group of about 60 Chinese soldiers waving white flags and handkerchiefs. The Chinese motioned to the GIs to halt, which they did, Lt. Perry Davis reported.

Sergeant Clarence C. Catlett said the tanks halted and the GIs tried to take the Chinese prisoners. That was not part of the enemy's plan. Catlett noted that "The guy leading them spoke English. He shook hands with my lieutenant and said, 'Friends.'

The lieutenant, Perry Davis, told the Chinese leader to have his men lay down their arms. That started an argument between the two. Meanwhile, according to Pvt. Gilbert Tilton, a Chinese soldier shook hands with one of his buddies—and dropped a grenade behind him as he did so. Then, Tilton said, "All hell broke loose."

Tilton shot the grenade thrower. After that things became, in Tilton's words, "a point blank mess." The Chinese soldier who had shaken hands with Lt. Davis shot him. The U.S. tankers buttoned up their vehicles and opened fire with their machine guns. The Chinese began shooting at the outnumbered GI with their burp guns as the Americans fought their way back to a little stream.

Lt. James E. Howden, a tank platoon commander, verified that the enemy "were Chinese all right. Some with their hands up and some carrying their weapons, but waving white flags.

It didn't look right, somehow, so I told my tanks to stay buttoned up. After the grenade went off we gave 'em hell." That was neither the first, nor the last, time, the Chinese stooped to foul play to annihilate the UN troops. The Dutch troops became a target as well.

The Netherlands battalion was the main security force for the headquarters and artillery installations in and below Hoengsong. But, Coughlin was not sure if he could employ it for his own purposes. He was sure that only Corps could order any changes in the Netherlanders' assignment. Coughlin had no way of knowing it at the time, but the Dutch troops were in for a devastating day, one that would be among the worst setbacks in the history of the Netherlands military.

Dutch troops were the victims of a Chinese ruse at Hoengsong. They could not easily distinguish between Chinese and South Korean troops, nor could the Americans. That was made clear in an account by Cpl James J. Lee, RA 43015015, Hdqs Co., 38th Regt., in an April 4,

1951 after action interview on 4 April 1951.

Lee recalled that on the morning of 12 February, at approximately 8 a.m., the Security Platoon of which he was a member was providing close-in security for six tanks from the 38th Infantry Tank Company. The platoon's mission was to break through an enemy encirclement and road block, approximately 1,000 yards long, and make contact with friendly forces that had been cut off in the vicinity of Saemal. They discovered during their operation just how devious and daring the Chinese could be.

The force crossed the river north of Hoengsong and advanced up the MSR. Its commander notified HQ via radio that there were approximately 200-300 oriental soldiers gathered in the road. They were wearing white scarves tied to their heads and waving white slips of paper. He reasoned that the soldiers were ROK troops retreating from the north. He was wrong.

The commander approached the troops and determined quickly that they were Chinese. He figured that they desired to surrender, so he walked to within a few feet of the enemy force and asked if they wanted to surrender. They stated that they did not. In fact, they indicated that they desired the Americans to surrender. They two groups were at an impasse.

Next, a solitary Chinese soldier approached the Americans. They did not fire at him, because they believed that he at least was going to surrender. That was not what he had in mind, though.

The Chinese soldier raised his hands in a fighting fashion as if he was indicating that he wanted to fight Lee's platoon leader, Lt. Uzzo, one on one. Suddenly, he grabbed for the weapon he had slung over his shoulder in an attempt to shoot Uzzo. But, the lieutenant was too fast for the Chinese soldier.

Uzzo shot and killed his brave, but foolhardy, foe. That was not the first time Uzzo, Lee, and the rest of the platoon would get up close and personal with the enemy that morning. The two groups separated from one another to a distance of 100 feet, at which time they opened fire on each other. The friendly forces withdrew after being completely surrounded by the enemy company.

They continued toward Saemal, crossing a river en route. Five more enemy soldiers appeared in front of them unexpectedly and opened fire on the Americans. Then they attempted to withdraw over a hill. They were too slow; the Americans killed all five of them.

After the brief firefight ended the Americans moved out again. They hadn't gone more than 150 yards before they saw approximately 200 soldiers in front of them, who started waving their hands to show that they were friendly. Despite their harrowing experience a while earlier, the Americans had no reason to believe that they were not. After all, ROK units had been passing through this area throughout the night. So, the Americans let them approach.

The ensuing friendship and conviviality was enough to take the Americans' minds off their plight, but not for long. When the "ROKs" were within six yards of the Americans, one of them said in English, "We are friends." While the handshaking and greetings continued, Uzzo noticed that many more men were appearing on the hills to his right, left, and front. So did the tankers.

The sixth tank, the last one in the column, opened fire at a group of men who had gotten around to the Americans' right rear. The tank's .50 caliber gunfire was now holding the group at bay; they were unable to move in any direction. As the tank fired, one of the "ROKs" threw Uzzo a piece of paper on which was written, "Surrender. Give up your arms and cartridge belts and we will allow you to keep your personal effects. We will give you safe passage to your lines." This was proof to the Americans that the soldiers mingling with them were enemies—and far from friendly.

THE CHINESE WERE DEVIOUS AND DARING

Uzzo told the Platoon Sergeant to withdraw the men and put them in position ready to fire. At that moment the lead tank, which was only two feet from the platoon leader and six feet from the enemy, opened fire on the group with its machine gun. Immediately, a bugle call sounded nearby. That was the signal for the enemy to fire at the lead tank and Uzzo. The Chinese soldiers went into action.

Individual Chinese soldiers attempted to drop grenades through the hatches of the two leading tanks. The tankers saw what was coming and closed their hatches. They tried to get away from the battle, but they could not turn around on the narrow road. So, all the tanks started at once to move to the rear in reverse. The second tank driver misjudged the side of the road and turned over. It was out of action, and its position put the rest of the troops in an awkward—and dangerous—position.

The Americans started firing furiously. But, the enemy force had increased to an estimated 500 soldiers. One burst from an enemy machine gun hit Uzzo in the back. He fell into a ditch alongside the first tank. The crew members tried to rescue him. The lieutenant told them not to bother. He said that he was hit too badly and that they should continue to withdraw.

Lee and his comrades could not get to Uzzo because of the intense enemy fire saturating the ditch in which he was stranded. Then, another burst of machine gun fire struck him in the chest. The Security Platoon had no choice but to leave him, albeit reluctantly. Lee said, "He was still firing his weapon at the enemy when I last saw him."

As the platoon withdrew, the third tank in the column attempted to contact TACP by radio, but was not successful. The enemy on the hills continued to move to the southeast in an attempt to encircle the group. Fortunately, one of the tanks had crossed the river to the east side and was directing heavy fire onto the Chinese. Miraculously, the Dutch came to the rescue.

The Netherlands Detachment, positioned on the northwest outskirts of Hoengsong, added its fire to the tank's, and kept the Chinese pinned down. That allowed the Security Platoon to complete its withdrawal without further fire.

CHAPTER 19

General Ruffner Assumes Command Of The General Confusion

"Confused, bitter fighting swirled all day and night yesterday throughout the Hoengsong area. Finally two United States 2d Division battalions and a South Korean regiment fought their way out of the Communist trap north of Hoengsong." (Washington Evening Star)

ON THE MORNING of February 13th General Almond issued orders to 2nd Division headquarters to reconstitute the 38th as a regimental combat team. (The regimental combat team, or "RCT," comprises a regular infantry regiment with smaller tank, artillery, combat engineer, mechanized, cavalry, reconnaissance, Signal Corps, air defense, quartermaster, military police, medical, and other support units to enable it to be a self-supporting organization in the combat field.) He instructed the 2nd and 3rd Battalions to remain in place until further orders.

Almond's instructions did not get to 2nd Div. HQ until about 11 a.m. They had hardly sunk in before Almond lifted the restriction on the 2nd Battalion. Then, all Almond's orders became moot when General

Ruffner took direct control of the unit. He left the RCT directive in place, however, and ignored Almond's directive re the 2nd Battalion.

Ruffner advised the battalion to prepare to repel a Chinese force, apparently from the 117th Division, which had been spotted two miles southwest of Hoengsong. He included Almond's RCT directive order with the "be prepared" alert to the forces at the road junction where they were expected to confront the Chinese. Then, he ordered SF 21 to withdraw to Hoengsong, and placed Coughlin in charge of the withdrawal. All the instructions were confusing to officers and troops alike. To make matters worse, since the availability of the 2nd and 3rd Battalions was limited, there was virtually no one to help SF 21 in its withdrawal.

While Ruffner was ordering troops to and fro and reorganizing, Almond discovered that he had been in the dark about Keith's earlier movements during the withdrawal. Almond asked his artillery officer, Colonel Ennis, for the current locations of both SF 21 and SF 7. Ennis informed him that SF 7 was three miles north of Hoengsong and a mile and a half east of Route 29, where it had set up to support the ROK 3d Division, which had been under attack by the Chinese 197th Division. The battle had started as an attack by the ROKs, but the Chinese had driven them back—and surrounded one of the 3rd Div.'s forward regiments.

Ennis, like Almond, was unaware that Ruffner had ordered Keith to continue his withdrawal. He told Almond that SF 21 had joined the 3d Battalion, 38th Infantry. So, Almond ordered both SF 7 and SF 21 to withdraw to Hoengsong immediately, even if they had to fight their way out. Ennis dutifully issued Almond's order through artillery channels around noon.

Almond's order to the support forces was wise under the circumstances. The Chinese were gaining ground, and the North Korean V Corps had joined them. The situation was becoming more precarious for the friendly forces, so withdrawal was the safest strategy at the

GENERAL RUFFNER ASSUMES COMMAND OF THE GENERAL CONFUSION

time, particularly since the news for Almond and Ruffner seemingly grew worse by the minute.

Not only was the ROK 3rd Division in trouble, but so was the ROK 5th Division on its right. It, too, had attacked enemy forces earlier in the day with no more success than the ROK 3rd Division experienced.

So, both ROK divisions, along with SF 21, began to fight their way back to Hoengsong. For them it was a race to escape encirclement, and the enemy forces appeared to be winning early in the afternoon. There was one saving grace for the allies, though: the enemy force which had attempted to cut the Wonju-Hoengsong MSR had been stopped by continual air strikes and friendly forces moving along this road. That did not allay one of the command's principal worries: losing even more artillery to the enemy east of Route 29.

The seriousness of the situation all around Hoengsong was growing. One of the signs was the number of high level meetings. Around noon General Matthew Ridgway flew into Wonju to meet with Almond at his headquarters. They discussed Corps operations and made a significant decision.

Almond announced that he planned to give up Hoengsong and defend nearby Wonju. He issued an order later that day for the 2nd Division, with the 187th Airborne RCT attached, to establish a stretched-out line that would be anchored west of Chip'yong-ni and extend to the southeast and east. The line Almond drew passed two miles north of Wonju and continued nine miles beyond the town.

The Special Task Force Almond created comprised one battalion of the 18th ROK Regiment, one Platoon of 72nd Tank Bn., and one company from the 187th Regimental Combat Team (RCT). The force jumped off at approximately 5 p.m. in an attempt to break the roadblock and link up with SF 21 and 3rd Bn, 38th Infantry. This effort was under the command of the Assistant Commanding General, 8th ROK Division. Active liaison and coordination was provided by an X Corps staff officer. The action was supported by fires of the remaining two artillery guns and Heavy Mortar Company 38th Infantry.

Almond's plan looked good on paper. The ROK 3d and 5th Divisions would be located in the right portion of the Corps' sector. They would be positioned between Route 29 and the Corps' east boundary, which was about seven miles farther north. According to Almond's thinking, positioning the South Koreans on this forward line would tie the X Corps to the left of the ROK III Corps, whose line extended to the north, well beyond the X Corps' front.

Almond did not plan to leave the South Koreans or the Corps' east flank unprotected. So, he assigned the 31st Infantry of General Ferenbaugh's 7th Division to positions at Todon-ni, a road junction four miles below P'yongch'ang. Moreover, Ferenbaugh's 32d Infantry, which was at that time holding positions between Chech'on and Yongwol, would add its support, and the 17th Infantry, which was supposed to be in reserve near Wonju, was advised to stand by to help.

That wasn't all. Almond also requested that the ROK I Corps headquarters be attached to X Corps to assume command of the ROK 3d and 5th Divisions. He did so partially because of his respect for General Kim. The general and his staff had worked with Almond in northeastern Korea. Consequently, they were experienced in joint operations and intimately acquainted with the X Corps staff.

Ridgway thought that was a good idea. He arranged to have Kim and some of his staff members flown into the X Corps sector on the 13th. The rest of Kim's staff would follow by truck. Finally, the ROK Capital Division would be assigned to ROK III Corps control.

Most of those movements were scheduled to take place later in the afternoon, and the way things were going for the friendly forces tomorrow might be too late. And, before any of these events occurred, the embattled support forces and ROK troops had to get out of their predicaments in order to play a part in Almond's grand scheme. While

Almond and Ridgway discussed strategy, Keith got SF 21 on the road.

Around noon SF 21 headed south from the road junction. By that time the enemy had succeeded in cutting the friendly forces into many small units. The 1st Bn. was surrounded by an enemy regiment. The 3rd Bn., too, was surrounded by an enemy regiment. A third enemy regiment was attempting to cut the MSR behind the Regimental CP and road blocks had been set up between the 1st and 3rd Bns and between the 3rd Bn and the regimental CP.

At the outset of SF 21's trek south, two companies of Keleher's infantry attacked the enemy along the high ground on both sides of Route 29. Their orders were to protect the vehicles and troops on the road. ST A and ST B remained with Maxiner to defend the perimeter, which was still under assault.

Coughlin had arranged for mortar and artillery fire and air strikes to support the withdrawing troops. Aircraft bombarded the ridges ahead of the troops, but that did not faze the enemy. They attacked Keleher's troops the moment they stepped off. What had started like a textbook withdrawal came to a grinding halt after a one-mile march. Keleher threw the rest of his battalion into the fray, but even that was not enough to deter the enemy from attacking. Fortunately, help was on the way.

Coughlin learned that Almond had ordered the 18th Regiment, ROK 3d Division, assembled about three miles east of Hoengsong, to move north along Route 29 to help open the road and facilitate SF 21's withdrawal. There was a hitch: they weren't expecting to step off until 2 p.m. The enemy was not operating on a time clock and would not wait for the ROK troops to swing into action—or inaction, as the case might be.

Another support team, this one labeled Support Team E (Company G, 187th Airborne Regimental Combat Team, and a platoon from the 72d Tank Battalion), was assembled nearby. ST E was assigned to accompany the South Koreans, who would be led by the ROK 3rd Division's assistant commander.

Almond added to the command confusion in the overall battle by assigning the Corps armored officer, LtCol Jack F. Wilhm, to coordinate the organization and opening of the infantry-armor advance. That took Coughlin out of the picture altogether. He might as well have returned to Hoengsong by himself. But, the move was only temporary.

A Short Rescue Attempt

The South Korean battalion started late, and managed to advance only a half-mile north of Hoengsong into the first hills above the Twinnanmul Valley. ST E didn't even get that far. It reached the river's lower bank and then stopped. Coughlin's operations officer, Maj. Warren D. Hodges, asked the South Korean commander to continue the advance. But, he refused.

The ROK commander insisted to Hodges that his orders were to take the hills he occupied at that point and hold them until dark. He promised that his troops would remain in position until the forces withdrawing from the road junction passed through. That was something, even if it wasn't what Hodges wanted.

Once again command issues surfaced. Coughlin did not have the authority to order the South Korean-American force farther up Route 29, or anywhere else for that matter. Once again luck came to his side. At 2:30 p.m. Almond released the 3d Battalion to aid in the withdrawal from the road junction. It was too late for many of the soldiers still engaged with the enemy.

CHAPTER 20

Never Go Back
The Way You Came

"United Nations forces are still engaged in a war of maneuver designed to inflict maximum casualties on the enemy and keep him off balance." (General Douglas MacArthur)

GENERAL MACARTHUR OFFERED that conclusion at about the same time the Chinese attacked Hoengsong. It did not seem as if the UN troops were keeping them off balance or inflicting maximum casualties on them. At least it didn't seem that way to LtCol Barney D. White.

SF 7, commanded by White, stepped off at 3 p.m. White had no intention of going back to Hoengsong along the same route he used to reach the ROK 3rd Division's position, which led west to the bridge on Route 29 where Keith's forces ran into trouble. That route was infested by enemy soldiers. Instead, White decided to use his ingenuity and his engineers to traverse a safer route.

Before he made any decisions, White sent a reconnaissance party west towards the bridge. It was ambushed almost immediately. As a result, he opted to move east toward the Twinnan-mul River, which flowed southwest past the northern edge of Hoengsong. The route hooked up with a more primitive road that meandered through the Twinnan-mul Valley. He duly notified Corps headquarters of his plan and moved out.

The beauty of the road he intended to cover was that it was not used often. On the other hand, it was ice coated and in rough shape. But, that worked both ways. The enemy wouldn't have it any easier along the route than would SF 7. Besides, White's engineers could make repairs to the road as they traveled. He posted a rear guard and off they went. Happily, there were no enemy troops to harass them. The rear guard pulled out about 5 p.m.

The roads were alive with withdrawing and repositioning troops that afternoon. The 674th and 96th Field Artillery Battalions, which had been supporting the ROK 5th Division from six miles east of Hoengsong, also began to move about 3 p.m. They were moving to new firing positions four miles south.

General Bowen, the commander of the 187th Airborne RCT and co-ordinator of these two artillery battalions, anticipated that the ROK 5th Division would hold fast above the new artillery positions to defend Hoengsong. However, the ROK divisions did not always do what their allies—or their own officers—expected them to do. Hoping they would this one time, Bowen moved the 1st Battalion of the combat team which had been in a blocking position below the ROK 5th Division back with the artillery units.

Coughlin received word of the 3d Battalion's release about 4 p.m. He instructed Maxiner and Keleher to force their way through the roadblock while he moved north to facilitate their withdrawal. According to Coughlin's plan, the 1st Bn. would attack on the east side of the road. The 3rd Bn. would do likewise on the west. The column of vehicles would stay between them.

Two hours later Maxiner and Keleher began the attack. The two battalions made some progress, but it was slow at best. The Chinese were less interested in the attacking troops than they were in the column of vehicles. They employed their "stop the vehicles and you'll stop their troops" strategy successfully.

They poured a steady and effective stream of the usual mortar, machine gun, and small arms into the column. As usual, individual soldiers stepped up to demonstrate outstanding bravery and leadership. One of them was Major Leonard Lowry, the commanding officer of Co., C, 1st Bn., 38th Inf. Regt.

Co. C's mission was to cover the withdrawal of a road-bound artillery battalion along a road infested by enemy soldiers along the hills and ridges. Lowry's company endured ten consecutive hours of heavy fighting, knocking out several enemy roadblocks designed to trap the battalion as they moved. Finally, the company reached the regimental assembly area and joined the 3rd Battalion.

The two battalions began assembling and reorganizing. Just then, a strong enemy force occupying positions on a ridge adjacent to the assembly area placed a heavy barrage of mortar and automatic weapons fire on the friendly troops. The enemy attack resulted in numerous casualties. Lowry seized the opportunity to stop the attack.

He quickly organized a group of men from his company and led them in an assault on the nearest enemy held hill. The attackers killed all the enemy troops on it. Lowry sustained a serious wound during the fighting, but he stayed on his feet and led his troops on assaults on other hills in the area.

Eventually, Lowry and his troops cleared the entire ridge of enemy troops. Their bravery notwithstanding, the friendly forces were unable to deflect the Chinese attacks in their effort to help SF 7. Overall, their slow progress was hampering, not helping, the withdrawal. That was the story of Hoengsong in a nutshell: individual acts of bravery could not overcome the devastation caused by superior enemy numbers.

Shortly after 6 p.m., per Corps HQ, Wilhm arrived at the 38th Infantry command post to instruct Coughlin to take charge of all American troops in the Hoengsong area. He had learned about the change in command when he reported the short South Korean advance above Hoengsong. Unfortunately, Coughlin still could not employ the South Korean battalion to help his withdrawing forces. There was some good news, though: he could use ST E.

Coughlin named his regimental tank company commander as the head of the support team and ordered him to link with the forces coming from the north. The commander, utilizing two of his own tanks, started the tank-infantry team up Route 29 at once.

Darkness had set in, which was apropos. Coughlin was somewhat in the dark about SF 7's whereabouts or exact withdrawal route as he dispatched ST E. Then, around 7 p.m., he noticed elements of SF 7 led by LtCol Baker, commanding the 2nd Battalion, 17th Infantry, moving through Hoengsong. Baker's contingent, which included infantry and artillery troops, moved into an assembly area southeast of town.

Baker's appearance surprised Coughlin. He had not been aware of SF 7's withdrawal through the Twinnan-mul Valley, even though it had been coordinated with Corps HQ through artillery channels. He thought White's force was behind him along Route 29. But, Baker's arrival was a positive change for Coughlin, who could use his troops to help other forces withdrawing over Route 29.

Once again command confusion manifested itself. Baker did not know about the new command structure until Coughlin informed him that his artillery should keep on moving to Wonju, while his infantry battalion would head north to help clear Route 29. Baker radioed Coughlin's orders to White, who was northeast of Hoengsong with the rest of SF 7.

White had some bad news for him. A 155mm Howitzer and its tractor had slipped off the road about a mile northeast of Hoengsong because of adverse road conditions. The road had become nothing more than an icy ledge along a steep ridge bordering the Twinnanmul River. As a result, the entire column of vehicles was blocked, and it would take engineers a considerable amount of time to clear the jam.

There was nothing Baker could do to alleviate the problem, so he waited at Coughlin's command post for an update about the attack north. While he was worried about troop movements north, a parade of South Korean troops moved through in the opposite direction.

The ROK 3rd and 5th Divisions were moving southward east of Hoengsong with elements of the North Korean V Corps hot on their tails. The ROK troops were on their way to take up their new line of defense. Meanwhile, Bowen was relocating his infantry battalions and the 674th and 96th Field Artillery back to Wonju. Even though friendly forces were on the move everywhere around Hoengsong, the enemy didn't seem to be having too much trouble keeping up with them.

A KMAG officer with the passing ROK troops nearest Hoengsong told Baker that the enemy forces following the ROK 5th Division had cut the lateral road stretching eastward from Hoengsong. That was the route the leading troops of SF 7 had used to reach their assembly southeast of town. The news should not have been particularly disconcerting to Baker, since the enemy forces had cut the road beyond the support force assembly. Nevertheless, he began to pull the leading troops and trucks back into Hoengsong and reassemble them along Route 29 south of town.

Things had not settled down even as February 12th neared its end. It was 10 p.m. and Baker was still shifting forces around. About that time the rest of SF 7 began to straggle in from the northeast. They were in limbo; Baker still had not gone back to Coughlin's CP to get his attack order. But, it didn't seem all that important at the time.

ST E was making steady progress in its attack up Route 29. They did not need Baker's support—or so it seemed. Even though it had taken a few casualties and lost one tank, ST E had fought its way up Route 29 for about a mile and a half. At 11 p.m. it linked up with Coughlin's forces coming south. That was as far as ST E needed to go. Its remaining tanks turned around, got out in front of the combined force, and headed south. They had to fight their way through the same ground they had just covered, and it wasn't any easier this time.

The Chinese still occupied positions on both sides of the road and continued to pour fire into the combined columns from both sides. The friendly forces attacked the Chinese with success, albeit limited. Their progress south was slow, but steady. Finally, they connected with the ROK battalion's position about a half mile above Hoengsong—but it was vacated. The South Koreans had withdrawn to rejoin their division. That did not seem to matter at the time. In the long run, it did.

ST E and Coughlin's forces just kept moving. Along the way they passed behind the Netherlands Battalion's positions along the upper edge of Hoengsong. Coughlin's plan was for his forces arriving from the north to proceed through Hoengsong, reorganize in an assembly area three miles south of town, and continue to the new defense line at Wonju. SF 7 would follow the same plan as it arrived from the northeast. All they had to do was follow Coughlin if they weren't sure of where they were supposed to be going. His HQ personnel and other troops, except for the Netherlands Battalion and part of the regimental tank company, were already leaving Hoengsong.

The Netherlands Battalion was assigned to cover the withdrawing forces, then serve as a rear guard en route to Wonju. The regimental tankers were positioned just below town. Their assignment was to attack any roadblock the Chinese might establish between Hoengsong and Wonju. Somebody forgot to tell the Chinese.

No sooner had the leading units coming down Route 29 entered Hoengsong than the Chinese launched a major attack all along the line of the Netherlands Battalion. They had some initial success, which allowed them to put heavy pressure on the flanks and rear of the troops withdrawing on Route 29, primarily at the position from which the ROK battalion had withdrawn prematurely earlier. If it had stayed in place, it might have been able to repel the Chinese attack—or at least delay it. In any case, the early withdrawal put the Netherlands Battalion at risk, and the Chinese took advantage of that situation.

Chinese attackers forced their way inside the Netherlands Battalion's perimeter and reached its CP. Other Dutch line companies held on against the Chinese at the edge of town. As they fought off the Chinese, SF 7 rushed toward town from the northeast and Coughlin's other forces fought hard to get in over Route 29.

The Chinese did not let up on SF 7. They continued to attack White's troops with the never-ending small arms, machine gun, and mortar fire. Their relentless attacks led to some confusion when SF 7's columns reached Hoengsong and got entangled with the vehicles Baker was moving through town. Baker came to White's rescue.

Baker held part of his infantry back to push enemy troops away from White's flanks. That gave the artillerymen at the rear of White's column an opportunity to repel enemy forces trying to roll up the column. Those two battles within the battle, combined with effective cover fire from the Dutch battalion, minimized losses. More importantly, they made it possible for SF 7 to pass behind the Netherlands Battalion by 11:30 p.m.

The indefatigable Baker kept his battalion in Hoengsong for another hour to cover White, who was marshalling his artillery units down Route 29 toward Wonju. Once they passed, Baker's troops mounted their trucks and became the support force's rear guard. The teamwork and tactics employed by Baker and White worked—somewhat.

Part of White's artillery reached Wonju with little opposition from the Chinese. Another segment was not so fortunate. As this group

THE HOENGSONG VALLEY MASSACRE

reached a point about a mile and a half below Hoengsong, Chinese troops covered the road from the west and opened fire. The friendly forces had no alternative but to press forward. About twenty vehicles managed to get through the roadblock before officers decided it was too dangerous to risk any more attempts.

Baker acted quickly to alleviate the danger. He ordered forward some infantry and a few of Coughlin's tanks. They destroyed the Chinese roadblock. Finally, the entire column reached Wonju. The cost of the battles near Hoengsong was high for SF 7. Troop casualties numbered 12 killed, 125 wounded, and 53 missing. Equipment lost included 35 vehicles, the 155mm. Howitzer that slipped off the road, and an M-16 antiaircraft weapon that threw a track above Hoengsong. Coughlin's forces took a beating as well.

His column approaching Hoengsong on Route 29 was battered. An enemy mortar round hit a two-ton truck towing a 105mm Howitzer; both vehicles jackknifed across the road. Unfortunately, the vehicles were in the middle of the column, which did not bode well for the troops and equipment behind them.

The truck's occupants were killed or escaped, and the Chinese made sure nobody reached the truck to get it upright or moved out of the road. One Chinese machine gunner poured continuous fire on the cab to prevent anyone from trying to reach and restart the vehicle. None of the friendly forces seemed particularly interested in trying to be a hero.

Moving the jackknifed vehicles off the road would be tough under the best of circumstances. It would take too many troops to do it by hand, and they would be running too great a risk to try it. They needed a heavy vehicle to help push the vehicles. Miraculously one arrived—and kept right on going.

Mace's two tanks approached the wreckage en route to Hoengsong. They were the only two tanks that had not made it into the town yet.

But, they simply drove over high dikes protecting a rice paddy bordering the road, through the paddy, and into Hoengsong. The trucks trapped behind the wreckage could not do that. To make matters worse, many of them were towing Howitzers, which made it even more impossible to negotiate the dikes. The enemy, taking advantage of the situation which they had created, began to attack the stranded column from the sides and the rear.

The troops caught behind the destroyed vehicles were forced to abandon them and continue south on foot. Many of them were killed, injured, or captured along the way. The killed included Colonel Keith—contrary to stories that he had been taken prisoner. The troops who escaped did so circuitously, and avoided the ongoing battles as they did. Some of them got close to Hoengsong and saw the Netherlands Battalion fighting the Chinese, so they kept drifting west to get away from the engagement. They bypassed Hoengsong and returned to Route 29 below town.

Soldiers realized that they could not fight the Chinese by themselves or in small numbers. Adhering to the adage of safety in numbers, they reorganized behind the Netherlands Battalion and drifted into Wonju. The Dutch were not far behind. They disengaged and reached Wonju just about 1 a.m. on February 13th.

The Chinese did not let them go without a fight. They entered Hoengsong after the Dutch left, but stayed there. That could have been because Baker's troops had eliminated the only enemy position south of town during their successful withdrawal to Wonju, and the Chinese were not sure what to expect between Hoengsong and Wonju. They, too, were heeding the adage about discretion being the better part of valor. That would not deter them for long.

CHAPTER 21

The Netherlands Detachment At Hoengsong

One of the first enemy jabs at the Dutch penetrated their line and reached the battalion command post. Lt. Col. M. P. A. den Ouden, the battalion commander, led headquarters troops in a successful attack to eliminate the penetration but was killed by a grenade. Members of Colonel den Ouden's staff also were killed or wounded. Despite these grave losses at battalion headquarters, the Dutch line companies held at the edge of town while Support Force 7 scurried toward town from the northeast and Coughlin's other forces struggled to get in over Route 29. (Gen M. B. Ridgway to Mrs. M. P. A. den Ouden, 20 Mar 51)

THE DUTCH SOLDIERS were a valuable asset to the allies. When the government of The Netherlands issued a call for volunteers in late 1950, 16,225 people stepped forward. Because of the Dutch Army's demanding standards, only 3,148 of them were accepted and eventually sent to Korea. They were assigned to Regiment Van Heutsz, which was established on October 15, 1950. The regiment became a part of the Netherlands Detachment United Nations (NDVN). (The Dutch navy also assigned one ship to Korea.) The detachment was assigned to the American 2nd Infantry Division, 38th Infantry Regiment.

The first contingent of Dutch troops deployed to Korea comprised 636 men, who started their trek on October 26, 1950. Their adjustment wasn't easy. Because they were assigned to an American division, they had to be organized and equipped to conform to American military practices—and they were given only ten days of training to adapt. That was not long enough for them to get used to the tactics, equipment, and operations employed by American units. So, the first detachment had to train themselves.

To compound their problem, the Dutch had to integrate 100 ROK soldiers to fill out their detachment, which still didn't bring it up to full strength. Fortunately, most of the Dutch soldiers had already acquired combat experience, which they gained from fighting guerrillas during the 1945-50 Indonesian war for independence.

The Dutch battalion received its first mission on December 26, 1950. Their assignment was to secure the main supply route between Chunju and Hamchang. In the first week of 1951, the 2nd Infantry Division was ordered to defend the area around Wonju and Hoengsong. The division's defensive lines collapsed under enemy pressure and it had to retreat to the south of Wonju.

On January 5, 1951, the Dutch troops covered the retreat, just as they would at Hoengsong a month later for ROK troops and members of the 38th Regiment. During that month they engaged in a good deal of heavy combat, lost 100 men—and welcomed the miraculous return of one member they had given up for lost.

For a couple weeks in early January the battalion enjoyed a respite from combat while the UN forces geared up for their first offensive operation of 1951, named Operation Roundup. They recaptured Suwon and Wonju in the middle of the month as part of their offensive. As the UN troops kept advancing, the Dutch battalion moved to Noda-ri, a small village located near the mountain pass between Chongju and Wonju. They stayed there for one night, then relocated to Mannang-po, another small community located on a railroad line, via a road that engineers had just constructed out of necessity. The friendly forces had to build roads as they moved from one place to another, which the enemy did not have to do because of its strategy of traveling light—and on foot.

The Dutch sent out patrols from Mannang-po to keep tabs on enemy movements. One patrol from B Company got trapped in an ambush, during which two of its members were killed and several others wounded. Another patrol sent north discovered a large number of dead North Korean soldiers on a hill near a frozen lake.

The dead North Koreans, who had fallen victim to an allied air attack, had a significant stock of weapons and ammunition in their possession. The patrol also found some valuable information in the clothes of the dead North Korean commander and took one wounded survivor as a prisoner.

The battalion continued its patrols to gather information on enemy troops. The results showed without a doubt that there were numerous Chinese and North Korean forces in the area, and they were well armed. The Dutch troops stayed on guard, literally and figuratively.

Life was relatively peaceful for the battle-tested Dutch troops in the days leading up to the Hoengsong massacre. Once they reached Hoengsong, companies A and B were placed to the north and west of the town. A Company took up residence on a mountain near a river. There were several high mountains on the other side of the river. B Company was placed to A's right. B Company located its command in a pair of houses that were damaged, but usable. The houses were close to the river crossing, half way up a hill on which the troops lay in position.

The busy road to Honchon, over which South Korean and American troops traveled to attack the enemy, bisected Company A's position, through a narrow valley with mountains on each side. The well-selected position gave Company A control over the valley and the road. The two companies were supported by two platoons of 4.2 mortars, one platoon of tanks, and one section of AAA.

Battalion Command established its quarters in a small church in the town, the only building in Hoengsong that had escaped destruction in the fighting around it. The battalion's staff members set up tents around the church. The S-2 unit occupied an outpost from which it kept in contact with ROK units and participated in combat patrols. Their positions gave them an excellent view of the ROK attacks against the Chinese in the hills—and a great sense of foreboding.

According to the plan, two ROK divisions would conduct a pincer move northward and try to cut off the Chinese; American tanks and artillery were assigned to support them. The Dutch troops watched with a bit of amusement as the ROK units begin their attacks against the Chinese. Van Schilt wrote, "You see them move out in endless lines. It is a strange Army to us. There are women among them who accompany them to the front, cook and wash for them, and spend the night with the soldiers. Also they have cattle with them. That is their food reserves running on its own feet."

The Dutch troops had a front row seat to the action as it unfolded. B Company had a panoramic view of the combat area. They watched the ROK soldiers climb the mountains one by one and oust the Chinese from their positions. Heavy artillery and aircraft fire helped the ROKs considerably. But, what started well fell apart quickly.

For some reason, the Dutch soldiers didn't feel comfortable as they watched. They couldn't explain their sense of foreboding; they just sensed an undetermined danger. As it turned out, their fears were justified.

Five minutes after midnight on February 12th the 38th Regt. notified the

Dutch command that the Chinese had turned the situation around. The ROK 10th and 13th Regiments that had been the attackers were now withdrawing—and quickly. It wasn't until 6:30 a.m. that Dutch commanders made plans to assist the withdrawing ROKS.

They repositioned Co. A to Co. B's left flank to facilitate a rear guard action should one become necessary. The Dutch were observing an increasing number of ROK troops flowing past their position. But, they still weren't in any great danger as far as they could observe. At 3 p.m. two events occurred that would have a great impact on the detachment, neither of which was particularly fortuitous.

First, detachment commander LtCol den Ouden was notified of a friendly forces counterattack along the main road north of their position by one ROK battalion and one company of the U.S. Army's 187th Airborne Regiment. That operation put the Dutch troops on heightened alert and brought them some unwanted attention.

As the counterattack began, den Ouden received orders from the 38th Regiment to send one part of his unit to recon a new position about 4,000 yards west of Wonju and to relocate his medical section to a spot just south of Hoengsong to establish a collecting station for all the wounded soldiers expected to pass through the area. That left den Ouden a bit shorthanded. A half hour after he dispatched the selected troops, the remaining soldiers were under deadly attack.

At 3:30 p.m. den Ouden was inspecting Co. A's position. Suddenly, mortar fire rained down on the company's position, killing 4 and wounding 8 Dutch soldiers. Den Ouden realized just how vulnerable his detachment's position was. There was nobody on either of its flanks, which he perceived correctly as a significant problem. The detachment's move to its new position would alleviate that problem, but it did not remove them from danger.

Another 6-8 mortar shells hit A Company about 5:45 p.m. This time there were no casualties, but a familiar problem resurfaced: friendly

THE NETHERLANDS DETACHMENT AT HOENGSONG

troops' inability to distinguish between ROK and enemy troops.

The action heated up for the Dutch. A few more shells and small arms fire hit their position, again with no casualties. The Chinese may have had a lot of ammo to expend, but the friendly forces did not. Early in the evening, ROK forces asked the Dutch to send them more ammunition. The Dutch passed on the request to 38th Regt. personnel, who informed them that there wasn't any extra ammo available. Instead, they said, the ROKs should withdraw. Another part of the Dutch detachment did as well.

The Dutch started to relocate their CP to the MSR near Wonju in preparation for the entire detachment's move. One 4.2 mortar platoon remained in place to cover the other as it moved. As the soldiers prepared to step off a few minutes after 9 p.m., they heard small arms fire just northeast of the CP. The unit's Motor Transport officer informed den Ouden that there was a large group of approximately sixty stragglers coming down the road, and he wasn't sure who they were.

The details of what happened next are murky, depending on who is telling the story. In any case, the incident was deadly for the Dutch troops, who lost their commander and several other men.

One account, provided by Col James W. Edwards, who commanded the U.S. Army's 2d Battalion, 23d Regiment, suggests that at dusk on February 12th a group of enemy soldiers dressed in South Korean uniforms and carrying U.S. weapons approached the Dutch CP. One of the enemy soldiers explained in English that he and his comrades were South Koreans, and they had run out of ammunition fighting the Chinese. He requested some ammunition from the Dutch, which they gladly provided.

The English-speaking enemy soldier thanked the Dutch as the pseudo "ROKs" slipped off into the gathering darkness. Once they got about 50 yards from the CP they calmly loaded their weapons and fired into the surprised Dutch soldiers, killing several of them. Then, they withdrew. As they disappeared they started a brush fire, which served as a marker for an enemy mortar barrage which fell on the CP with devastating effects.

Other accounts explain that CP guards didn't wait to find out who the approaching soldiers were: they just opened fire in a "shoot first, ask questions later" fashion. The soldiers in the column on the road yelled immediately, "OK, ROKS. OK, ROKs."

Den Ouden ordered the Dutch troops to stop firing and ordered S-2 Sergeant Pakker and an interpreter to find out who the troops actually were. As the interpreter approached the group, he heard them speaking Chinese and relayed that information to Pakker. The sergeant yelled to den Ouden, "There's something wrong here." The Chinese opened fire immediately, arousing the rest of the CP personnel. That was the last anyone saw of Sgt. Pakker.

In any case, Den Ouden took charge of the situation immediately. As Captain Tack, the Dutch S-3 officer, alerted the other companies that the Chinese were firing on them, den Ouden ordered everyone to pull back about twenty yards to form a consolidated defensive position with the rest of HQ Co. As he did, a hand grenade fell about five feet from him. The blast wounded him mortally.

The Chinese could not have picked a better place for a firefight if they had scouted it beforehand. The Dutch soldiers caught in the open tried desperately to get back to the protection of the HQ Co., but a steep embankment hampered their approach. The Chinese wounded several of the Dutch as they scrambled to get away.

Four soldiers, SgtMaj Wiessenekker, Sgt. I. Sonke, Sgt Wagner, and Pvt van de Water, dragged the now dead den Ouden's body with them to the company area. The heavy fire they were enduring impeded their progress. Nevertheless, they reached the embankment and tried to pull den Ouden up the embankment, albeit unsuccessfully.

As more Dutch soldiers sustained wounds, Tack, who was seriously wounded himself, contacted B Co. and requested them to come and help HQ and CP Companies. A patrol from the company arrived at 9:35 p.m., about a half-hour after the firefight began. By that time the Chinese had cleared out the area and established a position above the fleeing Dutch troops. They were firing down into the group with horrendous results.

Two Dutch soldiers in particular, Sgt I. Snoeys and Pvt Opmeer, were doing their best to repel the Chinese as the B Co. patrol prepared their wounded comrades for evacuation. Snoeys was ordered to retrieve or destroy two .50 caliber machine guns to prevent them from falling into Chinese hands. He was wounded in the process, but he destroyed the guns.

Opmeer, a switchboard operator, had a similar responsibility. He stayed at his switchboard as the battle continued around him until his position became completely untenable. He did not leave his equipment until ordered to do so. Before he did, he destroyed the switchboard. He, like so many of his comrades, was seriously wounded in the action. As a result of the firefight, den Ouden and 5 other headquarters personnel were killed, 14 were wounded, and 8 disappeared and were listed as missing in action.

HQ Co. reorganized and withdrew to the south of Hoengsong toward the Dutch contingent's final assembly point at the air base at Wonju. Heavy Weapons Co. assumed a position to the northeast of the CP and sent out a recon patrol to check out a large body of unidentified troops on an opposite ridge. Once again the troops raised their hands and delivered the by now familiar words, "South Koreans. Don't shoot." The group consisted of only five members, in comparison to the much larger group of Chinese the Dutch had encountered earlier. Once again the Dutch soldiers were taken in by the ruse.

As soon as the patrol got close to the group, one of the members threw a hand grenade in the Dutch soldiers' direction. The patrol retreated quickly, with no casualties. The grenade served as a signal to a much larger body of enemy troops, who initiated a large-scale attack on the HQ Co. Once again a Dutch soldier distinguished himself as he and his comrades repelled the attack.

Cpl Stenges stood on top of a ridge, fully exposed to the enemy. With little or no regard to his own safety, he threw a barrage of hand grenades in the enemy's direction, holding them at bay. He was wounded in the hand, but that did not deter him. In true John Wayne fashion he pulled the pins from the grenades with his teeth and kept on throwing them. Finally, his comrades dragged him to safety before he sustained any additional wounds.

During the melee HQ Co. lost communications with the CP group. Captain De Vries, the Heavy Weapons Co. commander, and new senior officer of the detachment after den Ouden's death, assumed command of the group, just as A Co. came under heavy machine gun and small arms fire from its rear. More than likely the attackers were the same enemy group that had attacked the Dutch CP earlier.

De Vries learned from A Co. that the last Americans withdrawing had passed through the detachment's area. So, he ordered A Co. to withdraw as well while he stayed behind with Heavy Weapons Co. as a rear guard. De Vries named a bridge south of Hoengsong as the assembly point for the withdrawing Dutch troops. Getting there was not easy, especially for Co B.

A Co. had to fight its way through Hoengsong in a series of firefights at road blocks the enemy had established, but they succeeded in clearing the town. Strangely enough, while A Co. had been engaged with the enemy, B Co. had been uninvolved in the fighting. That period of inaction ended when De Vries ordered it to withdraw as well. Once again Heavy Weapons Company stayed in place to protect B Co.'s withdrawal.

As it passed through the town the Chinese bombarded Co. B with mortar, machine gun, and small arms fire and hand grenades. Company B finally reached the bridge, but the fighting in the town was far from over.

Weapons Co. still had to get through the town. De Vries waited until 10:30 p.m. to start his withdrawal just to make sure A. Co. and B. Co. had reached the assembly point. He had a problem that neither of the other two companies experienced. He had 81mm. mortars and vehicles to marshal through the gauntlet. There was no shortage of volunteers to do the job.

Eight members of the company stepped forward. They successfully maneuvered the mortars and vehicles through the road blocks, despite heavy mortar fire from the Chinese. The surviving members of the Netherlands Detachment assembled at the Wonju airfield the next day, minus ten soldiers killed in action, 28 wounded in action, and 9 missing. The latter number was not as bad as it seemed, as stragglers arrived at the airfield throughout the next day.

The UN command ordered the U.S. 2d Army Division and other units to make a stand at Wonju. It had been a harrowing time for the division, which had fought a delaying action against the Chinese in the rugged mountain passes around Hoengsong while five South Korean divisions passed through. The UN forces gave ground begrudgingly through Hoengsong but that ended at Wonju. There the communist offensive ended.

The Dutch Detachment did not win any special praise or any rest for its actions on February 12th. Captain Manning, S-3 of the 38th Regt, did not waste any time assigning the Dutch with a new mission that was different from its support mission of early February. The next day it was thrown right back into the fray. At least this time the 38th Regt. provided it with trucks to get the members to their next mission.

CHAPTER 22

Goosens Gads About

"American and Dutch dead still lie where they fell more than two weeks ago when the Chinese caught units of the Second Infantry Division in an ambush...At the site of what seemed to have been a command post lay the bodies of three Dutch soldiers. A fourth lay nearby." (Gene Symonds)

ONE DUTCH CORPORAL named Goosens had a strange experience at Hoengsong. It involved the Chinese penchant for collecting watches and treating allied soldiers in an unpredictable manner. Goosens was the only Dutch soldier among those missing at Hoengsong who was found alive after eighteen days. He was rescued by U.S. Marines passing through the valley.

Goosens was wounded in the leg during the battle at Hoengsong on the night of February 12th. Unable to move on his own, he lay in the snow for 18 days after the fighting ended. Throughout that period he was exposed to the bitter cold blanketing the ruins of the town—and to Chinese soldiers who came by almost every day and provided him with food and tobacco.

He had vivid memories of the battle. Goosens felt like he had been in hell. Dutch, American, and Chinese soldiers swirled around him, shooting in all directions. At one point a group of Chinese soldiers stood near him as vehicles around him burned. Mortar rounds and phosphorous grenades hit the little church the Dutch troops had been using as their command center. What was left of it caught fire immediately.

Mortar rounds and hand grenades continued to explode at an alarming rate. Goosens theorized that the Chinese were being hit by their own fire. "It was as chaotic for them as for us," he said.

The shooting increased in intensity. Later, a couple of Chinese soldiers stopped and took Goosens' wristwatch. "I thought I was dead," he admitted.

He heard tanks rattle in the distance. He hoped that the Americans had initiated a counterattack, but the sounds became weaker and weaker. Disappointed, he hoped his comrades would launch an attack to free him. If they did, he would not have been hard to see. He was lying in the open, visible to friend and foe alike.

"I tried to crawl to a place less in sight," he said. "It did not work. My leg was completely stiff, and the wound hurt horribly. This condition lasted for hours. I lived under an unbearable nervous strain. What would the troops do, retreat and leave me behind? I did not know at all what was going on and how serious the situation was."

Goosens did not give up hope. "When it gets bright, the Chinese will find me," he thought. "I cannot do anything."

He lay in place hopelessly. Then, his worst fears were realized.

"I lie here, powerless. In the light of burning fires I see Chinese soldiers running, a bad sign for me. Our troops have left Hoengsong."

He got the feeling that he was on his own, among all those dead people, completely helpless. The first night passed slowly. His wound hurt badly. He suffered from the cold. Then, daybreak came and brought hope with it. The Chinese moved on, fearing an allied air attack. That did not alleviate his discomfort, however.

The cold was unbearable, and Goosens suffered intense thirst. Then, among the smoking ruins, he saw a sole person walking toward him. It was a South Korean soldier. He, too, was wounded, but not seriously.

"I signaled him to come over," Goosens noted. "I was lying in open terrain. Should the Chinese come back, they could see me lying there from the road. On the opposite side of the road stood our motor vehicle fleet, burnt out."

Goosens guessed that if he could lie under one of these vehicles he would be less visible and, as an added bonus, somewhat protected against snow or rain. With the aid of the South Korean soldier and an outpouring of uttermost exertion, he reached the vehicles, completely exhausted. They remained there for a few hours.

Goosens took up residence under a three-ton truck, where he crawled under the loading platform. After darkness set in the Korean left him. He also left a roll of sour drops behind.

"Never in my life had anything been that valuable to me than this roll of sour drops," Goosens explained. "The producer had christened them 'Lifesavers,' which is what they have been to me."

Later that day, when evening set in, the Chinese returned. They attempted to get some of the cars started to take them with them. Tens of them walked between the cars. Goosens did not dare to move, fearing they might find him. They tried to start cars and drive them away. Some of the vehicles came so close to Goosens that he could have touched them.

"I feared most that someone might succeed in starting the truck under which I lay, run me over, and leave me lying there openly exposed," Goosens declared. "What I feared happened. After a couple of failed attempts a Chinese managed to start the engine. The fumes blew into my face."

The soldier drove a little forward and backward to drive the car out.

"Every time I saw the car's bottom move over me, with all my energy I tried to get away from the wheels," Goosens continued. "Then the car moved forward. I felt a crack in my leg and severe pain. He had driven over my wounded left leg with the left back wheel. I wanted to yell because of the pain, but had to constrain myself so as not to alarm the other Chinese."

But, he told himself, it could have been worse. The truck could have rolled over his body or head. Luckily for him, the Chinese still did not dare to make a light or stick around long. They still feared the appearance of allied aircraft.

"Afterwards, I must have lost consciousness," Goosens reported. "When I regained consciousness, most of the cars had disappeared, and so did the Chinese." His misery did not.

The following days were horrible for Goosens. He suffered from never-ending hunger and thirst, not to mention the cold. But the thirst was the worst. Nature stepped in to help.

After 4 or 5 days, rain arrived. A considerable puddle formed next to him. He scooped the water out with his hands and drank as much as he wanted. That was refreshing, but it did not solve his need for food. The hunger worsened. At times it was so severe that he put sand in his mouth, but he spit it out immediately.

At times the aircraft that the Chinese dreaded flew over. Goosens waved at the planes with a neckerchief, hoping they would see him. They apparently did not. Time dragged on.

On the seventh day of Goosens' ordeal, snow set in. That was a relief for him. He could eat the snow to fight hunger and thirst. Unfortunately, snow meant cold. The cold was the worst, especially at night.

"I lost the feeling in my legs," Goosens said. "I feared they were both frozen. I also saw Chinese patrols approach, and sometimes felt the urge to call them. Then they could end my suffering. But there was always something preventing me from calling. I still had hope that our troops would return to Hoengsong and find me. I had a feeling that I should come out of this alive."

Hope gave way to depression. On the ninth day he could not take it any longer. His wound hurt horribly, as did his broken leg, which he feared might be infected. He decided to call the next Chinese patrol and see what would happen. After all, he theorized, being a prisoner of war would be better than dying in that forsaken spot from starvation and dehydration. He even thought that if he were lucky, he might be exchanged eventually. He acted on his perception.

"At noon, when I saw the first Chinese, I yelled as loud as I could," he observed. "The patrol stopped and looked into my direction. I waved with my neckerchief. The Chinese came over, circled around me, and looked at me from all angles while they spoke to each other. My impression was that they meant no harm.

"When I told them I was hungry and thirsty, one of them gave me a drink from his canteen. Another gave me something looking like birdseed; it helped against the hunger. I also was given some tobacco. They cared for my wounds and bandaged them. Then they carried me to a Korean house where I was protected somehow, at least against the weather.

"In any case I owe my life to these Chinese. At times they came back and gave me a little to eat and drink. They never were hostile. What puzzled me is that they did not transport me off to a prison camp. I assume they did not know how to get me there."

Once the Chinese left, Goosens was on his own again. He couldn't get captured even if he wanted to. Then, on what he believed was the sixteenth day, he heard tanks on the road southward. There was heavy firing in the area. He felt renewed hope that friendly troops would come back. But it was only an armed patrol, assisted by a few tanks, which retreated after having made contact with the Chinese. They did not stop for Goosens.

Finally, two days later some Americans passed by and found Goosens.

"I still see them coming, U.S. Marines with bayonets," he said. "They slowly proceeded among the ruins and approached the house where I lay. I heard them talk, but I was too weak to move, or to crawl out of the house. I yelled with all the energy I had left."

The Marines heard him and entered the house. Goosens did not remember much about what was going on. The Marines told him later that he had embraced them like a mother does her children. "But everybody will understand that," Goosens concluded.

Corporal Goosens had experienced a miracle. Sadly, he was one of the few Dutch survivors who lived to tell their stories. Many others could not. None of those stories, however, was as miraculous as that told by Corporal Goosens.

The Goosens story spread quickly among members of other military units. One U.S. Navy pilot, CDR Robert F. Abels, who had been assigned to destroy American equipment during the massacre, remembered it vividly. It buoyed his spirits considerably, even though Abels could not forget what he and his fellow pilots had witnessed on the bombing mission.

"No "High Fives" Or Laughter

"On 13 February 1951, a flight of eight F4U-4 Corsairs (could have been more, but this was the group I was in) was launched from the U.S. Navy carrier Valley Forge to conduct close air support for the troops in contact with Chinese troops pushing down the South Korean nation. We had one napalm bomb and eight 100 pound bombs on each aircraft.

"On contacting the air controller, we were directed to an area northwest of Hoengsong, where a long convoy of American trucks had been trapped. We were instructed to destroy all the trucks and supplies to prevent the Chinese from utilizing them.

"As we started our runs, we could see many bodies lying in the area and we requested if all friendly forces, including wounded, had left the area. We got an affirmative and made our runs, destroying an estimated 10 trucks and damaging 20 more.

"On our return to the carrier, there were no "high fives or laughter," as we felt pretty sick. It was hard to ever forget seeing so much of our material and fellow military destroyed."

Later, after Abels learned that a Dutch military man lived through all the chaos, he remarked that it was most uplifting to hear. "I am proud to learn that the Dutch military is also made up of steel men," he said. Indeed, that was true of all the men who fought and died at Hoengsong.

CHAPTER 23

Survivors

"Time and the retreating Reds have fully disclosed one of the bitterest stories of the Korean War—the battling march three weeks ago of half an American regiment through "Massacre Valley. Of 2,400 men at Changbong and Saemal, scarcely half got back to Wonju as unwounded survivors." (John Randolph)

GOOSENS WAS ONE of the lucky warfighters discovered by the Marines as they entered and retook the valley. In terms of numbers, however, few of the thousands of allied warfighters survived the Chinese ambush or the subsequent murders at Hoengsong. Many of those who did were captured and sent to prisoner of war camps, where they succumbed to their initial wounds and/or the harsh conditions there.

Some survivors filtered in through the allied lines days and weeks later. A few were discovered quite by chance and saved from captivity and almost certain death. They were welcomed not only as survivors, but as witnesses to what horrors had befallen the massacre victims.

A small number of soldiers fought their way back to friendly lines. That process was as fraught with danger as was the original ambush. In one case, of a group of twenty American soldiers cut off from their unit, only three managed to fight their way back, and it took them almost a week to do it.

The twenty soldiers were trapped three miles north of Hoengsong after the ambush began. As they started their return to friendly lines they encountered an equal number of communist troops. The Americans engaged in a firefight and killed twelve of the communists. But, they lost three of their own members. The rest kept moving.

The next day they encountered scattered groups of Chinese soldiers and snipers all along their route. The Chinese kept attacking them in small groups of 6-8 members. By the end of the day only twelve Americans were still alive. And their troubles continued.

They passed a small house outside guarded by a Chinese soldier. He alerted his comrades, who rushed from the building and opened fire on the Americans, who fell back slowly, firing as they went. After that skirmish they were down to six members. They lost three more the next day.

Those three kept moving towards friendly lines in freezing temperatures, eating nothing but rice. To stay warm they huddled together, rotating places as they rested. The soldier in the middle of the resting group would get warm, then they would switch to let another one warm up.

Ironically, the Chinese weren't the only troops they had to worry about. They made it a point to hide from UN aircraft as well. They were afraid that friendly pilots would mistake them for Chinese and drop napalm on them. They did not welcome being burned to death, as were many of the large numbers of dead Chinese troops they saw scattered along their route.

Finally, after six days of fighting, starving, freezing, and hiding, the only surviving three members of the original twenty soldiers reached

American lines. Their will to survive, persistence, and luck had saved them. They comprised only a few of the handful of UN soldiers who managed to fight their way back to relative safety.

One of the saddest survival stories involved a 20-year-old soldier from Long Beach, New York named Robert J. Phillipen. He was engulfed in a "gasoline bath" and several clubbings at the hands of Chinese soldiers at Hoengsong, who then held him as a prisoner. He was an indomitable young man though. Phillipen attempted to escape twelve times. Finally, on his twelfth try, on February 21st, he succeeded and got back safely to UN lines.

He told doctors about his experiences as a Chinese prisoner. They were amazed that he had survived. Unfortunately, his wounds and near starvation proved too severe for him to overcome. Phillipen died at the U.S. Army 4th Field Hospital on February 24th from burns and exhaustion. At least he died a free man, and freedom was the driving force behind other survivors' will to live.

The survivors told tales of heinous acts perpetrated by the Chinese, interspersed with stories of occasional enemy benevolence, some of which contributed to their rescue. The latter accounts, however, were few and far between. One theme revealed that courageous Korean civilians were instrumental in saving soldiers' lives, often at great personal risk.

One 38th Infantry Regiment, 2d Division Army medical officer, Lieutenant Darrell Wayne Dutro, gave thanks to an elderly Korean couple for providing him with succor after 1st Division Marines rescued him—as they did so many survivors. Dutro, who was wounded four times in fifteen minutes, told his story in a letter dated February 27th to his brother Clifford. The letter didn't arrive in his home town of Portland, Oregon until March 8th.

The massacre was a rude welcome to the Korean War for Dutro. He was not new to the Army, but Hoengsong was his first taste of combat. Dutro had been commissioned in June, 1945, upon graduation from officer candidate school at Carlisle Barracks. Pennsylvania, but he did not go overseas. After being recalled to active duty for the Korean War, he left the United States on January 9th and joined the 2d Division on January 20th near Wonju. It was only 23 days later that he was caught in the "Massacre Valley" ambush.

Here is how he explained his adventure to his brother.

"I will give you a quick resume of the awful ordeal. Our outfit got caught in an eight-mile road block north of Hoengsong. It lasted all day and all night and I did fine until the night. In an effort to retreat and help treat wounded en route, about 9 o'clock February 12, I got hit four times in 15 minutes.

"First bullet went in my right thigh, rear, and came out the front side. Next one lodged in my right inner ankle. Next one came through my helmet and right ear and the last one hit my left thumb. I pulled myself into a shack and was captured by the Chinese next morning. They let me go after a day and a half (fed me rice, but no medical treatment).

"After that, I made my way to Hoengsong and was cared for by an old South Korean couple for 11 days, at which point the 1st Marine Division took the town back. I was evacuated by tank to our own lines. God led me through this every step of the way. I have proven to myself the power of prayer."

Dutro was one of the lucky survivors. His family did not have to wait for years to learn his fate, as did others—some of whom are still waiting. His brother had been worried about him for nearly two weeks. The adjutant general of the Army promptly informed the family he was listed as missing in action on February 12, but a second telegram February 24 said he had been returned to military control. Other survivors had similar stories to tell about how lucky they felt to survive the massacre.

One civilian, a thirteen-year-old boy dubbed the Korean "Huckleberry Finn" by Associated Press War Correspondent Stan Swinton, was particularly daring. His real name was never revealed for security purposes, lest the Chinese find out who he was and retaliate against his family. Swinton called him Kim, which was a common name among Koreans.

Almost two weeks after the massacre the youngster led an American combat patrol including tanks and infantry into Hoengsong to rescue two wounded American soldiers who had been hiding there since February 13. The patrol was delayed a bit in its return to the town. It engaged in a three-hour firefight with Chinese troops entrenched on both slopes of the pass leading north from Hoengsong.

Kim had concealed the two men, a lieutenant and a technical sergeant, in a shack for ten days. The youngster appeared needier than the soldiers were. His clothes consisted of blue rags held together with a safety pin and patched canvas sneakers. And he did not have a lot of food or water to share with the two survivors, whose names were not revealed. They would have to wait at least one more night for them—and drugs to treat their wounds. Remarkably, the two Americans weren't the only soldiers Kim was hiding.

On February 23rd he slipped through the allied lines late in the day with three escaped South Korean prisoners in tow. Kim informed U.S. Army 2nd Lt. James Adair about the two Americans and explained that their wounds and frostbitten feet prevented their escape from Hoengsong by themselves. Adair decided it was too late to send out a patrol to rescue the pair. Another officer stepped in with a plan.

Lt. Leo T. Delaney, a medical doctor, asked Kim if he would return to the shack with medicine and food for the two escapees. The young Korean said he would. The soldiers furnished Kim with two blankets, two boxes of C rations, cigarettes, and drugs for the lieutenant and sergeant. Kim promised to return the next day to guide the American patrol and left.

True to his word Kim returned the following day. He left shortly thereafter with the patrol to retrieve the two Americans. Needless to say, they were overjoyed when their rescuers arrived. The pair told patrol members that they had eagerly taken the medicine Kim brought them the night before, eaten part of the rations, and enjoyed their first cigarettes in ten days. Then they were returned to the rear for medical treatment—along with Kim. Lt. Delaney was so effusive with his thanks he said the Americans hoped to adopt the boy.

The lieutenant and sergeant had a lot to thank Kim for. They were the sixth and seventh Americans to make it back safely to UN lines from enemy territory. Nineteen other soldiers and a South Korean nurse also made it back. Sadly, civilians said the road leading north of Hoengsong was strewn with dead American soldiers still lying where they fell—and they would remain there for a least another week. It wasn't until March 5th that another combat correspondent, John Randolph, reported that the bodies had all been removed.

There is some question as to why the bodies lay there so long. After all, unwritten U.S. military policy dictated that warfighters never leave their dead and wounded comrades on the battlefield barring the most exigent circumstances. Such circumstances may have existed around Hoengsong, where there was heavy fighting going on almost continuously during February, which prevented retrieval of the bodies. Meanwhile, rescue attempts continued.

Kim had been lucky. One of his countrymen had not, as two Americans picked up by U.S. Marine tankers revealed in their terrifying story of survival. Their remembrances involved the treachery and kindnesses of the unpredictable Chinese and the lengths to which survivors went to stay alive and return to friendly confines. The two, an unnamed 19-year-old private first class and a 35-year-old corporal, both members of the same artillery unit that had been assigned to support the South Koreans, also unidentified, told their story to John Randolph.

Both men were badly wounded in the ambush. The corporal, a member of the artillery's infantry guard, sustained a bullet wound in his leg during the attack. It was the second time he had been wounded in combat. In fact, he had just returned to active duty four days before the ambush. He had been shot the previous fall in an operation 15 miles from the Manchurian border. In addition to the bullet wound, his feet were badly frostbitten.

The PFC, an ammunition carrier, had been shot in both legs, in the kneecap, and in the back. Doctors said his frostbitten feet were worse than the corporal's. But, they were still alive and their prognosis for recovery was favorable. Here's part of what they told Randolph.

"We were ordered north from Hoengsong to back up the South Koreans," the corporal related. "Our convoy with guns started about 10 a.m. and made about 7 miles through the passes. I went on outpost guard that night for the battery. The Chinese hit us about 2 a.m.

"There was shooting all over the place. The ROKs were streaming back all around us, some walking, some running. They sent me and 14 other riflemen out to secure the guns. We helped get them in convoy, but only three of us came back.

"We started back down the road about 8 a.m. with the infantry fighting the Chinese off from the rear. I got hit in the leg about noon and they put me in a jeep trailer. The idea was to fight south so that someone could get through to us before we were surrounded on all sides. A helicopter came in to get the wounded, but it couldn't take them out because the Chinese fire was too heavy."

The following day the Chinese kept the convoy pinned under constant rifle and machine gun fire. As soon as darkness fell the convoy tried to move south without any vehicle lights showing. That did not fool the Chinese, as the private explained.

"It was about 8 p.m. the second day. We were through the pass and thought we were over the worst. That's when all hell busted loose.

The Chinese hit the driver in the front machine and that stopped the column. Everybody got rattled. I did, too. They were shooting from all sides. As soon as somebody fell, the Chinese would grab his weapon.

"It was all at close quarters. I was behind a jeep. I saw a larger truck and ran over. I thought it offered better protection. There were lots of my buddies there. Some were dead. Somebody yelled, 'Let's get out of here.' I turned around and the world seemed to explode at my feet. Blood gushed everywhere. I knew I had had it then and there. I got under the jeep."

Both soldiers sought refuge under vehicles. While the private dived under a truck the corporal climbed aboard a truck filled with wounded comrades. Neither place was safe, particularly aboard the truck, especially after the shooting stopped. The corporal, who had lost his weapon in the commotion, continued his story.

"Some Chinese climbed up on the truck and started to punch us with their rifle muzzles. They were American M-I rifles. We yelled, 'Wounded,' but they threw us out on the road. One Chinese came up, put his M-I against my head and pulled the trigger. The bullet creased my skull—I could feel it going through my hair. The muzzle blast nearly tore my eardrum out. I flopped over and pretended I was dead. The Chinese thought I was, and went away."

The private shared a similar experience.

"The Chinese put a pistol to my head as I lay under the jeep. I felt the blast and something went right down past my cheek," he said. "I threw myself into a gully and prayed. I don't know whether God answered my prayers or whatever, but after a while they went away and I crawled about 500 feet to a Korean mud hut."

Eventually the Chinese left the scene without checking for survivors. They drove away in every truck that was still operable. Yet, neither American moved. They remained apart for several hours in the wreckage of the convoy before they found one another. Then, miraculously, a Chinese soldier spotted the two and directed them to a nearby hut. Soon, a third wounded soldier joined them. But their ordeal was far from over.

They were trapped in the hut with several Chinese soldiers who for the most part ignored them. Whereas the Chinese had singled out and executed many of the wounded Americans during the ambush they left this trio alone—apparently because they were wounded. They appeared indifferent to the third man's plight, whose name the corporal never learned.

"I don't know his name," the corporal said. "He was a headquarters man. He had a gut wound and wanted water all the time. He was always crawling out of the hut to get water. We knew he was going to die. He lasted four days.

"Toward the end he was green and yelling out. He was talking to his pal. He'd say, 'Hey, Bronc, hey. Bill, pass me the water.' We went to sleep. Next morning he was dead.

"Some Chinese took his body outside. The first day someone took his field jacket. The next day they got his pants. The next day they took his boots. And the next day some Chinese took his underwear. I thought they'd take his body away then, for he was naked, but they left it there. It was there to the end."

That was the point at which Kim's fellow civilian fell prey to the Chinese. The difference in their treatment was stark, and explained why the Americans were reluctant to reveal Kim's name. The corporal said, "The first day we were in the hut a South Korean kid, about 19, helped take care of us. He was making us some powdered coffee that we had from some old C rations when the Chinese came in. They saw we were wounded and left us alone, but they shot the Korean through the head with a carbine."

As quickly as that the civilian was dead. Yet, for some inexplicable reason the Chinese left the Americans alone. They did not even detain them. They simply left them unharmed. The two soldiers stayed in the hut in below freezing temperatures for fifteen days as the Chinese worked around them. They fed them scraps which they traded for the Americans' clothing. That was another sign of the Chinese penchant for unpredictability.

They had stripped the mortally wounded headquarters soldier of his clothing as he died. Yet, they traded food for clothing for the private and the corporal. "I suppose we were lucky. They could have just taken our clothes if they wanted them," the corporal said.

As the days passed the pair prayed for a rescue. Their account of how it happened was touching.

"I dreamed how we might be rescued," the corporal recalled. "I always thought a tank would come down the road and it turned out just that way. When I first heard the engine, I thought it was an airplane."

Then I turned and said, 'Is that a tank outside?'

"We looked out and saw a wrecker man carrying away burned-out trucks down on the road, making a path for the others. Then we heard the tank's .50-caliber machine gun firing. We were almost nuts.

"We crawled down a path on our hands and knees, waving our hands and trying to scream at the tank driver.

"'Have you got any room?' we yelled.

"The driver waved and yelled, 'Hurry up.'

"They picked us up and put us inside. It was crowded, but how glad we were to be there.

"Our tank took us to an aid station and they brought us down here in an ambulance. We're waiting now for the morning plane to Japan."

They made it to Japan. The Marines had arrived, but they did not find many survivors as they progressed up the valley. They located a couple more, though—one of whom had well over a year to think about his experience at Hoengsong while he recuperated in a hospital.

Army Corporal August Goeldner of the Second Infantry Division sustained serious shrapnel wounds from artillery and a broken arm and was taken prisoner on the first day of the communist assault. He was with a group of prisoners being marched northward when he tried to escape on the second day. His captors caught him almost immediately and refused to treat his wounds. Since he was exposed to sub-zero temperatures he added frostbite to his list of ailments.

Luckily, on February 23rd a contingent of Marines rescued Goeldner and transported him to one of their field hospitals. Eventually, he was sent to Percy Jones Army Hospital in Battle Creek, Michigan. He was still there recuperating as late as October 2, 1952—eighteen months after being wounded. Goeldner, like so many of his comrades, was not likely to forget Hoengsong. Neither were the other survivors who were fortunate enough to cross paths with rescuing Marines.

On March 4 Marines discovered a third survivor, an Army master sergeant. He, too, was in poor condition. The sergeant had leg wounds and a severe case of frostbite. There were more survivor stories to be told. One of them was, to say the least, unexpected.

On March 18, 1951 sixteen wounded American survivors of the massacre entered UN lines, two via helicopter and fourteen on foot. They were battered but alive. Unfortunately, a seventeenth died before he could return. The survivors, all members of the U.S. Army 2nd Division, had a remarkable story to tell.

Some of them had received medical attention from the Chinese. One soldier was wounded in the head. The Chinese had applied crude, but effective, bandages. Additionally, they reported, the Chinese had planned to return the wounded to American lines by truck, but Allied planes had disabled the vehicles. As a result, soldiers said, the Chinese had abandoned them after leaving food for them.

The soldiers set out in the direction of the American lines. A helicopter pilot saw two of the survivors walking along. He landed and picked them up. The two soldiers in turn directed the pilot to the rest of the group. That increased the total number of survivors, but it was pitifully low.

One of the last survivors rescued was found in early April. A First Cavalry Division patrol found Pfc. Ronald Sauer north of Chunchon. He was another example of Chinese unpredictability. They had captured him at Hoengsong on February 12th. For some reason they released Sauer in April and left him on his own. When the patrol found him he was still covered with straw from his hiding place.

Overall, excepting the few prisoners of war taken at the massacre, there was only a small number of survivors who made it back to friendly lines within a few weeks after the ambush. They may have been few in number, but they had an important story to tell. That was significant. At least someone was able to reveal what happened at Hoengsong—even if the Army didn't want the world to hear it, at least at first. It's still hard to listen to today.

CHAPTER 24

Hope Springs Eternal

"Cpl. James R. Hare, 19, of Cumberland, Md., will be buried Feb. 13, in Levels, W.Va. In February 1951, Hare and elements of the 2nd Infantry Division (ID) were supporting Republic of South Korea forces near the South Korean town of Hoengsong when Chinese forces launched a massive counter attack. During these attacks, U.S. and Korean forces were forced to retreat south. Over the next few days units of the 2nd ID were attacked again, suffering more than 200 casualties, including more than 100 servicemen being captured by enemy forces. Hare was reported as missing in action on Feb. 13, 1951." (DPAA Announcement)

SUCH ANNOUNCEMENTS FROM the DPAA have appeared frequently over the past few years as soldiers' remains repatriated from Korea have been identified. The identifications have provided closure to many soldiers' families who have waited decades for it. But, the numbers included in the announcement may be undercounted, and the persistent requests from family members for news of their loved one puts a focus on the human side of warfare.

History has proven that the number of casualties was well over 200.

There are still many soldiers missing who were suspected of being captured and transported to communist prisoner of war camps, where they died. Possibly many of them will never be identified. That means many families will never get closure. That's not for a lack of trying though.

The large number of missing from one battle is a hallmark of the Hoengsong battle. So is the number of people looking for them. The DPAA conducts in-depth searches for veterans of all wars, and has identified numerous MIAs from Hoengsong. Veterans service organizations offer what assistance they can. The Korean War Veterans Association often places requests for information about Hoengsong participants in its magazine or on its website. Many survivors of the battle have contributed helpful information about survivors or POWs who died in communist prison camps or custody. Requests such as this to POW-tracking agencies are common.

"A friend of my Uncle, Wayne Donald Austin, provided me with an article from The Graybeards [the bimonthly magazine of the Korean War Veterans Association]. I would like to know if you could research the archives to determine if there is any information on my uncle.

Uncle Wayne was taken prisoner at the battle of Hoengsong, Korea in 1951 and his remains have never been found. He was attached to 1st Battalion, 38th Infantry Regiment, 2nd Infantry Division (A CO 1 BN).

"All of my uncle's brothers and sisters have passed and my five brothers and myself have very little information about Wayne. Since I am not considered next of kin, I have not been successful in obtaining his service record as of this time. Any help you could provide in obtaining his records would be greatly appreciated."

Sadly, Austin's remains have never been identified. Other relatives have received news of their fates unexpectedly. Victoria Bolton was among them—after waiting 65 years. She not only learned the fate of her father, but that he had earned the Silver Star at Hoengsong. Both pieces of information set her heart at ease.

Victoria grew up without a father or any knowledge of what happened to him, nor did her mother. As far as they knew, Major William Murphy Bolton, U.S. Army, who listed his home as St. James Parish, Louisiana, had been missing in action since February 13, 1951. Mrs. Bolton went to her grave without ever learning what happened to her husband. Victoria, the Boltons' only child, at least got to travel to Arlington National Cemetery to attend an August 12, 2016 memorial service for her father.

She was two months old when Major Bolton disappeared during the battle of Hoengsong. Fortunately, a researcher named Merry Helm found out what happened to him. The truth was harsh, but at least it was uncovered. Helm also uncovered the controversy over the circumstances X Corps Commander General Ned Almond caused by trying to cover up the incident.

Helm, who has written extensively about the Korean War, is also the author of Prairie Boys at War, Volumes I and II. She discovered while researching Volume II that Major Bolton had been captured and executed on a death march three months after the battle. She contacted Victoria to find out if she had her father's Silver Star citation. Victoria didn't even know he had earned a Silver Star—nor did she know that he had been captured and killed.

Helm arranged for Victoria to receive the medal on her father's behalf on the trip to Arlington. His Silver Star was authorized by the Army in General Orders No. 268 (May 4, 1951). The citation read:

"The President of the United States of America, authorized by Act of Congress July 9, 1918, takes pride in presenting the Silver Star (Posthumously) to Major William Murphy Bolton (ASN: 0-398864), United States Army, for gallantry in action as a member of KMAG in action near Hoengsong, Korea.

"At approximately 2100 hours on 11 February 1951, the 16th Republic of Korea Regiment was attacked by elements of two Chinese Divisions. Major Bolton, a United States Advisor with the regiment, was at the regimental command post when a part of the enemy force made two successive attacks on the command group. Hastily organizing the headquarters personnel into a defensive force, he placed them in position and directed their fire, successfully turning back both attacks and inflicting heavy casualties on the enemy.

"When it became apparent that the numerical superiority of the enemy was too great for the forward elements of the regiment to hold their position, Major Bolton went to the front lines, and heedless of the intense enemy fire, organized stragglers into platoons, placed them in defensive positions and directed their fire on the enemy. He remained with these small groups, exhorting and encouraging them until their positions were completely overrun.

"When last seen, he was directing the efforts of one group in an attempt to extricate themselves from the enemy encirclement. The aggressive leadership, courage and devotion to duty displayed by Major Bolton reflect utmost credit on himself and the military service."

Victoria Bolton was one of the lucky family members of Hoengsong POWs or KIAs who learned about their loved ones' fates. One of the reasons many such families have never been privy to such information is that the majority of debriefings of ex-POWs, gathered upon their release in 1953, were long classified. That has encouraged determined civilians to pursue the declassification of those men who went to Korea and were lost to posterity.

Major Bolton is still carried on the DPAA's books as unaccounted for, as are many other participants in the Hoengsong massacre. Hopefully they will all be identified at some point. If that happens it will set a lot of family members' minds at ease—even if they have to wait decades for that to happen.

Bolton's experience opens another enigmatic door in the story of Hoengsong. There were not a slew of high-ranked military medals such as Bronze Stars, Silver Stars or Medals of Honor handed out to participants. (See the partial list in Appendix A.) That was because the Army's criteria for authorization are so rigid. One criterion in particular is that the recipients' deeds have to be witnessed by other combatants and signed off on by officers. The chaos at Hoengsong essentially inhibited either one from being met, since filling out and saving the required paperwork until after the battle ended was not a high priority for participants.

There is no doubt that many of the warfighters at Hoengsong performed heroically in their effort to survive. All accounts of the battle suggest that members of all the military units involved fought hard to repel the communist onslaught. Any soldier who earned a medal there had to do something truly exceptional, as did the aforementioned Medal of Honor recipient Charles Long. His medal was presented posthumously to his family by then President Truman on February 1, 1952. The citation was short:

"Sgt. Long, a member of Company M, distinguished himself by conspicuous gallantry and intrepidity above and beyond the call of duty in action against an armed enemy of the United Nations. When Company M, in a defensive perimeter on Hill 300, was viciously attacked by a numerically superior hostile force at approximately 0300 hours and ordered to withdraw, Sgt. Long, a forward observer for the mortar platoon, voluntarily remained at his post to provide cover by directing mortar fire on the enemy.

"Maintaining radio contact with his platoon, Sgt. Long coolly directed accurate mortar fire on the advancing foe. He continued firing his carbine and throwing hand grenades until his position was surrounded and he was mortally wounded. Sgt. Long's inspirational, valorous action halted the onslaught, exacted a heavy toll of enemy casualties, and enabled his company to withdraw, reorganize, counterattack, and regain the hill strongpoint.

"His unflinching courage and noble self-sacrifice reflect the highest credit on himself and are in keeping with the honored traditions of the military service."

No doubt many other participants in the Battle of Hoengsong performed acts of valor that might have risen to the level of Long's, but went unnoticed. The lack of medals was simply another fallout of the battle, as is the case during other massacres. If there is no one to witness deeds of heroism they cannot be recorded and awarded. There is no doubt that many deeds of extreme heroism went unrecorded and unrewarded at Hoengsong. As the old French saying goes, "C'est la guerre."

That is small comfort for the families of the Hoengsong warfighters whose valiant deeds were never recognized or whose fates remain unknown. But, as another old saying goes, "Hope springs eternal." Time may be fading but hopes for acquiring knowledge of Hoengsong warfighters' fates is not.

CHAPTER 25

It's No One's Fault

"It is more important that innocence be protected than it is that guilt be punished, for guilt and crimes are so frequent in this world that they cannot all be punished." (John Adams, 1770, Argument in Defense of the British Soldiers in the Boston Massacre Trials, Dec. 4, 1770)

THE SMOKE FROM the battle had hardly disappeared before the calls for an investigation began, as they do after most massacres. In a time-honored military tradition, the Army had to find someone to blame for the debacle—or at least go through the motions—and it wouldn't be the generals. Certainly there were plenty of things to investigate that went amiss, as noted in the following communique:

HEADQUARTERS, 38TH INFANTRY APO 248 C/O Postmaster San Francisco, California · 25 April 1951

SUBJECT: Commander's Evaluation of Command Report for Period of 1 thru 28 February, 1951

TO: Commanding General, 2nd Infantry Division APO 248

1. I desire to call special attention to the following items mentioned in the Staff Evaluation of the Command Report:

   b. Greatly improved handling of the mail by furnishing the mail section a copy of the roster of replacements and Company assignments direct rather than through the personnel section.

   c. Casualties and records lost in the HOENGSONG action illustrate the importance of having up to date rosters in several different places.

   d. The identification of friendly ROK forces continues to be a major problem, especially in a retrograde action.

   e. The control of refugees moving towards the front from the rear can be improved. It is recommended that a larger number of South Korean officials be employed on this problem.

   f. The failure to fire defensive artillery fires for the 3rd Battalion on request because the 8th ROK Division Commander would not clear them was a serious error. This ROK Division Commander was not in contact with his Regiment and was too far to the rear to know the situation. The caution on the part of the artillery was not justified.

   g. The shortages resulting from the HOENGSONG action were critical. The personal attention and action of the Division Commander corrected this situation. Without this Command Action, the delay would certainly have been much greater, for many items were flown in.

2. Basic replacements for a combat unit should be young and healthy. Some received during the period were not.

The impersonal nature of the report was not unusual. It was an assessment, not an obituary. More important, it was a recognition that some things had gone wrong—seriously wrong—at Hoengsong. At least it was a report. Years later Army records such as the above referring to the Battle of Hoengsong were hard to access.

Merry Helm, the 24th Infantry Association historian emeritus, recalled her experience in trying to track down information:

"I managed to conduct interviews with a wide assortment of survivors, and I'm recently in touch with a man who was with S-2 with the Dutch. I also tracked down the official investigation Almond ordered, and it's quite eye opening, as well. I thought it was interesting that the whole sheaf was unmarked, with no folder, stuffed in the back of a box that contained mainly court martial records. I credit a savvy archivist for helping me with that.

"Finding the awards given to the KMAG men up front – like Major Bolton — also confirmed what I had begun to suspect – that the majority of the South Koreans fought their hearts out. The investigation proved the ROKs didn't deserve to be Almond's scapegoat, but Gen. Stewart had few choices on which to place the blame."

On March 5, 1951 a spokesman identified only as a staff officer recapitulated the Army's version of what happened. The release of the summary took less than a month after the massacre occurred.

"It all started with the plan to let South Korean divisions lead the advance against the Reds on the central front supported by special American task forces of artillery with an infantry guard and with the main American line several miles behind. The ROK (Republic of Korea) outfit was the 8th Division advancing mainly toward Hongchon, about 15 miles north of Hoengsong.

"A special support force of one American field artillery battalion and a battery of medium artillery with an infantry battalion to protect the artillery was ordered north to support the ROK advance. The ROKs were also joined by a special support team of a platoon of tanks with an infantry company.

"The night of February 11-12 the Chinese hit the ROKs hard. By 2:30 a.m. the Chinese had cracked through the ROK line and were attacking our own American infantry perimeter defending the guns. We heard later that one ROK regiment had collapsed but two ROK regiments must have put up one helluva fight.

"The American support team was sent back down the road to secure a bridge near Haktam so we could withdraw safely. The tanks took a platoon of infantry. When they got near the bridge they ran into a Chinese ambush and the whole little force was practically annihilated.

"The American support regiment was strung out over nearly 20 miles of road. The regimental commander had very few forces under his hand at any one point. It was estimated the Reds had at least 33,000 men massed against the American regiment and the 8th ROK Division.

"The support force started down the road and managed to fight all the way back to Saemal with the Chinese firing constantly from the hills on both sides of the road. All this time the battalion in Saemal was under constant attack from Chinese rifle, machine gun, and mortar fire. Officers in Hoengsong had seen figures massing on Hill 303 that controlled the Hongchon road. They thought for a while they were retreating ROKs.

"The Orientals turned out to be Chinese setting a trap for the whole American force to the north. Regimental headquarters sent a security platoon of tanks to check the road. A wild fight flared up and three of the tanks managed to break out of the trap with the loss of several infantrymen. That was the first inkling anybody had that the support force and the Saemal battalion were trapped.

"Our people immediately ordered the heaviest air, artillery, mortar and tank fire onto the hill and began calling for a rescue group to rescue our surrounded battalions. The Dutch battalion guarding approaches to regimental headquarters at Hoengsong could hardly move. They were in action themselves.

"By midafternoon the support force and Saemal battalion had linked up and began to fight their way down the long narrow defile that leads 2 miles into Hoengsong. It was slow going against an almost overwhelming enemy and the two battalions with the trucks and the guns on the road didn't get quite a mile by darkness.

"The rescue force jumped off from Hoengsong in darkness. The ROK engineers stormed up Hill 303 and took it away from the Chinese. The Chinese fought like hell, but the southern force went on through and linked up with the convoy. As darkness fell the remnants of the trapped force found themselves in terrible isolation.

"One wounded survivor says someone ran to the truck, where he lay with other wounded and shouted, "Come on you wounded guys, get out and fight for your lives."

"The Chinese division poured in more men regardless of losses. Hopelessly surrounded, the men fired until they fell. Everything fired; 105 millimeter Howitzers shot up their ammunition at point blank range. One self-propelled twin 40-mm flak mount must have fired every few hundred feet. The long, slim cartridge cases still shone in the sun three weeks later.

"Almost everywhere along the road were rifle cartridges spaced out every few feet. There were heaps of them where machine guns had fired. When the end was clear and the Chinese closed in for the kill the gunners destroyed their artillery pieces. That part of the convoy that escaped before the Chinese closed in was pulled back through Hoengsong where the Dutch were fighting for their lives.

"But the Chinese came swarming in on Hoengsong too fast to give the wounded even first-aid treatment there. They had to go all the way back to Wonju while the remnants of the Dutch, the support force and the rescue group pulled back in fighting retreat. By 11 o'clock that night it was decided that all who could come through the pass had got through and the Dutch were ordered to fight a rear guard action while the rest retreated to Wonju.

"Next morning the battered regiment set up its new line 2 miles in front of Wonju. Then, dug in and supported by massed artillery, it stopped every Chinese attempt to crack through. And it turned the first Red retreat into a rout. Two Chinese divisions marched down the Som River valley and were destroyed by the concentrated fire of 60 pieces of artillery. This was the "Wonju shoot" that finally broke the Chinese drive."

There was no doubt that something had gone wrong at Hoengsong. A passage in the February 1951 Staff Section Report of G-3, 2d Infantry Division Command Report noted:

"Operation Roundup progressed slowly from the outset and heavy enemy counterattacks on 11-12 February produced the complete disintegration of the 8th ROK Division exposing 2d Division support forces to the main enemy onslaught. The breakdown of the ROK Division chain of command and communications marked the final stages in the loss of control. These support forces were compelled by circumstances to fight through enemy roadblocks to the south where a link up was effected with small northbound armor-infantry forces. Personnel losses of over 1400 men, four batteries of artillery, and vast quantities of equipment attest to the fallacy of this method of support."

In the EVALUATION and RECOMMENDATIONS section of the report was written:

"Cardinal principles to the efficient functioning of a combat unit are (1) Unity of Command, (2) Clear Cut Zones of Responsibility. Two actions occurring during the month of February clearly illustrated the value of these two principles.

"When the CCF commenced their Fourth Phase drive down the central corridor of the Korean Peninsula, they split their forces into two roughly equal groups at Hongchon; one group moving to the southwest toward Chip'yong-ni, the other moving down the Hongchon-Hoengsong Road. The 23d RCT (Regimental Combat Team), a cohesive, well-trained, smoothly functioning team, succeeded in smashing the enemy in its defensive action, at small cost in human life.

"Support Force 21, the special task force organized to give artillery support to the 8th ROK Division and assigned to the 8th Division for operational control, was forced to operate in a command vacuum for many crucial hours. The cost in lives and equipment was high. The lesson of the essentiality of clear-cut command responsibility and unified organization was very clear."

Two other factors that contributed to the debacle at Hoengsong and that required investigation were reminiscent of the problems the allied forces had encountered before the Chosin Campaign: an overreach by General Almond and poor intelligence. General Ridgway recognized the first problem early. The second was not as apparent to him until it was too late.

Ridgway expected the communists to launch an imminent full-scale attack at some point, but intelligence suggested that they were shifting their forces to the east, away from their base of operations at Hongchon. Almond had a plan to circumvent it by hitting them first around Hongchon as part of Operation Roundup. Ridgway was concerned that his plan was too complex and might stretch his forces too thin.

Actually, no one was sure of where the communists were. Once again they seemed to have pulled a disappearing act. There was some speculation that their supply lines had dwindled and they had to wait to replenish ammo, food, and other materials. Consequently, Ridgway instructed Almond late on February 11th to patrol around Hoengsong. However, he told him not to attempt further advances toward Route 24 in either the 2d Division or ROK 8th Division zones until the IX Corps had reduced the enemy's Han bridgehead below Yangp'yong.

Ridgway feared that moving forward with X Corps while the IX Corps was still held up could isolate and overextend Almond's leftmost units in the area where the Chinese 39th, 40th, 42d, and 66th Armies were obviously massing. And, he was concerned that the intermingling of allied units could get too confusing if—more likely when—the enemy attacked. He was right in his fears. To compound his concerns, Ridgway did not trust his intelligence reports.

Ridgway was a stickler for accuracy in intelligence reports. His main concerns were that they include clear, concise, and accurate surveys of enemy strategic capabilities and tactical courses of action to the highest level as possible. Even though he had such reports in before the massacre occurred, he had one nagging thought on his mind: the lull in communist offensive operations that started around January 4th. Where were they and what were they waiting for?

He asked Col. Robert G. Fergusson, the acting G-2 who prepared the estimate Ridgway had in hand, to answer those questions. Fergusson maintained that the lull was due to the problems the Chinese armies were experiencing with resupply, transportation, and reinforcement efforts. He predicted that they would resolve those problems quickly and resume their push to drive the United Nations Command out of Korea. Once they started their offensive they would be perfectly willing to sustain high levels of casualties and supply losses. Fergusson was right about the casualties and supply losses—but it was the allies who incurred the bulk of both at Hoengsong.

Fergusson's report was accurate up to a point. He mistakenly said that the Chinese would not attack until their IX Army Group was in position, and that would not be at least until February 15th. He was wrong on both counts. They did not wait for the IX Army Group and they attacked well before. The devastating statistics of allied losses at Hoengsong between February 11-13 attest to that.

ROK Units

3d Division	1,238
5th Division	1,141
8th Division	7,465
Total ROK casualties	9,844

U.S. and U.N.

2d Division

(Includes 38th Infantry, artillery with Support Force 21 tanks with Support Team B, Netherlands battalion, and Support Team A) 1,769

7th Division

(Support Force 7)   190

187th Airborne Regimental Combat Team

(Includes Support Team E, 674th Field Artillery Battalion, and 96th Field Artillery Battalion)   59

Netherlands Detachment   100

Total U.S. and U.N. casualties 2,118

Total casualties   11,962

EQUIPMENT

ROK 3d, 5th, and 8th Divisions (mostly by the 8th)

14 105-mm. howitzers, 901 other crew-served weapons, 390 radios, and 88 vehicles.

American units and the Netherlands battalion

14 105-mm. howitzers, 6 155-mm. howitzers, 277 other crew-served

weapons, 6 tanks, 195 radios, and 280 vehicles

The high losses of personnel and equipment upset General Ridgway. He attributed them to weak leadership.

"While there is nothing sacrosanct about a piece of artillery, compared to the loss of the lives of men," he wrote to General Almond on February 13th, "I don't expect to hear again of such loss as reported to me this morning of five 155 Hows of Battery A, 503rd. It is prima facie indication of faulty leadership of serious import in some echelon."

The next day Ridgway ordered his inspector general to investigate all "the circumstances attending the loss by X Corps of artillery pieces and other major items of equipment on or about 12 February 1951." And, for good measure, he sent a note of admonition to Almond.

Ridgway was not alone in lamenting the loss of the equipment. Almond's secondary concern was the loss of fourteen Howitzers by the 15th Field Artillery Battalion and five by the 503d. Neither general placed the value of the equipment over the high human costs. Neither did Army Major Cecil B White, Artillery, the commanding officer of the 15th Field Artillery Battalion. He was determined to retrieve some of the battalion's missing equipment, for which he earned a Silver Star. His citation read in part:

"[Major White] displayed gallantry in action against an armed enemy on 3 March 1951 in the vicinity of Hoengsong, Korea. Major White was accompanying a platoon of the 1st Marine Division out of Hoengsong with the hopes of recovering some of the equipment which the 15th Field Artillery Battalion had lost when its positions were overrun. Although heavy artillery, mortar, and small arms fire poured in around him, Major White was not deterred in his mission.

"Reaching the area where his battalion had been overrun, he detached himself from the Marine force and proceeded to inspect a large amount of equipment that was intact and undamaged. During a small arms fight with the enemy, Major White killed one enemy and captured an enemy officer. Returning to the battalion command post, he directed a recovery team to the equipment and back to safety. The gallant conduct and devotion to duty displayed by Major White reflect great credit upon himself and the military service. He entered the military service from Washington."

Ridgway took to heart the loss of the excessive personnel casualties among the 2d Division units that had supported the ROK 8th Division. He was quick to order an investigation into that aspect of the massacre as well.

On February 13th Almond instructed General Ruffner to look into the underlying reasons. Ruffner, in turn, assigned the task to General Stewart, the assistant 2d Division commander. Almond had his suspicions about what the investigation would find. He presumed that "aggressive leadership on the part of commanders concerned was lacking."

Almond was particularly critical of Support Force 21's halt at the road junction position of the 3d Battalion, 38th Infantry. He believed that losses would have been fewer had the support force continued directly to Hoengsong based on the idea that Support Force 7 had withdrawn immediately after being ordered back and that this prompt move accounted for its lighter losses.

On the 14th Almond expressed his preliminary conclusions—even before Ruffner had submitted his findings—in his response to Ridgway and his note of admonition. He avoided any specifics, but he told Ridgway that "in only one instance, now under investigation, have I found loss of U.S. equipment due to faulty leadership, and all the facts on this are not evident yet." He was apparently referring to SF 21.

In the same response Almond addressed Ridgway's earlier concern about Operation Roundup control arrangements. He assured Ridgway that "the operation, as conceived and coordinated, included the protection of the U.S. artillery units involved and was, in my opinion, all that could be desired. It worked out as planned except for 2 battalions of infantry and I of artillery which became enmeshed in the onslaught of Chinese who poured through the ROK formations. There has never been any loss of control of the major units."

It didn't take long for the investigations to conclude. The 2d Division report was issued on February 19th. It absolved Support Force 21 of any command deficiency. General Stewart found that there had been only "strong, courageous, and aggressive" leadership at all levels.

"Support force commander Colonel Keith had withdrawn from Ch'angbong-ni as soon as cleared to do so, had not yet received orders to proceed to Hoengsong when he stopped and joined the 3d Battalion of the 38th Infantry, and had made every effort to reach Hoengsong as soon as such orders reached him," he said.

"The cause of the losses in equipment and personnel among 2d Division units was the sudden and complete defeat of the ROK 8th Division with little or no warning to the 2d Division forces," he concluded. Stewart recommended that there be no similar intermingling of U.S. and South Korean units in the future.

An Army investigation confirmed Stewart's findings. The investigators determined that "All losses, in both men and materiel, stemmed from "the surprise and overwhelming attack of at least four CCF Divisions and two NK Divisions...against numerically inferior and widely spread forces of the 8th and 3d ROK Divisions."

Subsequently, the rapid disintegration of the ROK 8th Division "exposed the left flank of the [X Corps] salient and permitted the enemy forces in strength to advance rapidly to positions in the rear and along the MSR, thus blocking the only route of withdrawal for the tanks, artillery and motor elements caught north and west of Hoengsong."

In this unexpected situation, "there [were] insufficient US or other UN forces available to the X Corps Commander or the 2d U.S. Infantry Division Commander to form a task force of sufficient strength to defeat the enemy's efforts and to break...the roadblocks that delayed the withdrawal of the friendly units located north." Hence, the heavy toll was a result of enemy action and not attributable to the "fault, neglect, incompetence, acts or omissions of the U.S. Commanding Officers concerned."

Ridgway accepted the various investigators' explanations, but he did not withdraw a warning he had issued on the 14th. The "loss or abandonment to enemy of arms and equipment in usable condition," he notified all corps commanders and the KMAG chief, General Farrell, "is a grave offense against every member of this command. I shall hereafter deal severely with commanders found responsible and shall expect you to do likewise."

The matter was over. The loss of almost 12,000 allied troops was due to circumstances beyond anyone's control. The loss of equipment was egregious. The Army simply wrote off the massacre as a misfortune of war. The war would go on—and it did, for another two-and-one-half-years. The Korean War became known as "The Forgotten War." The Hoengsong Massacre, however, is still not forgotten, as its victims are still being identified in dribs and drabs. The debacle at Hoengsong truly deserved to be described as a massacre.

Epilogue

"Read. Think. Ask questions - and triple check before you start believing." Teru Kuwayama, War Correspondent

A FEW DAYS after the massacre ended and the allied troops gathered at Chip'yong-ni, they fought an epic battle against their communist foes. UN troops won a convincing victory and drove the communists back. Many military historians believe that the battle of Chip'yong-ni was the turning point in the war.

For the first time since June 1950 UN troops had blunted their enemies' offensives and counteroffensives. After that the war settled into a stalemate, with neither side having a particular advantage. That was how it remained until the cease fire was signed on July 27, 1953.

Bitter memories of the Hoengsong Massacre remain among the few soldiers still alive who survived it. Many of those who did not were not accounted for immediately after the fighting ended. Their bodies lay in unmarked graves for several decades after the troops on both sides left Korea. Some will never be found or identified.

The remains of some of those located are just being identified today through the efforts of the Department of Defense's POW/MIA Accounting Agency. They are remembered in short, concise announcements such as this. (The soldier's real name is not used.)

Defense POW/MIA Accounting Agency

Department of Defense

The Department of Defense POW/Missing Personnel Office (DPMO) announced today that the remains of a U.S. soldier, missing from the Korean War, have been identified and will be returned to his family for burial with full military honors.

Army Pfc. Anthony R. Too-young, 18, of Midtown, N.Y., will be buried Dec. 15, 2022, in Farmingdale, N.Y. On Feb. 11, 1951, Too-young was assigned to Company L, 3rd Battalion, 38th Infantry Regiment, 2nd Infantry Division, as part of Support Force 21. They were deployed near Changbong-ni, South Korea, when their defensive line was attacked by Chinese forces, forcing the unit to withdraw south to a more defensible position. Too-young was reported as missing in action Feb. 13, 1951.

Reports received after the battle indicated that Too-young had been captured by Chinese forces and died while in captivity, but these were not substantiated by any eyewitness accounts of American POWs who returned. His remains were not among those returned by communist forces after the Armistice in 1953, or in Operation Glory in 1954. When no information regarding Too-young was received, a military review board declared him presumed dead and his remains unrecoverable.

Between 1991 and 1994, North Korea turned over to the U.S. 208 boxes of human remains believed to contain more than 400 U.S. servicemen who fought during the war. North Korean documents, turned over with some of the boxes, indicated that some of the remains were recovered from the vicinity where Too-young was believed to have died.

To identify Too-young's remains, scientists from the Joint POW/MIA Accounting Command (JPAC) and the Armed Forces DNA Identification Laboratory (AFDIL) used circumstantial evidence and forensic identification tools, to include mitochondrial DNA, which matched his brother.

Today, 7,567 Americans remain unaccounted for from the Korean War. Using modern technology, identifications continue to be made from remains that were previously turned over by North Korean officials or recovered by American recovery teams.

For additional information on the Defense Department's mission to account for Americans, who went missing while serving our country, visit the DPMO web site at www.dtic.mil/dpmo or call (703) 699-1169.

No, the victims of the Hoengsong Massacre have not been forgotten. The U.S. government is still working to identify as many of them as possible. Slowly, ever so slowly, the number of Americans who fought in the Korean War and are unaccounted for is dwindling. Many of those who fought and died or who were captured at Hoengsong may yet be returned to the country they represented for a proper homecoming and burial. That will be a small consolation for their families—and a further reminder that "Freedom is not Free."

The almost 12,000 allied soldiers killed at Hoengsong could certainly attest to that.

APPENDIX A

Partial list of military awards authorized for Hoengsong heroes

NOTE: This list does not include awardees mentioned specifically in the text of the book, nor is it a complete list. It highlights a few of the soldiers who were recognized for their valor at Hoengsong.

The SILVER STAR is awarded to PRIVATE FIRST CLASS LEWIS R BARNES, ER36748659, Infantry, Army of the United States, a member of Company C, 38th Infantry Regiment, 2d Infantry Division, who displayed gallantry in action against an armed enemy on 12 February 1951 in the vicinity of Saemal, Korea. Infiltrated enemy forces had set up machine guns, automatic weapons and mortars on both sides of a road and were delivering accurate and devastating fire upon elements of a vehicular column moving south toward Hoengsong. After sixteen long, weary hours of fighting this enemy as a member of a recoilless rifle squad, Private Barnes was attached to a rifle platoon which had the mission to wipe out several hostile machine guns emplaced on high ground overlooking the road. During this attack, Private Barnes picked up an abandoned automatic rifle and delivering heavy machine gun fire, fearlessly advanced frontally upon one of the enemy positions at which time he was seriously wounded. Though barely able to walk, he nevertheless proceeded with his assault until he had gained the hostile position where he killed the entire enemy crew with automatic rifle fire. His audacious action enabled his comrades to eliminate the remainder of the enemy and was responsible for saving many lives. The gallantry displayed by Private Barnes reflects great credit upon himself and the military service. Entered the military service from Wabash, Illinois. GO 100, 8 May 1951 (WIA, RTD FECOM 11 Apr 51)

———◆———

Lt. William R. Exley of Syracuse was awarded a Silver Star for heroic actions at Hoengsong. (His award is listed as unconfirmed on the Military Times Hall of Valor List, https://valor.militarytimes.com/hero/104046.) The Exley entry reads:

CITATION:

(UNCONFIRMED - Citation Needed): William R. Exley, United States Army, is reported to have been awarded the Silver Star under the below-listed General Orders for conspicuous gallantry and intrepidity in action against the enemy while serving with the 7th Infantry Division in Korea.

However, the following information appeared in the Syracuse, NY, Herald-Journal, April 7, 1952, p. 62:

"Lt. William R. Exley has received the Silver Star for gallantry in action near Hoengsong, Korea, February 1951…The award was presented at Ft. Sill, OK, last week…

"At the time of his heroic action Lt. Exley was serving with the 23rd ROK Regiment as a forward observer when enemy troops came within 20 yards of his position.

"He led his men to safety through intense fire and organized a new team to return and guide artillery fire on the enemy refusing aid for himself despite the fact that he had been injured."

APPENDIX A

The SILVER STAR (Third Bronze Oak Leaf Cluster) FIRST LIEUTENANT JOSEPH GREENES, 01176983, Artillery, Army of the United States, a member of Headquarters Battery, (then Battery C), 15th Field Artillery Battalion, 2d Infantry Division, who displayed gallantry in action against an armed enemy on 12 February 1951 in the vicinity of Changbong-ni, Korea. On that date, Battery C was overrun by a strong enemy force. After a brief firefight, march order was given. The battery had withdrawn approximately one mile when the head of the column came under heavy small arms fire, forcing it to stop. Enemy bugles sounded from nearby ridges in preparation for an attack on the remainder of the column. Lieutenant Greenes ordered the howitzers uncoupled and supervised the delivery of over 400 rounds of direct fire. With utter disregard for his personal safety, he moved from gun to gun pointing out targets and danger points, all less than 200 yards from the convoy position. Many times he would take a wounded gunner's place until a new gunner could be found. After the main attack was stopped, Lieutenant Greenes rallied as many men as he could and led them in a counterattack, clearing the hills on each side of the road. Upon returning to the column, he supervised the loading of all wounded on trucks. The gallant leadership displayed by Lieutenant Greenes reflects great credit upon himself and the military service. Entered the military service from Ohio. GO 270, 7 July 1951

The First Bronze Oak Leaf Cluster to the SILVER STAR is awarded to CAPTAIN REGINALD J HINTON, 01313094, Infantry, Army of the United States, Commanding Officer of Tank Company, 38th Infantry Regiment, 2d Infantry Division, who displayed gallantry in action against an armed enemy on 12 February 1951 in the vicinity of Hoengsong, Korea. Captain Hinton was in the company of his regimental commander, witnessing the operation of a tank-infantry task force whose mission it was to break through enemy lines, effect a junction with surrounded friendly units, and support their withdrawal. When the advance of the task force was halted by hostile mortar fire at a defile, the regimental commander ordered Captain Hinton to assume command. Unhesitantly and without question, Captain Hinton rushed to the point where the tanks were halted and, placing himself ahead of the lead tank, assumed command of the task force, utterly heedless of the heavy enemy fire around him. Inspired by his example of fearlessness, the tankers and infantrymen immediately resumed their advance while he led them on foot, pointing out targets and directing tank fire on enemy emplacements. Under his aggressive leadership the task force effected a link-up with the surrounded forward units. He then disposed his men to act as a covering force and, under the screen of his fire, led the units back through the enemy roadblocks until friendly lines were reached. The gallantry and inspirational leadership displayed by Captain Hinton reflect great credit upon himself and the military service. Entered the military service from Minneapolis, Minnesota. GO 62, 18 March 51

The DISTINGUISHED SERVICE CROSS (Posthumous) is awarded to MASTER SERGEANT JIMMIE HOLLOWAY, RA34201485, U.S. Army, for extraordinary heroism in connection with military operations against an armed enemy of the United Nations while serving with Battery A, 15th Field Artillery Battalion, 2d Infantry Division. Master Sergeant Holloway distinguished himself by extraordinary heroism in action against enemy aggressor forces at Changbong-ni, Korea, on 12 February 1951. On that date, the beleaguered battalion, heavily engaged against a numerically superior foe, was attempting to effect a withdrawal and Sergeant Holloway, constantly vulnerable to hostile fire, directed the defense and retrograde action of his battery. Learning that a wounded soldier had not been evacuated from the area just vacated, he dashed approximately 150 yards across open, fire-swept terrain to rescue him. Later, as the battalion proceeded to move back, it was halted by a roadblock and came under vicious fire. In the ensuing action, a mortar burst ignited one of the ammunition trucks. Sergeant Holloway, braving a withering barrage of fire, directed removal of the ammunition from the burning vehicle and then pushed it off the road. As enemy fire increased in volume and intensity, forcing the battalion into hasty defensive positions, he again raced through devastating fire and, uncoupling a howitzer from a truck, placed protective fire on a hill to enable a company of infantry to effect a withdrawal. After the executive officer was wounded and unable to respond to a call for artillery fire, Sergeant Holloway rushed forward to an exposed vantage point and, with mortar fire bursting within fifteen yards, fearlessly directed deadly accurate fire into the opposing force. Upon orders to secure commanding terrain and establish defensive positions for the night, he volunteered to act as point for the combat patrol and was last seen moving up high ground toward the enemy. Master Sergeant Holloway's extraordinary heroism and devotion to duty were in keeping with the highest traditions of the military service and reflect great credit upon himself, his unit, and the United States Army. Home Town: Orange (city or county?), Florida. Department of the Army GO 107, 14 Dec 1951. (Master Sergeant Holloway was captured and died while a prisoner on May 10, 1951. His remains were not recovered.)

The DISTINGUISHED SERVICE CROSS (POSTHUMOUS) is awarded to SERGEANT ALAN R. JASTRAM, RA17249836, U.S. Army, for extraordinary heroism in connection with military operations against an armed enemy of the United Nations while serving with Headquarters Company, 3d Battalion, 38th Infantry Regiment, 2d Infantry Division. Sergeant Jastram distinguished himself by extraordinary heroism in action against enemy aggressor forces in the vicinity of Hoengsong,

Korea, on 12 February 1951. On that date, the Battalion Command Post was subjected to a fanatical attack by a numerically superior enemy force. Successful defense of the area depended on control of high ground one hundred yards to the rear of the command post, which was occupied by the enemy. Twice the Headquarters Company troops assaulted the ridge and were beaten off by the enemy. On the third attempt, when the attack seemed doomed to failure and his comrades were wavering under the intense enemy fire, Sergeant Jastram singlehandedly attacked the hill, shouting words of encouragement to his comrades as he moved forward. Inspired by the boldness of his action, his comrades followed him in the attack, overran the enemy, and secured the commanding terrain. During this action Sergeant Jastram was killed by a burst of enemy fire. Eighth Army General Order #501, 3 July 1951. Home Town: St. Louis, Missouri. (B 1930)

The SILVER STAR is awarded CORPORAL PETER G KUTSUGERAS, ER15417545, (then Private First Class), Infantry, Army of the United States, a member of Company M, 38th Infantry Regiment, 2d Infantry Division, who distinguished himself by gallantry in action on 12 February 1951 in the vicinity of Hoengsong, Korea. Company M was moving in a vehicular column flanked by rifle elements on foot when a group of enemy hiding in a culvert ambushed the column and halted its forward movement. Corporal Kutsugeras, with complete disregard for his safety, crawled over other soldiers who were held down by the intense enemy fire and ran through direct small arms fire to the mouth of the culvert, where he engaged the enemy inside, killing or wounding all but three of them. Seeing that these three were about to escape, he ran to the other end of the culvert and killed them as they were attempting to escape. The gallantry displayed by Corporal Kutsugeras reflects great credit upon himself and the military service. Entered the military service from Indiana. GO 215, 24 June 1951

APPENDIX A

———◆———

The SILVER STAR is POSTHUMOUSLY awarded to PRIVATE FIRST CLASS CHARLES W LAUDERDALE, RA18331507, Infantry, United States Amy, a member (truck driver?) of Company I, 38th Infantry Regiment, 2d Infantry Division, who distinguished himself by gallantry in action on 12 February 1951 in the vicinity of Saemal, Korea. Although wounded while his unit was fighting its way out of enemy ambush, Private Lauderdale refused to leave and requested permission to return to the fight as a rifleman. When that permission was refused because of his serious wound, he nevertheless insisted that his place in a litter jeep be given to a man who was more seriously wounded than himself. Private Lauderdale was solely responsible for seeing to his [comrade's] evacuation and thus saving his life. When last seen, Private Lauderdale was returning to the scene of the fighting. The gallantry and selfless devotion to a wounded comrade displayed by Private Lauderdale reflect great credit upon himself and the military service. Entered the military service from St. Francis, Arkansas. GO 297, 16 Jul 51 (born 1930; listed as MIA then KIA)

———◆———

The DISTINGUISHED SERVICE CROSS is awarded to MAJOR LEONARD LOWRY, 01302026, Infantry, U.S. Army, for extraordinary heroism in connection with military operations against an armed enemy of the United Nations while serving as Commanding Officer of Company C, 1st Battalion, 38th Infantry Regiment, 2d Infantry Division. Major Lowry distinguished himself by extraordinary heroism in action against enemy aggressor forces in the vicinity of Hoengsong, Korea, on 12 February 1951. On that date, Company C had the mission of covering the withdrawal of a road-bound artillery battalion along a road paralleled by enemy-infested hills and ridges. After ten consecutive hours of heavy fighting, during which Major Lowry heroically led his men in knocking out several enemy roadblocks designed to trap the battalion, the column reached the regimental assembly area and joined the 3d Battalion. As the two battalions began assembling and reorganizing, a strong enemy force occupying positions on a ridge adjacent to the assembly area placed a heavy barrage of mortar and automatic-weapons fire on the friendly troops, inflicting numerous casualties. Quickly organizing a group of men from his company, Major Lowry personally led them in an assault on the nearest enemy held hill and succeeded in killing the enemy occupying it. Although seriously wounded during this engagement, he continued to lead his men in assaults on the others hills in the area until the entire ridge had been cleared of hostile forces. 8th Army GO 419, 10 June 51. Born: May 16, 1920 at Milford, California; Home Town: Blackhawk, Iowa (RTD 20 Mar)

The Second Bronze Oak Leaf Cluster to the SILVER STAR is awarded to MASTER SERGEANT VITO E PERRONE, RA32000574, Infantry, United States Army, a member of Tank Company, 38th Infantry Regiment, 2d Infantry Division, who displayed gallantry in action against an armed enemy on 11 and 12 February 1951 in the vicinity of Hoengsong, Korea. On those dates, Sergeant Perrone was serving as platoon sergeant of a tank platoon in support of a rifle battalion. The battalion, under pressure of overwhelming enemy attacks from its front and flanks, was forced to withdraw through terrain already infested by large hostile contingents. The tank platoon, with two tanks leading the infantry and with two tanks commanded by Sergeant Perrone bringing up the rear, covered the gradual retrograde movement. Throughout two days and nights the cut-off forces fought bitterly and suffered heavy casualties in their efforts to penetrate the hostile encirclement. The two lead tanks were destroyed by the enemy and only the two tanks led by Sergeant Perrone remained. Directing the fire of his tank weapons at every target of opportunity and frequently dismounting from his tank in order to discover hidden gun positions from which the enemy was blocking the movement of the friendly troops, he effectively covered the withdrawal and assisted in keeping the column moving. Whenever he saw the route obstructed by an abandoned vehicle, he would rush forward on foot to remove the obstacles. At one point, he observed two 155mm howitzers that had slid into a ditch. In order to prevent them from falling into enemy hands, he delayed his withdrawal long enough to ram and destroy the two field pieces with his tank. Near the town of Hoengsong the road was completely blocked by abandoned and destroyed vehicles. Determined not to abandon his two tanks, which meanwhile had run out of ammunition, he led them down a steep bank around the obstacle and, proceeding on foot in defiance of heavy enemy mortar and small arms fire, succeeded in getting them back to friendly lines. The gallantry and heroic leadership displayed by Sergeant Perrone reflect great credit upon himself and are in keeping with the fine traditions of the military service. Entered the military service from New York. GO 62, 18 Mar 51

The Silver Star is POSTHUMOUSLY awarded to MAJOR ELWIN IRVING WHALEY, 0453764, Infantry, United States Army, for gallantry in action as a member of the United States Military Advisory Group to the Republic of Korea, in action against the enemy near Hoengsong, Korea. On the night of 11 - 12 February 1951, the 10th Regiment, 8th Republic of Korea Division, while advancing toward Hongchon, Korea, was attacked by elements of two Chinese Communist divisions. Major Whaley, Senior United States Advisor with the regiment, immediately went to the front to assist and advise the combat unit commanders in the deployment of their troops. Without regard for his personal safety, he repeatedly exposed himself to the intense hostile fire in order to direct and coordinate the fire of friendly forces more effectively. Fully aware that Chinese Communist Forces had penetrated other units and were operating in rear areas, Major Whaley, by personal example of courageousness and intrepidity, instilled in the Republic of Korea troops the will to hold their positions at all costs, despite the overwhelming odds against them. While under heavy small arms and mortar fire, he established collecting points for stragglers, organized them into fighting units and directed their efforts against the enemy. The regiment continued its gallant stand until the preponderance of enemy strength broke the defense lines and the regimental positions were overrun. When last seen on 13 February, Major Whaley was directing the efforts of a group of Korean and American soldiers in trying to establish a new defense line approximately four miles north of Hoengsong. The gallantry displayed by Major Whaley reflects great credit on himself and the military service. (Home of record: Hartford, WI) POW/MIA (8th Army GO 336 (May 24, 1951) (Captured and died as POW 7 May 51. Born 1914.)

APPENDIX B

The Chinese Phases of the Early Stages of the Korean War

INTELLIGENCE

Staff Section Report of G-2, 2d Infantry Division for February 1951

Identification of enemy units in the 2d Division area had been a primary concern during the month of January. The efficiency of the collecting agencies was reflected during the month in the speed and accuracy with which the Enemy Order of Battle was prepared. During the month of February, dissemination of information on projected plans and combat efficiency was greatly increased. As in the past month, the medium for the dissemination of special information was the Annex to the daily Periodic Intelligence Reports.

Many of the prisoners captured during the month spoke of an impending "Fourth Phase Offensive." A document captured during the period gave what is considered the most accurate interpretation of the Phases in the enemy scheme of operations and this document (a staff officer's notes of an address given on the 4th of February by CCF General Peng, Tuh Huai, Commanding General of the joint NKPA-CCF Headquarters), is here briefly summarized:

Three phases of the Korean War were completed during the period between the 25th of October [1950] and the end of January [1951]. The 1st Phase ranged from the south bank of the Yalu River to the line along the Chongchon River.* The Second Phase ranged from the Chongchon River Line to a line south of the Taedong River below Pyongyang. The Third Phase ranged from the line south of the Taedong River to a line south .of the Han River.

1. The supporting documents for this report are the PIRs contained in Appendix C-2.

*The heavy assault against the 2d. Division in the Kujandong and Kunuri sectors was the climax of this phase.

It had been the intention of the CCF to destroy the entire UN Forces during the 1st Phase and then complete the subjugation of all ROK sympathizers on the Korean Peninsula. In order to accomplish this, the Communists purposely fell back in front of the advancing Eighth Army hoping to lure the attacking unit so deeply into their trap that extrication would prove impossible.

It was the Chinese plan to offer just enough opposition initially to exhaust the advancing troops. The eventual offensive, although inflicting heavy losses in men and materiel, failed in its ultimate objective and the UN Forces were successful in their withdrawal. Lacking mobile equipment, the Chinese were unable to follow up their initial advantage and the offensive ground to a halt.

The Chinese then stopped to strengthen the liberated areas, establish coastal defenses, and replenish supplies. Recognizing the need for haste, they launched their Second Phase before they had succeeded in building up adequate reserves of personnel and supplies. This again forced a halt at the Taedong River, although UN opposition to this advance was minimal.

The Chinese were successful in crossing the Han River during the

Third Phase and establishing strong beachheads but, again, the phase was a tactical rather than a strategic success because they were unable to destroy UN Forces and lacked the mobility to keep up with the withdrawing units.

The Chinese began to propagandize their Fourth Phase Offensive toward the end of January. This was to be a decisive attack which was to end with the destruction of all UN Forces and the complete occupation of the Korean Peninsula. The CCF and NK units were informed that armor, artillery, and air would support the units in the attack. It was intended that there should be a three to four month rest between the Third and Fourth Phase but the "Limited, Objective Offensive," initiated by the UN Forces during the last week of January forced the Communists to move up the time of the attack.

The Communist strength for this attack was assembled in the central sector and the major effort was expended down the Chunchon corridor splitting into two prongs at Hongchon, one attacking down the road to Hoengsong and Wonju, the other driving southwest in the direction of the Chip'yong sector.

It was this attack which stopped the 8th ROK Division and inflicted the heavy losses on the Support Force 21 made up of 2d Division units. This attack ended in complete failure because of the magnificent defensive effort of all 2d Division units, particularly of the 23d RCT in Chip'yong.

When it became obvious that further offensive effort would destroy the combat potential of the CCF without accomplishing the purpose of the attack, the CCF again withdrew to await reinforcements and to permit the units to regroup prior to again renewing the attack in a projected Fifth Phase Offensive.

APPENDIX C

Enemy Forces In Action Around Hoengsong

CHINESE

42d Army

Corps Troops	2,500
124th Div	9,500
125th Div	6,500
126th Div	6,000
	24,500

40th Army

Corps Troops	2,500
118th Div	10,000
119th Div	6,000
120th Div	4,500
	23,000

39th Army

Corps Troops	2,500
115th Div	10,000
116th Div	6,000
117th Div	8,500
	27,000

66th Army

Corps Troops	2,500
196th Div	10,000
197th Div	9,000
198th Div	8,000
	29,500

37th Army

Corps Troops	2,500
109th Div	7,000
111th Div	8,000
	17,500

NORTH KOREAN

V Corps		II Corps	
12th Div	5,000	31st Div	4,000
7th Div	4,000	9th Div	3,000
6th Div	3,500	2nd Div	4,500
	12,500	27th Div	2,500
			14,000

TOTAL = 148,000

APPENDIX D

This poem was written by a prisoner in Camp #5 in North Korea. It expresses well every Korea War POW's feelings about those bitter times.

A TIME TO REMEMBER

Not a bugle was heard
Not a funeral beat
Nor even a drum sounding retreat
As over the ice the corpses were carried
To that hill where our G.I.s were buried.

Six feet by two feet and one foot deep
In a Korean hill they sleep
Both young and old, perhaps one wonders,
"Why?" These 1600 had to die.

No little white crosses to bear their names
But they were not buried in shame
Although they lie in unknown graves

APPENDIX D

They were 1600 American brave.

There were no useless caskets
To enclose their breast, only G.I. clothing
For their last rest
All colors of men, black, brown and white
Now 1600 faded lights.

A pill, a powder, or medicine of any kind
May have saved them from that yonder hill.
Those 1600 now laying still.
In their illness, tossing and turning
Most of them knew there would be no returning.
Some went easy, but most in pain
Did these 1600 die in vain?

For those of us who may go back
To enjoy life's fill, they will still
Be there on that lonely hill
Forgotten by some, yet remembered by most
They will be "The 1600 in their last post".

Author Unknown
Source: Rowley, Arden A. Korea-POW: A Thousand Days With Life On Hold, 1950-53. Pp. 53-54.

Sources

Introduction

Crossville, TN, Chronicle, Nov. 5, 2013 (Military authorities tried to hide the extent of the disaster.)

"A Distressing Description," The Graybeards, Sept/Oct 2012, p. 69

Source: http://www.2id.korea.Army.mil/history

Sobieski, Anthony. 1,127 Days of Death, Part II. The Graybeards, July/Aug. 2020, pp. 68-69

Boone [IA] News-Republican, March 3, 1951, p.1 (headline/Milne)

Moore, Tom. Email to author.

Richmond, VA, Times Dispatch, Mar 4, 1951, pp. 1 & 3 (Abell)

Cumberland [MD] News, March 1, 1951, p.1 (description of Hoengsong)

Boston, MA, Traveler on February 12, 1951, p. 6 (mountain goats)

The Dunn, NC, Daily Record, March 5, 1951, pp. 1 & 4 (scenes of carnage)

SOURCES

Chapter 1

Washington D.C. Evening Star, June 26, 1951, p. B-7 (Chinese & prisoners)

San Diego, CA, Union, Mar. 6, 1951, p. 1 (massacre valley/pathos)

Chapter 4

Austin, MN, Daily Herald, Apr. 10, 1951, p.2 (Emmerick)

Chapter 7

38th Infantry Regiment Command Report, http://www.koreanwar2.org/kwp2/usa/2id/004/USA_2ID_060003_0251.pdf

Chapter 9

http://cooljapan1.blogspot.com/2013/06/korea-yeosu-suncheon-rebellion-life-15.html (Yeosu–Suncheon Rebellion)

Chapter 10

https://www.findagrave.com/memorial/118097137/jimmie-holloway

Chapter 11

"Bad Day at Hoengsong," The Graybeards, Jan/Feb 2015 (Burgess)

Sexton, Scott. "Winston-Salem man who died in POW camp 64 years ago will get final resting place," Winston-Salem, NC, Journal, July 21, 2015.

https://www.honorstates.org/index.php?id=251085 (Sawver)

https://www.facebook.com/dodpaa/posts/1052038391573288 (Perreault)

"Korean War veteran's remains return to Licking County," Bethany Bruner, Reporter, Newark, OH, Advocate, Nov. 15, 2016

Chapter 12

Paris, TX, News, Apr. 10, 1951, p. 1

Chapter 13

McGrath, John J: The Korean War: Restoring the Balance. https://history.Army.mil/brochures/kw-balance/balance.htm

Chapter 16

Detailed Evasion and Escape Interrogation of Return: PFC Freeman, William D. Jr.

Chapter 17

"What really happened at Hoengsong?," The Graybeards, May/June, 2012, p. 67

Coshocton, OH, Tribune, March 18, 1951, p. 1 (Chipman)

The Dunn, NC, Daily Record, March 5, 1951, pp. 1 & 4 (105th Artillery Bn.)

Chapter 18

Washington DC Evening Star, Feb. 12, 1951, p. 1 (white flags)

Chapter 21

"No High Fives Or Laughter," The Graybeards, Jan/Feb 2012, p. 68

Chapter 22

Memphis, TN, Commercial Appeal," Mar. 3, 1951, p. 1 (Symonds)

Chapter 23

Boston, MA, Traveler, Feb. 19, 1951, p. 8 (three survivors)

Washington, DC, Evening Star, March 12, 1951, p. 6 (Phillipen)

Portland, OR, Oregonian, March 13, 1951, p. 10 (Dutro)

Washington D.C. Evening Star, Feb. 25, 1951, p. A-8 (Huck Finn)

Washington DC Evening Star, March 4, 1951, PP. 1 & 7 (Randolph)

Cincinnati, OH, Times-Star, Oct. 2, 1952, p. 3 (Goeldner)

Towanda, PA, Daily Review, March 5, 1951, p. 1 (Third survivor)

Baton Rouge, LA, Advocate, March 19, 1951, p. 1 (Nineteen survivors)

Chapter 24

Washington DC Evening Star, March 5, 1951, p. A-6 (staff officer report)

http://www.koreanwaronline.com/history/EbbAndFlow/Ch13.htm (Fergusson)

https://history.Army.mil/books/korea/ebb/ch14.htm (losses/investigation results)

GENERAL

http://www.koreanwar-educator.org/topics/casualties/p_casualties_hoengsong.htm:

Army Casualties at Hoengsong & Vicinity - February 12-14, 1951; Hoengsong, Wonju, Chip'yong-ni, Chaum-ni

Korean War Project, www.koreanwar.org

Elie Van Schilt, Dutch Volunteers fighting in the Korean War, https://www.zum.de/whkmla/documents/ndvn/ndvn05.html